Language Adaptation

Language Adaptation

Edited by

FLORIAN COULMAS

Professor of Linguistics, Chuo University, Tokyo

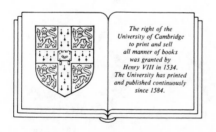

The right of the
University of Cambridge
to print and sell
all manner of books
was granted by
Henry VIII in 1534.
The University has printed
and published continuously
since 1584.

CAMBRIDGE UNIVERSITY PRESS

Cambridge

New York   Port Chester

Melbourne   Sydney

Published by the Press Syndicate of the University of Cambridge
The Pitt Building, Trumpington Street, Cambridge CB2 1RP
40 West 20th Street, New York, NY 10011, USA
10 Stamford Road, Oakleigh, Melbourne 3166, Australia

First published 1989

Printed in Great Britain at the University Press, Cambridge

British Library cataloguing in publication data

Language adaptation.
1. Language change
I. Coulmas, Florian
410

Library of Congress cataloguing in publication data

Language adaptation / edited by Florian Coulmas.
p.   cm.
Includes index.
ISBN 0-521-36255-5
1. Linguistic change.   2. Language planning.   3. Terms and
phrases.   4. Language and languages – Foreign words and phrases.
I. Coulmas, Florian.
P40.5.L54L36   1989
409 – dc19   89-508 CIP

ISBN 0 521 36255 5

AO

To the memory of
Muhammad H. Ibrahim, one of us

Contents

Contributors

Peter Braun
Gesamthochschule Essen

Florian Coulmas
Chuo University, Tokyo

C. J. Daswani
National Council of Educational Research and Training, New Delhi

Konrad Ehlich
Universität Dortmund

Muhammad H. Ibrahim[†]
University of Jordan

David P. B. Massamba
University of Dar es Salaam

Wolfgang Nedobity
Infoterm, Vienna

Fritz Pasierbsky
Gesamthochschule Paderborn

Uwe Pörksen
Albert-Ludwigs-Universität, Freiburg

Chaim Rabin
Hebrew University of Jerusalem

Seiju Sugito
National Language Research Institute, Tokyo

Makoto Takada
University of Tsukuba

Preface

This book explores the process of making languages suitable for the communicative purposes of their speech communities. The central notion which is used here to describe and analyze this process is that of 'language adaptation.' 'Language development,' 'language cultivation,' 'language modernization,' and 'language planning' are related notions which are more familiar, but they do not mean quite the same. Unlike the other notions, 'language adaptation' refers both to deliberate and to unguided processes of linguistic change. Language is seen, in other words, as a system which tends to evolve in such a way that it serves the needs of those using it, but whose development can also be influenced by conscious intervention if need be.

The authors of this volume agree that conscious intervention is to be reckoned with as a factor of language change. However, the processes they describe are not necessarily the same. This is so for two reasons: (1) structural differences between individual languages account for different adaptation strategies and patterns; and (2) conditions of socio-historical development and language use account for different kinds of adaptation needs. The purpose of this book is to compare how different speech communities adapt their languages to their communicative needs, and how different languages lend themselves to adaptation processes. Thus most of the chapters offer detailed analyses of individual languages – Arabic, Hebrew, Chinese, Japanese, German, Kiswahili, Kannada, Telugu, and several other Indian languages. The other chapters discuss problems of a more general significance – the role of a classical language for language adaptation, the emergence of a lexical stratum of internationalisms which become increasingly important in adaptation processes, general principles of terminology formation, and attitudinal problems of deliberate language cultivation.

The idea for this book grew out of a conference held in Bad Homburg in the summer of 1985 which was generously sponsored by the Werner Reimers Foundation. Additional support was provided by the German Academic Exchange Service (D.A.A.D) and by the German Foundation for International Development. Most of the authors took part in this conference, which was conceived and organized by Professor Konrad Ehlich of the

University of Dortmund and the present writer. However, without the readiness of the contributing authors to take notice of and discuss each other's views this book would not exist. It is offered to the critical reader in the hope that the notion of language adaptation will prove useful and stimulate further discussion.

F. C.

1   *Language adaptation*

FLORIAN COULMAS

Introduction

Introducing a new concept in a field of scientific inquiry is sometimes embarrassing because we could kick ourselves for not having thought of it sooner. 'Language adaptation' is one such concept. It is not our purpose here to investigate the question of why it has taken so long to give consideration to a linguistic phenomenon that seems both obvious and important for a better understanding of what speech communities do with their languages. Rather, it is to discuss in some detail what the notion of language adaptation is all about and what its significance for a socio-historical understanding of language is.

To begin with, some clarification is in order as to how the notion of language adaptation relates to similar notions in the pertinent literature, such as 'language modernization,' 'language change,' and 'language development.' The first one of these, language modernization, would be suitable for present purposes if it was not for the fact that the term 'modern' has largely lost its relative meaning of 'up to date.' Accordingly, 'modernization' is usually understood as referring to the process of making something suitable for the present time. Language adaptation, by contrast, is a process not restricted to modern times. For example, when in the fifteen century the Koreans decided to use their language for purposes of written communication, it had to be adapted to a variety of new functions, and new genres came into existence. Similarly, in the nineteenth century a number of European languages, such as Czech and Finnish, were charged with the new task of becoming national standard languages and had to be adapted accordingly. And in our present century, language adaptation processes can be observed in several languages, such as Arabic, Swahili, or any of the literary languages of India, which, like their respective speech communities, have come into contact with the realities of modern life rather suddenly. Obviously, then, 'language modernization' is not the most suitable term to cover all of these phenomena.

On the other hand, it seems prudent to make a conceptual distinction *vis-à-vis* 'language change,' the proper object of historical linguistics. Most

1

students of historical linguistics have traditionally found it difficult to recognize deliberate intervention into linguistic evolution as a component of what they are investigating. To them language change is something that happens rather than something that is done. The possibilities of artificially influencing it are considered to be about as great as those for altering the course of the planets. Language adaptation is a kind of language change, but it has both natural and intentional aspects. Also, it focusses on what in historical linguistics are sometimes called 'external factors' of language change.

Finally, as 'language development' is mostly used, this notion concerns first and foremost external factors of language change. In a widely quoted paper Ferguson (1968) has identified graphicization, standardization, and modernization as the elements of language development, where 'modernization' is used in the above mentioned sense of adjusting to modernity rather than bringing up to date. In this sense, language development, unlike language adaptation, does not encompass unintentional language change.

Thus the notion of language adaptation to some degree overlaps with each of the three notions discussed, but is congruent with none of them. As will become more apparent in the following, it provides the conceptual foundation for a theory of how languages adjust when they come under pressure resulting from new or changed functional requirements.

Languages are often said to reflect the social realities of their speech communities. Serving as they do the particular communicative needs of individual speech communities, they must be able to deal with whatever needs to be dealt with in linguistic communication. Normally this is exactly what languages are: symbolic systems providing an adequate means of fulfilling all communicative functions relevant in a given community. One reason, or rather one explanation of why languages differ is that speech communities differ with respect to the ways they use their language(s) and the communicative functions that languages fulfill.

Plausible as such a general statement may appear to everyone who favors a functionalist approach to the study of language, it is not easy to substantiate it in more specific terms. It is easy to say that a language is ideally suited to the communicative needs of its society, but it is quite difficult to show what exactly it is that makes it suitable. Therefore the general claim that languages meet the communicative demands of their societies is hard to substantiate in a non-trivial way.

An alternative approach to the question of how suitable a language is for its speech community is to start at the other end, that is to look at languages that in one way or another are not adequately equipped to serve their societies properly. Just as we can learn something about understanding where understanding breaks down or is inhibited, we can throw some light on the notion of the suitability of a language by looking at languages that are wanting and unable to fulfill all of their societies' communicative needs. One reason why languages may suddenly seem wanting is that, for political or ideological reasons, they are suddenly assigned new tasks.

Multilingual societies typically use languages in a functionally specialized manner, which is why not all of their languages or varieties are equally suitable for all communicative domains. This is often seen as a sign of, and/or reason for, underdevelopment, for the advanced countries have cultivated the idea of the national standard language which encompasses registers for all communicative purposes. As I have argued elsewhere (Coulmas 1988), the 'national language,' like the nation state, is a European invention. Since the rather successful implementation of this idea co-occurred with Europe's phenomenal development since the Renaissance, it is tempting to assume a causal relation between social development and a unified language suitable for all communicative purposes. With the advent of decolonization, the former colonies, most of which became multilingual states, have therefore come under much pressure to assign to one of their languages the status of 'national language,' which should then be adapted in such a way that it could satisfy all of the communicative needs of its respective society.

Since a unified, all-purpose language is a standard attribute of advanced countries, it has often been argued that making such a language available would be a significant step for the advancement of developing countries. The question is whether this is not putting the cart before the horse. Languages cannot be made suitable for serving new functions in thin air. That the functional range of a language is first expanded and that that language is then used to carry out the respective new functions is less likely than that it gradually becomes fit to serve new functions as a result of the speech community's desire to employ it for tasks that it used to carry out with other languages or not at all. It is using a language for purposes of modern communication which generates the necessary registers and thus leads to functional expansion. Not all languages are subject to this kind of pressure to adapt, especially in multilingual societies, where only some languages are used in all domains of modern life. Languages, therefore, differ on a large scale.

While this is not a very popular notion in modern linguistics, much can be said in favor of an approach that recognizes socio-functional differences between languages. Linguistic research in this century was shaped by the general positivist trend in the social sciences and by the value attributed to democracy by Western intellectuals. In conjunction with each other these tendencies generated an implicitly egalitarian perspective on the study of language: all languages are equal. At the beginning of this century, such a claim meant genuine progress in linguistics, which was still in the grip of European ethnocentrism. Realizing that languages are, in principle, of equal complexity was, however, a very abstract insight. Linguistic research of the last fifty years has proceeded on the basis of this insight and has led to a remarkable understanding of the fundamental structural make-up of languages; but, as a consequence of the egalitarian perspective, much less has been done on the functions and functionality of languages in society. In this regard languages are clearly not equal.

It is an undeniable fact that social development and language change are not always well attuned. For a variety of reasons social development may sometimes proceed at a quicker pace than linguistic development, especially when speech communities are subject to external influences such as war or colonization. As a result a situation arises where a language cannot satisfy in all respects the communicative needs of its speakers. Such a language is in need of adaptation. If it is not adapted to the new social conditions, it risks decay and eventually replacement by another language.

In the course of history, languages have been known to adapt successfully, thus recovering their full communicative potential after a period of retardation or degeneration. At present, a great number of languages, especially in Third World countries, are faced with demands to fulfill new functions that meet needs for educational, social, economic, scientific, and technical development. They are not yet well adapted and fit for the job.

While it is not surprising that a contemporary social phenomenon – the maladaptedness of vernacular languages in developing countries – has its predecessors in history, it remains to be seen in what respect language adaptation processes of the past are comparable with those of the present. In order to study the mechanics of language adaptation, it will be necessary furthermore to supplement this historical question with the typological question of how different languages and their speech communities react when they come under pressure to adapt under comparable circumstances. Let us first consider a historical example.

An attempt at enlightened language adaptation: the German case

Three hundred years ago, the German language was badly in need of adaptation. After the Reformation had stimulated the development and standardization of the vernacular varieties to a unified *Hochdeutsch*, the destruction of religious and political unity in the seventeenth century brought first standstill and then corruption and decay. The language was neglected by those whose support and care it needed most – the intellectual and power elites – who adjusted to the language and culture of their more highly developed neighbors. The situation became so critical that there were serious reasons to question the ability of German to survive as a medium of expression for more than the lowest and most ordinary functions. However, some concerned scholars and politicians realized the ever growing contrast between the boorish German and the cultivated languages of adjacent countries – French, Italian and Dutch in particular, but also Spanish and English. They also realized the political dimension of linguistic neglect and decay. Thanks to their attention and concern, the case of German language adaptation is well documented.

The most prominent witness was Gottfried Wilhelm Leibniz, one of the greatest scholars of his time. He was not a neutral bystander, however, but an active promotor of German language adaptation and cultivation. He was concerned about the fate of the German language, because he was convinced that the well-being of language and nation went hand in hand: 'it is found in all history that usually nation and language bloom together' (Leibniz 1683/1916: 19).[1]

The fact that Leibniz himself wrote about ninety percent of his works in French or Latin may seem ironic in the light of his pressing for the improvement and use of German. Yet this very fact vividly illustrates the calamity. In order to reach his audience, that is the intellectual elite, Leibniz had to publish in either French or Latin. As Pörksen explains in more detail (see chapter 9), scientific or philosophical writing in German was almost unheard of at the time, and Leibniz was quite bitter about it: 'There are few straightforward books written in the German language that have the right taste or savor ... Usually we write books containing nothing but a hodgepodge of copies from other languages' (Leibniz 1683/1916: 12).[2]

Educated people did not care to write in German, and as a result the language developed a deficit in abstract terms which in turn made it ever more difficult to use for expository writing:

There is, however, a deficit in our language in those things that you cannot see or feel, but attain by contemplation only: such as expressions of emotion, virtue and vice, too, and other matters of morality and government: further those relating to more refined and polished insights that are brought into circulation under the names of logic and metaphysics by those who strive for wisdom in their act of thinking and the general doctrine of things.[3]   (Leibniz 1697/1916: 27)

Leibniz's diagnosis of the weaknesses of German was very specific. While the language was well adapted to the communicative needs of trades, such as mining, hunting, and navigation, it could not function adequately in the higher domains of communication: 'Just as one would have expected, we experience the worst insufficiency in words referring to morality, passion of the mind, social intercourse, governmental matters, and all sorts of affairs of civil and public conduct; as one cannot fail to notice when translating from other languages into our own' (Leibniz 1697/1916: 29).[4]

Leibniz was aware that the insufficiencies he could not 'fail to notice' were not unalterable intrinsic traits of the German language. Every language, however poor it may be, can, after all, express everything, but unless a language is cultivated or if it is neglected it may not lend itself so easily to the expression of complex thoughts (Leibniz 1697/1916: 41). The heart of the problem was therefore not to be found in the linguistic substance, but rather its speakers were to blame, many of whom had 'forgotten their German without learning French properly' (Leibniz 1683/1916: 66). Leibniz's critical judgment is unambiguous. He concludes that 'the Germans do not lack the ability, but the resolution to elevate their language throughout' (1697/1916: 27f).

An appropriate attitude towards language adaptation is vital for its success. This insight was at the bottom of Leibniz's concern and the reason for his two pleas quoted here, 'Admonition to the Germans' (1683) and 'Of German Language Cultivation' (1697). He knew that the only chance of redirecting the unfortunate course of development on which the German language was set was to change the snobbish attitude of the intellectual and political elites, whose preference for French was a means of dissociating themselves from the lower classes and defending their social privileges. As he could hardly argue that the elites would themselves profit directly from cultivating German, he had to convince them that it had to be done for the benefit of the nation as a whole.

Leibniz was not content with pointing out the shortcomings of the German language and pleading for its reform. He also proposed specific remedies. First of all, the language needed to be enriched. In order to be an elaborate means of higher forms of communication, the vocabulary had to be as voluminous and diverse as possible. In the 1697 article he suggested four steps towards that end: '[1] search of good words that already exist, but do not come to mind in time because they occur so rarely, [2] further, the recovery of old and forgotten words of special quality; [3] also nativization or naturalization of foreign names where they are deserving of it, [4] and finally, where other means fail, careful coinage or composition of new words' (Leibniz 1697/1916: 42).[5]

Enriching the vocabulary was important. However, upgrading the language was not confined to the lexicon. A normalized grammar was just as important: 'The purity of language, speech and writing consists in that both words and phrases have a proper German sound and that the grammar or art of language is seemly observed' (Leibniz 1697/1916: 46).[6] A codified grammar was necessary because it would make the language a more precise and potent instrument and because it would enhance its status:

While we Germans thus need not be surprised or ashamed that our grammar is not yet in a welcome state, methinks it is still too far off the mark and, therefore, greatly in need of improvement. This would serve our glory and destroy the delusion entertained by many that our language is incapable of rules and has to be learnt almost entirely through usage.[7]   (Leibniz 1697/1916: 51)

A norm was deemed necessary for both linguistic and political reasons, but Leibniz's conception of how to arrive at a proper norm again shows great insight in matters of language. While he explicitly states that rules must be there so that he who learns the language is provided with guidelines other than just usage, he nevertheless recognizes usage as the final authority and source of rules: 'Usage is the master' (Leibniz 1697/1916: 52). His aims for adapting the German language were thus greater uniformity and exploitation of the available resources rather than adherence to rules for the rules' sake and narrow-minded purism.

Enrichment and normalization were the two points Leibniz stressed most. He was, however, by no means a bigoted purist as many of his less enlightened followers were. Rather, he acknowledged the necessity and positive effects of foreign loans: 'I am, therefore, not of the opinion that one ought to become a puritan in language and, for superstitious fear, avoid a foreign but handy word as a mortal sin, thus debilitating oneself and depriving one's words of emphasis' (Leibniz 1683/1916: 29).[8]

As a matter of fact, he explicitly commended the introduction of educational and cultural achievements from Italy and France, emphasizing their beneficial influence on development. However, he was strictly opposed to uncritically copying neighbors and adopting their language, because 'taking over a foreign language normally has brought with it loss of freedom and a foreign yoke' (Leibniz 1697/1916: 30). In his proposals Leibniz was eager, therefore, to strike a balance between purism, on the other hand, and alienation, on the other, recognizing, as he did, the multiplicity of resources a language can and should exploit for its development.

At the end of the seventeenth century, the German language was in a precarious state. The Thirty Years War had destroyed religious unity; the Holy Roman Empire of German Nations had disintegrated; there was a vacuum where other European nations had a capital defining standards of conduct, fashion, language, and the like; and finally, the elites were blinded by the glamor of the culturally more advanced neighbor and prone to despise their own heritage, including their national language. Those were very unfavorable conditions, all of which Leibniz clearly recognized (1683/1916: 12). He was convinced, nevertheless, that the German language could be improved and adapted to the needs of all communicative functions. However, this was a major task, much too heavy for individuals to carry out. It needed political support and an institutional frame.

Leibniz, therefore, recommended the foundation of a society or academy whose members would occupy themselves with cultivating and guiding the German language, much like the Accademia della Crusca in Florence and the Académie Française in Paris did for Italian and French, respectively. No institution of similar authority ever came into existence in Germany, but in 1700 the Königlich Preussische Akademie der Wissenschaften was founded with Leibniz as its *spiritus rector*. This body, however, never had anything like the impact of the French Academy. Political disunity in Germany did not allow for a language academy to evolve that could claim nationwide recognition. So much more important was the role of the grammarians and lexicographers who devoted themselves to implementing Leibniz's ideas about language reform. Gottsched, Adelung, Campe, and later the brothers Grimm, are only some important names. It can be argued that the German language would have adapted to the conditions of the changing world anyway – to urbanization, industrialization, and the general elevation of knowledge in the wake of compulsory education. To some extent this is undoubtedly true.

However, there is no denying that the process of adaptation was influenced by 'the language makers' (Harris 1980). Most of them must have known Leibniz's appeals; in some cases this is evident.[9] Their attention to what he said was, however, selective. It seems that he was best understood where he argued against the pervasive contamination of German and least where he advocated tolerance towards foreign investiture.

What needs to be stressed here again is that conscious intervention in the 'natural' course of language development is not a new phenomenon typical of the now underdeveloped post-colonial countries. What the chapters of this book illustrate, each in its own way and for a variety of different languages, is that language adaptation is a necessary condition for the survival of a language in a speech community affected by rapid social, economic, and technological changes. This may sound Darwinian to some: they may very well accept the challenge of coming up with a theory that explains the conditions of 'the survival of the fittest' in the realm of languages.

Admonition to the Indians

If Leibniz were to act as a language consultant to the government of India today he would very likely say about Hindi pretty much the same as he said about German three hundred years ago: it needs to be adapted, and it can be adapted. In spite of the fundamental and obvious differences between the language situations in seventeenth-century Germany and present-day India, there are some interesting parallels, parallels that are highlighted by our interest in language adaptation.

Consider, for instance, Gandhi's views on language problems in India. If 'English' is replaced by 'French', 'Hindustani' by 'German,' and 'Latin' by 'Sanskrit,' his words sound like a repetition of Leibniz's 'Admonition to the Germans.' He condemned the fact that the elites succumbed to foreign influence and accepted their cultural and linguistic domination: 'In slavery, the slave has to ape the manners and ways of the master, e.g., dress, language, etc. Gradually, he develops a liking for it to the exclusion of everything else' (Gandhi 1965: 101). Just like Leibniz with German, Gandhi recognized the attitude of the educated classes, rather than intrinsic properties of the language, as the main obstacle to the elevation of Hindustani: 'If the English-educated neglect, as they have done and even now continue, as some do, to be ignorant of their mother tongue, linguistic starvation will abide' (*ibid*.: 96). And just like Leibniz, Gandhi regarded the neglect of the native heritage as a national disgrace, 'a loss to the nation' (*ibid*.: 19). His criticism of the role of English in India is more than a little reminiscent of what Leibniz said about French in Germany: 'We have impoverished our mother tongue because of our love for English. We demean ourselves by insulting our language' (*ibid*.: 2).

We even find in Gandhi's appeals the same mixture of rational and emotional argumentation as in Leibniz's, and the same paradox, of which he was painfully aware. Both Leibniz and Gandhi used the foreign elite language while promoting the use of those native languages that should assume the functions of national languages: 'I have no doubt in my mind that Hindustani ... is the national language. But I have not yet been able to prove this in my own writing or speech' (*ibid.*: 98).

Like all intellectuals and figures of national prominence, Gandhi felt that he could not dispense with English. Also, he had no intention of confusing the issues at hand and using his pro-Hindustani arguments as a lever to stimulate xenophobia and provincialism. But he was as proud as he was sagacious, foreseeing, as he did, that a decline in the standards of English in India was an inevitable consequence of the end of British rule, and that it was therefore vitally important to adapt Hindi (and other native languages) to the functions of modern communication which they would have to fulfill.

At the time of independence neither Hindi nor any other Indian language was well adapted to the needs of education, technology, and management. To change this was a matter not only of national pride, but of economic necessity as well, and to bring about changes was a matter of urgency if further damage was to be averted:

English should not be allowed to transgress its rightful place. It can never be our national language, nor the medium of our education. We have impoverished our languages by using it as such. We have imposed a great burden on our students ... This slavery to an alien language has kept our millions deprived of a great deal of necessary knowledge for many years.   (*ibid.*: 131)

Just as the neglect of German by the intellectuals had been diagnosed by Leibniz as the major reason for its precarious state, Gandhi blames his compatriots. He echoes Leibniz's complaint, for instance, that no German grammar written in German and for Germans was available, when he says: 'I have not yet seen a single complete grammar of the Hindi language. Such as exist are in English and have been written by foreigners' (*ibid.*: 17). Not only was the language not standardized, it also lacked entire domains of vocabulary necessary for advanced communication because of the exclusive use of English for these functions: 'There are no equivalents for scientific terms. The result has been disastrous. The masses remain cut off from the modern mind' (*ibid.*: 5).

Like Leibniz, Gandhi realized that language adaptation could only be brought about by making use of a variety of resources. And like Leibniz, he was more enlightened and less of a purist than many of his successors. Coining new words on the basis of Sanskrit roots was not enough; foreign words, too, had to be accommodated in the language: 'The introduction of new words into any language enriches it' (*ibid.*: 104). To guide the language adaptation process, Gandhi called for 'language experts,' a request that was later met by the establishment of various institutions such as the Central Institute of

Indian Languages in Mysore.[10] Most important, however, for the adaptation of Hindi and other vernacular languages was their active employment for all purposes of higher communication. The point at issue was to break the vicious circle of linguistic degeneration caused by neglect and reluctance to use the native languages because of their thus produced shortcomings. The weaknesses of the autochthonous languages were, in fact, the greatest strength of English:

> The lure of English has not left us. And until it goes, our own languages will remain paupers. Would that the people's Governments everywhere do their work either in the national or provincial languages! But to attain this, they must have language experts and the public must be encouraged to write in their provincial or national language.
>
> (*ibid.*: 108)

Leibniz's goals for the cultivation and adaptation of German were not achieved overnight, but eventually they were. Hindi is still in the process of adaptation and has to overcome certain weaknesses such as its lack of generally accepted technical terms. Just how this should be achieved is a matter of considerable controversy. There is no doubt, however, that the process continues and that its success is important for the nation as a whole. Nobody would predict that in the foreseeable future English will be reduced to insignificance in India as French was in Germany, but Hindi will have to assume increasingly more functions of English, because 'it is now clear that the declining use of English at all levels of education and administration is both inescapable and irreversible' (Di Bona 1970: viii).

The path of Hindi is thornier than that of German in the Renaissance because it faces not only English as a formidable adversary, but also the other native languages of India, notably those of Dravidian stock, whose speakers are not yet all prepared to concede Hindi the privileged position that English used to occupy. Rather, these languages too are undergoing a process of adaptation which, Daswani argues, will eventually put them in a position to reclaim some of the territory now occupied by English (see chapter 5). Many more languages with highly respected literary traditions are involved in India than were ever spoken in Germany, and therefore the adaptation process of Hindi and its promotion as *the* national language for all Indians are so much more complex than was the case with German. Nevertheless, there are enough striking parallels in the two situations to invite a systematic look at the essential components of language adaptation.

The analogies between Leibniz's and Gandhi's arguments are especially noteworthy because the contexts of language adaptation in Germany and India are not analogous if we look at them from the point of view of social development. The adaptation of German was the result of the re-organization of the power structure over several centuries. As such it was both a by-product of, and a stimulating factor for, the full-fledged development of capitalism, which went along with urbanization, industrialization, general education, and the spread of literacy. The emergence of nationalistic and democratic ideas in the wake of the Enlightenment[11] also contributed to the ideas of a single linguistic standard which could become the language of all members of a nation. These ideas had time to grow, so that the work of grammarians and lexicographers could be absorbed by the society.

In India, on the other hand, the promotion of Hindi was first and foremost tied to the idealism that pervaded the anti-colonialist struggle. Once independence was achieved, the highest expectations were placed in Hindi and its role for creating a modern and democratic society. However, so far these expectations have only been partly met at best, which, given the short period of time, is not surprising. This makes the situation more difficult because advances in science, technology and other domains of modern life are rapid and do not wait for Hindi to catch up.

An additional complication is the fact that those who consider themselves guardians of the development of Hindi (and other major Indian languages) are deeply divided amongst themselves. Gandhi fostered the idea that what he called 'Hindustani,' that is a popular variety of Hindi/Urdu which developed rather naturally, starting in army barracks and bazaars where people from different regions and of different social backgrounds had to interact, could serve to bridge the gaps between regions and social strata so characteristic of Indian society. As a result of centuries of foreign rule, Hindustani contains many words of Persian, English, and other origins. This fact as well as its popular character as 'a language used by people of different social and regional background seems to have worked against its candidacy for official status' (Southworth 1985: 233). Instead those 'language experts' prevailed who advocated purism and Sanskritization, that is the substitution of many common loan words by Sanskrit-derived words. The result is much at variance with Gandhi's intentions, namely the language becomes 'less accessible to those who have no formal education' (*ibid.*: 230). Many progressive language planners, educationists and politicians are frustrated with the official policy of promoting high-standard Hindi, which is so much more unlikely to become a popular language of a modern state: 'Most standardisation devices in Indian languages today serve only to extend the "tradition-inspired" value system of small urban elites' (Khubchandani 1981: 27). It seems that Hindustani adherents are fighting a losing battle. In any event, it is clear that the adaptation of Hindi has not yet come to a final conclusion. While consciously relying on Sanskrit as a resource of vocabulary expansion can be said to be systematically consistent and preferable for nationalistic reasons inasmuch as foreign infiltration is held in check, the alienation of the language from the masses brought about by Sanskritization also has to be reckoned with.

The conservative policy of Sanskritization is a very controversial issue for the adaptation of Hindi as well as for the other major languages of India, including those of Dravidian stock. And it will be interesting to observe the success of those who favor it. More generally, it can be said that a controversy between 'popularists' and 'traditionalists' is characteristic of all language adaptation processes. If they were determined by enlightened spirits such as Leibniz and Gandhi, a middle-of-the-road course would be followed. However, language adaptation would hardly be so sensitive a matter if rational reasoning was all that was needed to bring about a practicable solution.

The role of writing

The transition from orality to literacy is an important historical event for every society. Recent work by scholars such as Ferguson (1971), Goody (1968, 1983), Graff (1979), and Heath (1980) has enhanced our knowledge of the history of literacy, its role in modernization, the control of bureaucratic institutions, industrialization, and the building of nationhood. In linguistics it has become abundantly clear that writing is not just visible speech, but rather a mode of verbal communication in its own right. Without writing, modern societies cannot function. While it has become clear that (1) literacy is not the same as a standard language and (2) literacy does not necessarily bring about or even stimulate modernization, it is safe to say that complex forms of societal organization require writing and a written language.

There is no justification for the assumption, however, that this language has to be the vernacular of the masses. Rather, a great many cases throughout history demonstrate that this was not the case. It was very common, indeed, that for a variety of reasons the written language of a community was not the same as that of the common people (Coulmas 1987).

When in the sixth century B.C. Darius, king of the then illiterate Persians, subjected peoples from the Nile to the Indus to the central administration of his empire, he adopted Aramaic, a foreign language, for the purposes of written communication, using scribes and translators (see Haas 1982: 32). On the other hand, *cuius regio, eius lingua* (see Coulmas 1985: chapter 5), that is the imposition of the language of the conqueror on the conquered, as, for example, the spread of Greek through Asia in the wake of Alexander's military expeditions (see Harris 1980: 118f), was a venerable principle throughout the ages.

In other cases, oral societies borrowed the written language, rather than the script only, form their more advanced neighbors. For example, the Koreans, Vietnamese, and Japanese all used the Chinese written language before adapting the Chinese script to their own languages and vice versa. When they finally began to write Korean, Vietnamese, and Japanese, they wrote a highly artificial language that had very little to do with the language of the people and which was nobody's mother tongue. *Kanbun*, the earliest form of written Japanese, for instance, is described as 'a language quite unlike Japanese which few of the writers could actually speak' (Sato Habein 1984: 8). This tradition began at about A.D. 600 and continued for many centuries. The stories of Korean and Vietnamese are very much alike.

Yet another kind of relation between writing and vernacular language can be seen where the written language was cultivated by a small caste of scribes and not allowed to change in the direction of the language of the people, whose speech, in turn, was not influenced by writing as they were largely illiterate. Restricted literacy of this kind may lead to either linguistic divergence and the subsequent emergence of new languages, or to a situation which is generally known as 'diglossia.' For example, when the gap between written Latin and the vernacular varieties spoken throughout the Western half of the Roman Empire became too great, the Romance languages evolved, a process which became irreversible once these varieties had begun to acquire a written form and were no longer regarded as corrupted spoken versions of the pure language, Latin.

A wide gap between written and spoken varieties, on the other hand, is the state of affairs of languages, such as Arabic, Tamil, or Sinhalese, which exist in diglossia. Their speech communities had developed a literary tradition in connection with great cultural achievements of a religious and/or artistic nature and subsequently did not allow the written language to deviate from the ideal and thus to adjust to the changes of the spoken language. The result was an unbridgeable rift between spoken and written language which did not lead to linguistic divergence only because the (for the most part illiterate) people continued to regard the written variety as the 'real' and correct manifestation of their language (see De Silva 1976; and Britto 1986). Ibrahim (see chapter 3) demonstrates that such a state of affairs creates considerable problems for the adaptation of Arabic because the spoken vernaculars are so far removed from the written standard that convergence is hard to bring about, and moreover that written standard is, for ideological reasons, not easily subjected to deliberate intervention.

As these examples may illustrate, the written language more often than not was not the same as the vernacular. In some cases this is more obvious than in others, especially where the written language is actually a different language and not only a different variety of the same language. In the latter sense, there is of course always a difference between spoken and written language, if only because speech and writing are different modes of expression and serve different communicative functions. Generally, writing enlarges the functional potential of languages. However, there are also cases where languages are gradually reduced to those functions usually carried out in writing, as for instance, Medieval Latin or Hebrew, while spoken registers degenerate. But in such cases writing holds a potential on the basis of which the dormant spoken registers of such a language can be re-established. What language adaptation means under such circumstances, and what kinds of problems have to be dealt with is discussed for the exemplary case of Hebrew by Rabin (see chapter 2).

What concerns us here is that writing, while potentially introducing diglossia into every speech community,[1][2] is always instrumental in language adaptation. That writing does not just duplicate speech is by now a common-place.[13] It changes the nature of verbal communication as well as the speakers' attitude to, and awareness of, their language. Writing makes a society language-conscious; it is a 'more advanced and specialized form of adaptive behaviour than speech' (Harris 1980: 13). Goody (1977) calls written language 'decontextualized' and stresses its importance for a discontinuous organization of the perceptual world. The entire meta-linguistic terminology – parts of speech, sentences, meanings, words, morphemes, phonemes, etc. – is a product of the 'language experts,' the *grammar*ians whose raw material is language in written form. The dictionary, this important institution of the Western tradition, is perhaps the most obvious example of how writing allows us to take a discontinuous view of language and to organize its parts in which-ever way we see fit.

Writing thus makes it possible to create or codify a standard which becomes independent of an individual or a group of speakers. Gottsched, the most prominent of German grammarians of the eighteenth century engaged in adapting the German language, explicitly acknowledges its importance in this respect. He had no doubts about the historical priority of speech, but, empha-sizing, as he did, cultivated rather than natural language, he conceded written language the role of the model spoken language should conform to: 'Before the invention of letters, all languages of the world were rugged and unshapely. Their first proper form they owe to writing' (Gottsched 1748, Section 3, §1).[14]

This attitude has been branded the 'tyranny of writing' by de Saussure because he failed to appreciate the fact that 'the emergence of *homo scribens* makes a radical and henceforward irreversible difference to what a language is' (Harris 1980: 14). In the present context this difference is particularly important as it implies, among other things, the possibility of depersonalized and consciously designed strategies for language adaptation: the cataloguing of grammatical rules, the compilation of word lists, the dissemination of such reference works throughout the speech community in the interest of establish-ing a unifying norm, as well as the coming into existence of entirely new genres of language use. *Homo scribens* created an educated world that requires teachers, schools, curricula, textbooks, methods, mother tongue instruction, and the like, a world, in other words, in which the systematic advancement of knowledge is cultivated, verbalized, and recorded. Furthermore, he created a symbol of identity, a powerful means of defining groups across social strata. Writing provides a previously low-status language with prestige and thus furnishes a major attitudinal pre-condition for adaptation attempts to suc-ceed. However, it also is an essential technical pre-condition inasmuch as it makes possible the systematic organization of word lists and thereby the differentiation and enlargement of vocabulary,[15] as well as the fixation of an authoritative grammar for schooling and deliberate language spread.

Writing thus plays a very intricate role for language adaptation. On the one hand, it introduces novel stylistic varieties and the possibility of freezing a given linguistic state, which, in a speech community with low literacy, will lead to diglossia whose low variety will then, at some point, make adaptation necessary; on the other hand, it provides the attitudinal and technical prerequisites that make language adaptation possible. At least for the purposes of modern communication in our times, there can be no language adaptation without writing.

Natural versus artificial

Written language was once called 'an unnatural substitute for the spoken word' (Jespersen 1933: 670). While we would call it an extension or supplement of speech rather than a substitute, we can accept Jespersen's qualification of 'unnatural.' As opposed to speech, writing is unnatural in the sense that languages do not develop a written norm without conscious effort. Writing itself is an artefact, and as such it is the main agent of introducing artificial elements into the so-called natural languages. The notion of 'artificial language' is most readily associated with computer software, but actually very much is artificial in natural language,[16] which is, after all, in keeping with the fact that culture is part of human nature.

To distinguish the natural from the artificial in human languages is not easy, but clearly there are tendencies of linguistic development that are more artificial than others. Many languages have been influenced by puristic attitudes. Reformers, who, usually under the impact of nationalistic ideology, are concerned about the purity of their language, set themselves the task of purifying the language by divesting it of foreign loans. In some cases such efforts are just part of the national culture and have long tradition, as in France where guarding the language against foreign influence is part of the routine of the Academy. In other cases they are tied to a unique political event such as the conception and adoption of the archaizing *katharevousa* as the 'pure' and formal variety of Greek at the beginning of the nineteenth century at a time of flourishing nationalism and liberation from Turkish rule. The *katharevousa* is a prime example of artificial features being deliberately introduced into a language.[17]

Innovation in language is necessary because there is a constant need to name novel objects, processes, and relations. When a speech community wants to express a concept for which there is no word in its language it can either borrow one from another language or coin a new one; it can, in other words, borrow the form and the meaning or the meaning only.[18] As the chapters of this book demonstrate for various languages, both of these borrowing strategies are very important in the context of language adaptation. They also show, however, that different speech communities have different preferences, and that these preferences may change in the course of time. In the present context one example has to suffice to illustrate this point. The lists of chemical elements in Table 1.1 reveal the preference of different

Table 1.1. *Terms of chemical elements in six languages*

Greek	Italian	English	German	Japanese	Chinese
μάλαμα	oro	gold	Gold	kin (金)	jīn (金)
ὀξυγὸνον	ossigeno	oxygen	Sauerstoff	sanso (酸素)	yǎng (氧)
οὐράνιον	uranio	uranium	Uran	uran (ウラン)	yóu (铀)
σαμάριον	samario	samarium	Samarium	samarium (サマリウム)	shān (钐)

strategies in different languages, as well as a curious transformation of words of different origins through the languages in question.

Just comparing the names of the above four elements across these six languages is very telling. The more recent the discovery, the more uniform the names. For elements such as gold that happen to exist in pure form in nature, one can expect to find old national words in practically all languages. For elements such as hydrogen and oxygen which are associated with chemical substances or reactions readily perceivable in, and of overt importance for, everyday life, some languages have terms composed of native morphological material, such as the German *Sauerstoff* and its Japanese translation *sanso*. Further, terms for elements that have no connection with everyday life are very similiar for most languages, except for minor morphological adjustments and formal differences betraying the immediate source or model language, for example German in the case of the Japanese *uran*. In Chinese, however, the nativization is complete. While the phonetic shape of the word is supposed to approximate to that of the first syllable of the English 'uranium,' the number of syllables is reduced to fit the monosyllabic pattern of all Chinese terms for chemical elements. The script, moreover, makes the word indistinguishable from naturally developed forms. Finally, the term for the last element is treated like a proper name in all languages. There is no composite meaning that could be translated, that is rendered in a different form in a different language. Again Chinese is the apparent exception, but *shān* is really a truncated form of 'samarium.'

The word *sanso* illustrates a very common process in Japanese involving three different languages: it is a Japanese loan translation coined on a German model making use of Chinese roots, *san* and *so* being the Sino-Japanese readings of 酸, 'acid,' and 素, 'simple,' respectively. Again, the foreign origin of the term is obscured by the writing system, which in both Chinese and Japanese plays an important role in word formation, determining adaptation strategies.

Interestingly, scientific terms have frequently been re-imported into

Chinese from Japanese, as the Japanese word for 'telephone,' *denwa* (电话) illustrates. The two characters literally mean 'electric speech' and are as such understandable to Chinese, too. In Chinese they are read *diànhuà*. This word has replaced the earlier, more cumbersome term 德律风 (*délyùfeng*), which was coined to imitate the sound shape of 'telephone.' The phonetic shape of re-imported character compound words in Chinese is different from Japanese, but in writing, the words are the same in both languages. The peculiar role Chinese characters play for language adaptation in both Chinese and Japanese is explained in some detail by Pasierbsky, and Sugito and Takada, respectively. From their three chapters it becomes obvious how important the writing system and the written language are for augmenting the vocabularies of these languages. Chinese characters in East Asia serve a function similar to that of Greek and Latin roots for terminology formation in European languages. Of 62 terms used in physics, Miyajima (1981) reports, 26 have the same written form in Chinese and Japanese, while 22 are similar in a way comparable with the similarity of French and English technical terms. The written language, this entirely artificial stratum of linguistic expression, thus constitutes an interlinguistic link and a multifunctional resource for terminology formation. For Chinese and for Japanese, too, this artefact has become the language's second nature, through which borrowing and vocabulary innovation is filtered.

Under such circumstances of intense mutual contact, borrowing is a multi-layer process making use of elements that are frequently recycled.[19] The direction of borrowing is variable. For many centuries Japanese has relied on Chinese loans for adapting to the communicative needs of more refined culture. Since modern times, however, it has begun repaying its debts, increasingly so since Japan's technological lead over China and the rest of Asia has been consolidated.[20] Through the medium of Chinese characters Japan has become an exporter of technical terms. On the other hand, it has turned away from Chinese as a source, absorbing instead an enormous influx of English loans. Again, this shift is not exceptional, but rather typical for language adaptation processes.

In Old English times, to cite another example, it was the fashion to form native words for new notions – for those of Christianity, for instance. Later, in the early Renaissance, the preference shifted to borrowing from French and using material from the classical languages (see Jespersen 1933: 667).

That languages, or rather, speech communities, at various historical periods should turn from one adaptation strategy and one preferred source of innovation to another is usually a reflection of social and political changes. Such strategy shifts are evolutionary answers to problems coming into existence through rapid changes in the socio-economic and politico-cultural habitat of a speech community. To some extent they are conscious, and thus there are guided as well as unguided phases or aspects of language adaptation.

Natural, unconscious development has sometimes led to a great similarity of forms which it is important to distinguish between. In such circumstances conscious intervention may be desirable. Jespersen (1933: 666) cites a British order of 1844 to use 'port' instead of 'larboard' because of the latter's similarity with 'starboard.' At a time when terminologies are becoming increasingly complex for a great variety of different fields of science, technology, management, and administration, and when international communication is increasing rapidly, the need is felt by some to co-ordinate language adaptation efforts on the level of terminology formation across languages. Braun (see chapter 11) discusses some of the requirements and implications of such efforts.

Notice, however, that adaptation processes are not restricted to vocabulary supplementation; grammatical changes may also be involved. Yanabu (1979: 14ff), for instance, observes that pre-modern Japanese texts did not usually consist of an array of complete sentences with subjects and predicates exhibiting a finite verb form at the end; rather, loose concatenations of clauses were much more common:[21] phrases merged into each other connected by parts of speech that would have one grammatical function in the first and another in the second. The finite sentence as the basic unit of Japanese texts, Yanabu contends, is really a result of the enormous amount of translations of Western books accompanying the opening of Japan to the West in the nineteenth century. In a sense, then, Japanese was influenced consciously and artificially in the Meiji period mainly by those intellectuals who devoted themselves to the difficult task of translating philosophical, scientific, and literary books from Western languages. Again, this amounted to creating new genres, notably scientific discourse and naturalistic prose, which had never before existed in written Japanese. As the modernization of Japan was so sudden and drastic, its linguistic repercussions are particularly obvious and thus promising for more in-depth research on language adaptation.

What the Japanese example highlights is the important role of translation, and hence of the bilingual individual, for language adaptation. Translating, of course, presupposes a very conscious attitude towards language and sometimes requires the conscious stretching of grammatical rules. It is also very revealing as to the limitations of a given language relative to the expressive power of another. A very interesting example is that of John Dryden. This man of letters who called his language 'uncultivated and unpolished' and as late as 1693 complained that no tolerable dictionary or grammar of it was available, in his 'Dedication to *Troilus and Cressida*' reports how he relied on translation for clarity:

I am often put to a stand, in considering whether what I write be the idiom of the tongue, or false grammar, and nonsense couched beneath the specious name of Anglicism; and have no other way to clear my doubts, but *by translating my English into Latin*, and thereby trying what sense the words will bear in a more stable language.

(cited in Bolton 1972: 44, emphasis added)

Dryden's mildly perplexing trick of translating sentences of his mother tongue into Latin and then putting them back into English in order to understand their true structure and meaning clearly reflects a belief (1) in universal grammar and (2) the fact that this universal grammar is incorporated in Latin rather than English. This belief that grew out of the general European esteem for the (written) classical languages in medieval and early Renaissance times brought into the Western grammatical tradition a number of concepts that could hardly have been derived from the study of European vernacular languages alone. More significantly, it is not a farfetched assumption that the practice of matching English against the 'more stable' model of Latin should have influenced its development. For one thing, the Latin standards of clarity and precision were imposed on English, and one obvious way of doing justice to them was to depart as little as possible from the grammar of the Latin text to be translated. Also, in the Renaissance, Latin and Greek were still held in high esteem and many writers continued to write Latin. Milton started his career as a Latin poet, and he continued to write in Latin until he was almost fifty. It seems most likely that both conscious and unconscious interferences from Latin influenced the grammar of written English (as well as other European languages).

The explicit Renaissance debate about English and its adequacy for literary purposes is a reflection of the intellectuals' dependence on the scaffold of Latin grammar. Throughout the Old and Middle periods English had developed quite naturally. In particular, the enormous absorption of French vocabulary after the Norman conquest happened without conscious attention or guidance. Significantly, English was hardly used in writing for several centuries after that, as government was conducted in French and learning in Latin. When in the Renaissance the desire grew to elevate the status of English *vis-à-vis* French and Latin, it was often felt wanting and its appropriateness as a literary language was in doubt. It is not surprising, therefore, that from that time on many learned men raised their voices, calling for a conscious regulation of English. It was discovered, for instance, that most writers of English were in the habit of placing prepositions at the ends of sentences – a pratice that was clearly at variance with both Latin authors and the etymology of the word 'preposition.' Dryden therefore established the rule that terminal prepositions should be avoided at all cost, a prescription that survives to the present day as the kind of linguistic pedantry, up with which, Churchill said, he would not put. Many other artificial features entered the language in that period. It was the spirit of the time that the English language was deficient in many respects and needed guidance. Samuel Johnson, the great lexicographer, understood his task as weeding out the most outrageous improprieties of the language:

Every language has its anomalies, which though inconvenient, and in themselves once unnecessary, must be tolerated among the imperfections of human beings, and which require only to be registered, that they may not be increased, and ascertained, that they may not be confounded; but every language has likewise its improprieties and absurdities, which it is the duty of the lexicographer to correct or proscribe.

(Johnson 1747/1963: 4)

It was in the Renaissance, with the spread of literacy, that dictionaries and grammars acquired an authority almost like that of the Ten Commandments (Harris 1980). By providing the insignia of upgrading the prestige of the vernacular languages and by bringing them out from under the shadow of Latin, they became institutions in their own right whose task it was to ascertain the language, to free it from impurities, and to stabilize it.

Again, the English example illustrates a rather general phenomenon. The need or desire to use a language in writing produces an awareness of its shortcomings relative to a standard defined by the usage of another, more advanced language. Writing, in turn, produces the remedies by stimulating the production of reference works whose authority is reinforced by the need to compete with the prestige of the model language. That way the course of development of a language is sometimes influenced in an artificial manner.

Conclusions

In this inquiry we have tried to show that languages at certain points of their historical development are found wanting by members of their own speech communities, and that with respect to certain communicative functions they *are* wanting. The reasons for such a state of affairs can be many; typically external socio-economic influences on a given speech community are highly relevant. Political domination, or the actual or alleged cultural superiority of neighbors, invaders, or colonizers may affect the language loyalty of the trend setters of linguistic conduct – the learned and affluent – in such a way that they adopt a foreign language for purposes of higher communication. As a result, certain registers of higher communication remain underdeveloped because the vernacular language is never used for such purposes. This being so, a language acquires a reputation of being inadequate.

Another reason for a language's inadequacy may be that communicative functions are introduced into a speech community very suddenly through external contact, so that the language cannot adjust gradually and develop the registers appropriate for these novel tasks.

That languages are not adequately equipped to fulfill the communicative needs of their speech communities is an abnormal state of affairs; however, a review of language histories reveals that it is not all that uncommon. If a speech community fails to react to such a state of affairs, its language may degenerate and eventually disappear. But if it does react the language may very well adapt and regain full communicative adequacy. The measures that can be taken to achieve this goal have here been subsumed under the concept of 'language adaptation,' a notion which may help us to appreciate the fact that the relative inadequacy of languages is not a modern phenomenon typical of developing countries whose languages are nowadays in need of adaptation. A careful look at languages, such as German, English, Japanese, and others which are now fully adapted to the needs of modern communication in science, technology, and management, reveals that, not too long ago, they too were felt to be deficient relative to the ideals of more highly developed languages. Yet they were successfully adapted to the demands of modern communication.

Language adaptation is, for the most part, a gradual and continuous process that takes place almost unnoticed by the speech community. In times of linguistic crisis, however, conscious intervention may be called for. Language adaptation then becomes a political goal whose substance exhibits remarkable similarities across languages and historical epochs. The values in question can be summarized as uniformity, precision, elegance, purity of form, allegiance to literary tradition, and elaboration through coinage of new terms. For achieving these goals, writing is always instrumental, and so are features typical of literate societies – depersonalized standards, reference works, and schools.

The well-adaptedness of a language is not necessarily a permanent state of affairs, and neither is maladaptedness. Just as a language may be a donor language in one period and a borrower in another, its relative adaptedness is a matter of potential change. While nowadays, with English hailed as the first really universal language, the chances of adapting the languages of post-colonial societies to the needs of modern communication are often seen to be rather poor, one should not forget that the prestige of Latin was a formidable obstacle for the adaptation of all modern European languages. The decisive factor of successful language adaptations has always been the determination of the speech communities concerned rather than the structural and lexical make-up of their languages.

Notes

1 'Einmal findet sich in allen Geschichten, daß gemeiniglich die Nation und die Sprache zugleich geblüht.' (All translations in the text are my own.)
2 'Massen wenig rechtschaffene Bücher vorhanden, so in deutscher Sprache geschrieben und den rechten Schmack oder Saft haben ... Wir schreiben gemeiniglich solche Bücher, darinnen nichts als zusammengestoppelte Abschriften aus anderen Sprachen genommen.'
3 'Es ereignet sich aber einiger abgang bei unserer Sprache in den Dingen, so man weder sehen noch fühlen, sondern allein durch Betrachtung erreichen kann: als bei Ausdrücken der Gemütsbewegungen, auch der Tugenden und Laster und vieler Beschaffenheiten, die zur Sittenlehre und Regierungskunst gehören; dann ferner bei den noch mehr abgezogenen und abgefeimten Erkenntnissen, so die Liebhaber der Weisheit in ihrer Denkkunst und in der allgemeinen Lehre von den Dingen unter dem Namen der Logik und Metaphysik auf die Bahn bringen.'

4 'Am allermeisten aber ist unser Mangel, wie gedacht, bei den Wörtern zu spüren, die sich auf das Sittenwesen, die Leidenschaften des Gemüts, den gemeinlichen Wandel, die Regierungssachen und allerhand bürgerliche Lebens- und Staatsgeschäfte beziehen, wie man wohl befindet, wenn man etwas aus andern Sprachen in die unsrige übersetzen will.'

5 '[1] Aufsuchung guter Wörter, die schon vorhanden, aber jetzt, weil sie wenig beobachtet werden, zu rechter Zeit nicht beifallen, [2] ferner durch Wiederbringung alter verlorener Worte, so von besonderer Güte; [3] auch durch Einbürgerung oder Naturalisierung fremder Benennungen, wo sie solches sonderlich verdienen, [4] und letztens, wo kein anderes Mittel, durch wohlbedächtliche Erfindung oder Zusammensetzung neuer Worte.'

6 'Die Reinigkeit der Sprache, Rede und Schrift besteht darin, dass sowohl die Worte und Redensarten gut deutsch lauten als dass die Grammatik oder Sprachkunst gebührend beobachtet.'

7 'Ob nun schon wir Deutschen uns also desto weniger zu verwundern oder auch zu schämen haben, das unsere Grammatik noch nicht in willkommenem Stande, so dünkt mich doch gleichwohl, sie sei noch allzuviel davon entfernt und habe daher eine grose Verbesserung nötig ... Dies würde zu unserm Ruhm gereichen ... und den von etlichen gefassten Wahn benehmen, als ob unsere Sprache der Regeln unfähig und aus dem Gebrauch fast allein erlernt werden müsste.'

8 'Es ist demnach die Meinung nicht, dass man in der Sprache zum Puritaner werde und mit einer abergläubischen Furcht ein fremdes aber bequemes Wort als eine Totsünde vermeide, dadurch aber sich selbst entkräfte und seiner Rede den Nachdruck nehme.'

9 Gottsched, for instance, rephrased Leibniz's words (quoted above – see note 7) in the preface to his *Deutsche Sprachkunst* when he says: 'here we have to join forces ... to free them from the prejudice that our language couldn't possibly be subjected to rules.'

10 It would be extremely interesting to compare the language movements in India (see, for example, Anamalai 1979) with the German *Sprachvereine* (see, for example, Blackall 1959).

11 See Fishman (1972), Weinstein (1983), and Coulmas (1985) for more detailed accounts of the nexus of language and nationalism.

12 Notice, for instance, what Pawley (1984: 36) remarks about English: 'Printed texts in English are normally in a dialect that departs more or less from the vernacular; this is particularly true of texts used at secondary school level. Children thus have the job of learning to read and write in a partly-new language.'

13 See, for example, Coulmas 1981; Coulmas and Ehlich 1983; Vachek 1973; Tannen 1982; and Feldbusch 1985. For reviews of the recent literature, see also Akinnaso 1982 and Slaughter 1985.

14 'Alle Sprachen der Welt ... sind vor der Erfindung der Buchstaben sehr rauh und unförmig gewesen. Ihre erste ordentliche Gestalt haben sie der Schrift zu danken gehabt.'

15 The early development of Castilian is a good example. Its adaptation for national purposes was fostered by King Alfonso X (1252–1284): 'These three decades marked a renaissance in science and letters around the court. A lexicographer himself, the king selected or adapted Castilian words to replace Latin or Arabic technical terms. A growing number of writers – particularly Jews who preferred

the spoken language rather than "Catholic" Latin – used Castilian in their trans-lations and original works; this effort made possible its use in government docu-ments' (Weinstein 1979: 347).

16 Cf. Paul's remark on the natural and the artificial in language: 'In addition to his natural language which, up to that point, he has used exclusively, an individual learns an artificial language closer to the [written] norm. In the modern countries this is brought about, for the most part, through school instruction whereby one learns the written language in the strict sense as well as a vernacular which approximates to the written language' (Paul 1886: 415).

17 Cf. Browning's (1969: 107) very harsh judgment on the Greek nationalists' attempt at purifying their language: 'The katharevousa was created in the second quarter of the nineteenth century by progressive "purification" of the new demotic, and introduction of more and more elements from the learned tongue. It is always macaronic in character, mingling together incongruously old and new, and studded with false archaisms, hypercorrect forms, and mere blunders.'

18 See Haugen (1950) for an insightful comparison of kinds of linguistic borrowing.

19 A similar situation is found in modern Greek. Scientific terminology consists to a large extent of compounds formed from Greem elements in a language other than Greek such as French or English. From there they are (re-)imported into modern Greek (see also Ehlich and Braun in this volume).

20 Cf. Kindaichi (1957: 164f): 'There are [in Japanese] two kinds of Chinese character words dealing with abstract expressions: (1) those borrowed from China, and (2) those coined in Japan as translations of Western words imported during the introduction of Western culture during the early years of the Meiji period ... Thus scientific essays can be written in Japanese thanks to the existence of such words; and in this regard Japanese is a civilized language, qualitatively different from the languages of primitive people' (my translation). While nowadays we would take exception to the qualification of languages as primitive, it is clear that Kindaichi put his finger on an important point distinguishing Japanese from many other non-Western languages.

21 'The Japanese felt uneasy about a sentence coming to a definite conclusion, rather admiring sentences that looked as if they would end but went on for several pages' (Kindaichi 1957: 173; my translation).

References

Akinnaso, F. N. 1982. On the Difference between Spoken and Written Language. *Language and Speech*, 25: 97–125.

Anamalai E (ed.) 1979. *Language Movements in India*. Mysore.

Blackall, Eric A. 1959. *The Emergence of German as a Literary Language*. Cambridge.

Bolton, W. F. 1972. *A Short History of Literary English*. London.

Britto, Francis 1986. *Diglossia. A Study of the Theory with Application to Tamil*. Washington, D.C.

Browning, Robert 1969. *Medieval and Modern Greek*. London.

Coulmas, Florian 1981. *Über Schrift*. Frankfurt am Main.

1985. *Sprache und Staat. Studien zu Sprachplanung und Sprachpolitik*. Berlin, New York.

1987. What Writing can do to Language. In S. P. X. Battestini (ed.), *Georgetown University Round Table on Languages and Linguistics 1986*. Washington, D.C.

1988. What are National Languages Good for? In F. Coulmas (ed.), *With Forked Tongues*. Ann Arbor.

Coulmas, Florian and Ehlich, Konrad (eds.) 1983. *Writing in Focus*. Berlin, New York, Amsterdam.

De Silva, M. W. S. 1976. *Diglossia and Literacy*. Mysore.

Di Bona, Joseph E. 1970. *Language Change and Modernization. The Development of a Hindi–English, English–Hindi Glossary of technical Terms in the Field of Education*. Ahmedabad.

Feldbusch, Elisabeth 1985. *Geschriebene Sprache*. Berlin, New York.

Ferguson, Charles A. 1968. Language Development. In J. A. Fishman, J. Das Gupta, and C. A. Ferguson (eds.), *Language Problems of Developing Nations*. New York.

1971. Contrasting Patterns of Literacy Acquisition in a Multilingual Nation. In W. Whitely (ed.), *Language Use and Social Change*. Oxford and New York.

Fishman, Joshua A. 1972. *Language and Nationalism*. Rowley, Mass.

Gandhi, Mohandes K. 1965. *Our Language Problem*, ed. A. T. Hingorani. Bombay.

Goody, Jack (ed.) 1968. *Literacy in Traditional Societies*. London, Cambridge.

1977. *The Domestication of the Savage Mind*. Cambridge, London.

1983. Literacy and Achievement in the Ancient World. In F. Coulmas and K. Ehlich (eds.), *Writing in Focus*. Berlin, New York, Amsterdam.

Gottsched, Johann Christoph 1748. Deutsche Sprachkunst. Nach den Mustern der besten Schriftsteller des vorigen und itzigen Jahrhunderts. *Ausgewählte Werke*, vol. 8, ed. H. Penzl. Berlin, New York 1978.

Graff, Harvey J. 1979. *The Literacy Myth. Literacy and Social Structure in the 19th Century City*. New York.

Haas, W. (ed.) 1982. *Standard Languages. Spoken and Written*. Manchester.

Harris, Roy 1980. *The Language Makers*. Ithaca, New York.

Haugen, Einar 1950. The Analysis of Linguistic Borrowing. *Language*, 26, 2: 210–231.

Heath, Shirley Brice 1980. The Functions and Uses of Literacy. *Journal of Communication*, 30: 123–133.

Jespersen, Otto 1933. Nature and Art in Language. In *Selected Writings*. London. *Samuel Johnson's Dictionary 1747*. A modern selection ed. E. L. McAdam and George Milne 1963. New York.

Kindaichi Haruhiko 1957. *Nihongo* [The Japanese Language]. Tokyo.

Khubchandani, Lachman M. 1981. *Language, Education, Social Justice*. Poona.

Leibniz, Gottfried Wilhelm 1683. Ermahnung an die Deutschen. In *G. W. Leibniz Deutsche Schriften*, ed. W. Schmied-Kowarzik. Leipzig 1916.

1697. Von der deutschen Sprachpflege (Unvorgreifliche Gedanken betreffend die Ausübung und Verbesserung der deutschen Sprache). In *G. W. Leibniz Deutsche Schriften*, ed. W. Schmied-Kowarzik. Leipzig 1916.

Miyajima Tatsuo 1981. A Study of Specialized Terminology: The Problem of Technical Terms. In *The National Language Research Institute Report 68*. Tokyo.

Paul, Hermann 1886. *Prinzipien der Sprachgeschichte*. Halle.

Pawley, Andrew 1984. School English is Nobody's Mother Tongue. *Papers from the 20th Extension Course Lectures*. Auckland.

Sato Habein, Yaeko 1984. *The History of the Japanese Written Language*. Tokyo.

Slaughter, M. 1985. Literacy and Society. *International Journal of the Sociology of Language*, 56: 113–129.

Southworth, Franklin C. 1985. The Social Context of Language Standardization in India. In N. Wolfson and J. Manes (eds.), *Language of Inequality*. Berlin, New York, Amsterdam.

Stubbs, Michael 1980. *Language and Literacy. The Sociolinguistics of Reading and Writing*. London.

Tannen, Deborah (ed.) 1982. *Spoken and Written Language: Exploring Orality and Literacy*. Norwood, New Jersey.

Vachek, Josef 1973. *Written Language. General Problems and Problems of English*. The Hague.

Weinstein, Brian 1979. Language Strategists: Redefining Political Frontiers on the Basis of Linguistic Choices. *World Politics*, 31, 3: 345–364.

1983. *The Civic Tongue*. New York, London.

Yanabu Akira 1979. *Hikaku Nihongoron* [Comparative Japanology]. Tokyo.

2 Terminology development in the revival of a language: the case of contemporary Hebrew

CHAIM RABIN

The historical background

Words meaning 'revival' or 'rebirth' ('renaissance') are often used to characterize processes of broadening the use of a language, whether this is by increasing the percentage of users of that language within a community historically associated with it, as in the case of the Irish revival, or by introducing it into new fields of use within its community, whether these uses were previously reserved for another language (e.g. in diglossia, or by employing a majority language within the political structure), or such uses had previously been non-existent among the users of that language, as is the case in societies acquiring for the first time the use of writing or of written literature of a prestigious type. The last-named type of 'revival' was typical of the rise of new nations in Europe in the nineteenth century. The use of the term 'revival' is attested by the development of Yiddish artistic, Western-style literature, and was employed in the first article, published in 1879, by Eliezer Ben-Yehuda (1857–1922), regarded as the orginator of the 'revival of Hebrew,' with reference to the Hebrew writings of his Jewish contemporaries in Eastern Europe.[1] At that time, Hebrew was in most Jewish communities only written, while the spoken activities were in the language of the country where that particular community lived as a minority, or in a Jewish language developed at some remote point in history out of that majority language, or in one completely different from the majority language because it had been carried by Jewish emigrants from the country where that Jewish language had developed.

Just as other 'high languages' in diglossia situations were occasionally spoken in contexts where the 'low language' could not be used (for instance, with strangers using the same 'high' language, but not the same colloquial medium) or by certain privileged social groups in formal circumstances, so Hebrew was used in the Middle Ages when Jews from different countries met, or when Jews wished to converse in the presence of non-Jews and not be understood. This is a natural consequence of the fact that command of a language as a written form of expression can, by an act of will, be applied also in speech (without acquiring thereby the registers of spoken language). In the case of Hebrew, in the two generations preceding the mass revival of the spoken language, such occasional spoken use had been intensified in the bigger cities in Palestine with large Jewish populations, where communities from many countries had settled in separate quarters. Each of them guarded their own Jewish language and traditional pronunciation of Hebrew for sacred purposes, but they bought and sold in markets frequented by all communities, and there, not having any other language in common, they spoke Hebrew in the pronunciation of Oriental Jews (see Parfitt 1972). This being a purely utilitarian lingua franca, we have no written records to show what it was like. It is therefore impossible to know whether any of it was absorbed into the Hebrew spoken after the revival, especially as the groups involved in it rejected the political implications of that revival. The Eastern European (Ashkenazi) part of this pre-Zionist population ('the Old Yishuv') still insist on using their former languages at home and in the community. The Oriental (Sephardic) part, while maintaining their former languages to some extent, speak Hebrew in a form basically identical with that of the Zionist population.

The idea of speaking Hebrew seems to have come to E. Ben-Yehuda about six months after he had composed his article – though before it was printed. In the article itself, spoken use of the language is merely mentioned as a possibility, 'if we want to do so.' It is possible that the contacts Ben-Yehuda had with exiled intellectuals from several new nations fighting for recognition convinced him of the role that spoken language played in the process of 'national rebirth.' As soon as his article appeared, it seems to have been interpreted by Jews in the Czarist Empire as a call for speaking Hebrew. Although most of the established Hebrew literary figures expressed their disagreement with this idea, as well as with the call for setting up a large settlement of a modern, secular character in Palestine, which is, in fact, the main message of his first article, societies for speaking Hebrew began to spring up in various parts of Eastern Europe. This was no doubt connected with the marked deterioration of the Jewish situation in Czarist Russia, which shattered the hopes of obtaining full citizen status and gave rise to mass emigration, mainly to America and Palestine. Ben-Yehuda, who had meanwhile moved to Jerusalem and started working towards the introduction of Hebrew as the language of instruction in the more modern schools, called upon the young emigrants from Russia to speak Hebrew. They responded by establishing all-Hebrew schools in the villages they founded and thus widening the circle of 'native Hebrew speakers,' the first of whom, in splendid isolation, had been Ben-Yehuda's first-born son.

I have not found out when the term 'revival' was first applied to the process of extending the use of Hebrew to everyday speech. Hebrew is, as far as I know, the only case where the 'high' variety of a diglossic language was expanded to replace the 'low' variety, or in this case the multiplicity of 'low' languages. It was in all probability this multiplicity which assured the success of spoken Hebrew in Palestine. There are other cases where 'high' languages in a more or less diglossic situation also became spoken registers. This happened with *Hochdeutsch*, literary German, in the nineteenth and twentieth centuries, and seems to be happening with literary Arabic in our own time. However, as the 'lower' language forms, though widely differing among each other, are closely related to the 'high' language, and are considered by the community as being 'the same language,' it would be more correct to speak in these two cases of a process of standardization rather than revival. The Jewish languages, by contrast, are all unrelated or only distantly related to Hebrew, so that in this case there is a real replacement.

This is the historical and social background to the adaptation of Hebrew to the needs of an advanced Western-type society. Hebrew in Israel now serves as the language of a sophisticated society – in a modern, often hyper-modern literature, in politics, newspapers, university teaching and research, and all the forms of expression customary in Western societies. The adaptation did not come as part of the Westernization of a traditional society, since the driving force were Jewish immigrants already Westernized, first from Eastern Europe, and afterwards also from central and western countries of Europe and from North America, who were willing, for ideological reasons, to adopt the Hebrew language, but required it to express their technical, intellectual, and literary needs, evolved in the use of the more developed European languages. The Jews from less developed countries were only drawn into this Western civilization gradually, and acquired the more sophisticated resources of the Hebrew language as part of their own Westernization. In this, as far as I am aware, Hebrew also stands more or less alone among the languages discussed in this book.

Three modernizations

Hebrew did not undergo a process of modernization for the first time in the nineteenth and twentieth centuries. It had done so at least twice in its long history. Once it happened during the period of the Second Temple and the Hellenization of the Middle East, that is roughly between 300 B.C. and A.D. 200, just before Hebrew ceased to be spoken. In this period it enlarged its vocabulary to deal with new tools, institutions and ideas introduced by Hellenistic Greek and Latin, the latter through the medium of Graecicized Latin words, and words created in Greek for Roman institutions and concepts. This was done by borrowing hundreds of Graeco-Roman words,[2] as well as by adapting the meanings of existent words and by forming new words. In this process, Hebrew was not alone: similar developments took place in Aramaic and Coptic, and some centuries later in Arabic, where the innovations were imported mainly through the medium of Aramaic, and again in the eighth and ninth centuries via Syriac, one of the Aramaic languages, when

Syriac scholars translated into Arabic Greek works of philosophy, natural science and medicine, using extant or specially prepared Greek–Syriac translations as intermediate stages. In Hebrew, the absorption of the new material was made easier by the contemporary abandonment of later Biblical Hebrew as the written standard and its replacement by Mishnaic Hebrew, a standardized form of the spoken language. It is possible too that the main innovation of Mishnaic Hebrew in the verb – the creation of a present tense based on the participle, where Biblical Hebrew had only two tenses, past and future, which shared the present between them – is due to the influence of Greek. The same development of the verb took place in Aramaic.

It is possible that a similar replacement of a classical form by a semi-colloquial one for modern subjects facilitated the penetration of loanwords and the formation of new Arabic words. The Syrian translators did not employ Classical Arabic, based upon the language of pre-Islamic poetry, controlled by grammarians and orthoepists, but 'Middle Arabic,' the form used by Christians and Jews, who were not admitted to the religious Muslim schools where the Classical language was taught. Middle Arabic, close to the colloquial language and without guidance by grammarians, easily absorbed new words and direct loans of Greek words.

The ideology of the Arab Classical language, however, as being the sole vehicle of poetry and artistic prose, influenced from the ninth century onwards the Jews, first in the East and later in Muslim Spain, to use their own ancient and grammarian-controlled language form, Biblical Hebrew, as the vehicle for poetry and artistic prose. This, in principle, should have left Mishnaic Hebrew (which by then had absorbed also many Biblical words) as the language for non-artistic prose, but the idea that Mishnaic Hebrew had in its time as a spoken language been the colloquial of the common people, or, as it was phrased, 'the language of the ancients,' looked too much like employing a colloquial for writing, a thing which by Arabic standards was out of the question. Biblical Hebrew could not be used because by definition new words could not be introduced into a Classical language and, in comparison to the extremely rich vocabulary of Classical Arabic, Biblical Hebrew, with its total salvaged vocabulary of about 7,000 words, was too poor to serve as a language for what was then modern scientific discourse. The 'insufficiency' of Hebrew is often mentioned by theorists as the reason why they had to use Middle Arabic, in Hebrew characters, to write scientific prose. In Christian Europe, on the other hand, where Medieval Latin was constantly being enriched with new words, and vernacular languages had started to be written, the enriched Mishnaic Hebrew continued to be written by Jews for all contemporary purposes.

The year 1135 saw the first mass expulsion of Jews from Muslim Spain. Many scholars went to the south of France and to northern Italy, and there some of them began to translate scientific Arabic writings by Jewish and Muslim authors into Hebrew for the local Jews. For this they used enriched

Mishnaic Hebrew, dealing with the need for technical terminology by forming calque derivations of Arabic words (which, as stated above, were largely calques of Greek words) and to a small extent by borrowing Arabic words, including loanwords from Greek (see Sarfatti 1968). The Hebrew language was extended by many hundreds of new words, as well as by grammatical constructions rendering Arabic ways of expression. The mixed language proved itself effective and viable, absorbing in the succeeding centuries concepts from European languages by calque formations, and also, increasingly, Aramaic words from the legal language of the Talmud.

In the eighteenth century, apparently under the influence of Western European classicism, Biblical Hebrew was taken up again as the language not only for poetry but also for modernist prose expressing European thought and literary genres. This so-called *Haskala* (Enlightenment) literature was cultivated and read by a small part of the Central and Eastern European Jewish population, while the vast majority continued to read the mixed Hebrew and even developed it into new literary styles. This was the situation at the time Ben-Yehuda published that first article, in 1879.

Since at that time the use of Biblical Hebrew was identified in public life with modernism and progress, and in principle no new words could be formed, but new concepts and objects could only be named by clumsy genitive constructions or by Biblical allusions containing several words, the revival of Hebrew speaking might well have been short-lived. However, soon after Ben-Yehuda's first article, we see Mishnaic words in otherwise Biblicizing texts of a discursive character, for instance in political articles in the press. The decisive innovation came in literature, through the rise of Realism. The novelist and short-story writer S. J. Rabinovich, better known under his pen-name Mendele Mokher Sefarim (Mendele the itinerant book hawker), had in 1863 stopped the publication of his own contemporary novel *Fathers and Sons*, written in Biblical Hebrew, and gone over to writing Yiddish, the language spoken by his characters in real life. In 1885, after writing in Yiddish for 22 years, he began to publish another novel in Hebrew, but this time in the mixed Hebrew of the majority of his readers.[3] It is significant that this innovation was taken up by almost all his contemporaries, and that by 1890 it had also penetrated into poetry. Already in the early 1880s, the majority of the new Hebrew speakers actually used this mixed language in speech. The new literary idiom had no barriers against new formations or foreign words. In particular, it was completely open to the absorption of Aramaic words. Thus, for reasons not directly connected with the spoken revival (which Mendele Mokher Sefarim opposed until the end of his life), Hebrew entered its period of total use in a shape which allowed for adaptation to the needs of the modern age.

Professor Uzzi Ornan, of the Hebrew University of Jerusalem, has prepared a dictionary of words added to the language between 1880 and 1920, comprising some thousands of words, both loans from European languages,

Arabic, and Turkish, and newly formed words from Hebrew elements. Ben-Yehuda himself invented hundreds of new Hebrew words, which he used in his newspapers, and there were some fertile word creators in the circle surrounding him, including his eldest son. Word invention came to be a kind of national sport, and was practiced by writers of Modern Hebrew literature, both in Palestine and in the Western part of the Jewish diaspora. The innovations of the better-known authors, whether nonce-words or accepted by other authors or the general public, were assiduously recorded by the dictionary makers, and in larger dictionaries, such as the one by Even-Shoshan (1966–1983), are given with reference to their first appearance.

From the Language Committee to the Academy for the Hebrew Language

As early as 1890, a body was set up to control and further vocabulary enlargement. Named the 'Language Committee,' it was composed of Ben-Yehuda and some teachers and natural scientists living in Jerusalem. The Committee ceased to function after six months, and the minutes we know were taken have disappeared. Fifteen years later, the Committee, under the same name, was revived as an enterprise of the Teachers' Union, who were worried that teachers in different places were inventing terminology for their subjects without contact with other schools, and pupils passing from one locality to another had difficulty in understanding the lessons. The first achievement of the new body was a dictionary of elementary mathematics. The method of dealing with word creation systematically for one subject at a time was continued, and is still the rule at present. Actually, most of the lists contain only a limited percentage of newly formed words (which are also not marked as such). Many of the words given which do not belong to the older stages of the language were created outside the Language Committee at various times, and their listing merely serves the function of official approval. Other words are taken from older periods of Hebrew, sometimes by changing their meaning. The saying of an early member of the Committee, the poet Ch. N. Bialik, is often quoted, that 'the best innovation is one that is not an innovation,' that is a word from the ancient texts, Hebrew or Aramaic. In 1953, the Language Committee was renamed the 'Academy for the Hebrew Language' (*Aqademiyah la-lashon ha-'ivrit*) and became an official body, whose decisions become law after they are countersigned by the Minister of Education and published in the Official Gazette *Reshumot*. The vocabulary lists are published as separate booklets and are supposed to oblige at least government departments to use the listed words in their publications. The Academy, like its predecessor, also engages in language standardization. It has produced rules for spelling, tables of transliteration of Hebrew proper names and place names into the Latin alphabet, rules for the transliteration of foreign names into Hebrew characters and for the spelling of foreign words, as well as rules for punctuation, and a variety of decisions on grammar, including rules for the inflection of all noun patterns. In actual fact, the legal authority of the Academy is largely illusory. Its rules for punctuation and for spelling unvocalized texts[4] are ignored by the public, and are not taught in the schools; the transliteration system was adopted for signs on inter-urban highways only after a long time and is still largely ignored in street names. The Academy's decisions on grammar are, at least officially, taught in the schools. The reason for this limited success is probably that the government has no machinery for forcing linguistic decisions upon the public or upon the schools, and relies on the Academy to work for the acceptance of its own decisions. The Academy, however, is a scholarly body without the inclination or ability to make propaganda or to persuade other bodies to carry out its decisions. The terminology decisions, on the other hand, enjoy great success. The public appears to believe that the Academy regulates everything in the language and are interested in its vocabulary innovations and grammatical decisions, even though they are mostly ignorant of what has actually been decided and often ascribe to the Academy decisions which are either different from the ones it made, or refer to matters the Academy has never dealt with. Yet the terminology booklets do not sell well and newspapers have proved to be unwilling to print word lists or to report on important innovations of the Academy. The most successful publication is a series of wall sheets giving selected terms established for a certain occupation or science, accompanied by some grammatical and spelling rules, and lavishly illustrated, which are put up in schools, offices, and workshops. The principal success of the Academy, however, lies in the rapid acceptance of its professional and scientific terminology lists by the practitioners of those activities. Apart from the need of professions for a unified and clear terminology, this success is also due to the way in which those terminologies are discussed and established.

Terminology work

Each terminology committee is composed of between one to three members of the Academy and a usually larger number of practitioners of the field in question. It is the latter who draw up a list of the terms required in the subject, in English, and accompanied by Hebrew terms already employed in the profession. In the meetings, each term is examined as to its correctness in Hebrew, that is its form and the meanings of the word in older literature. It is ascertained whether the same word is used in some other list by a different profession in a sense different from that needed in the list under discussion.[5] The professional members raise problems involved in the use of certain terms in their practice or in teaching. From time to time, partial word lists agreed by the committee are circulated to members of the Academy and to a large number of people in the profession. Criticism and alternative suggestions are received, discussed, and if accepted, incorporated in the list. The revised list is once more circulated among Academy members, and objectors are often invited to discuss their opinions with the Committee. The list, when complete, goes to a meeting of the Academy's Board of Terminology, which discusses items where Academy members insist on their objections, but the Board also raises objections of its own, which necessitate reconsideration by the Committee. In the next stage, the list and the points of dissension are discussed by a joint meeting of the Terminology Board and the Grammar Board. At one time, the list was discussed once more in the plenary meeting of the Academy, but this proved too time-consuming, and now only items where no agreement could be reached are presented to the plenum, who, after a discussion in which the professional committee members participate, and eventually after returning the list to the Committee for reconsideration, officially confirm the list by vote.

The future users of the terminology are thus involved at every stage of the discussion. The words have been seen by many members of the profession, and when the list is finally published most of it has already become familiar. It has often happened that terms came into professional use immediately after the first circular, but were in the future discussion replaced by others, as a result of which two different terms became current, each with a different shade of meaning. Only recently the Academy confirmed such a term which it had rejected, but this time in the changed usage given to it by the professionals.

Apart from the Academy, the army has its own language commission, and so have the police, the customs, and some other governmental bodies. There is some degree of co-operation. We can estimate, however, that the words created by all official bodies make up only a small part of word innovation when compared with those created by journalists, publicity experts, novelists, poets, and scientists. The way of creating new words is, however, the same in each case, even if certain procedures may be used more by one group than by another.

Some grammatical mechanisms

The vast majority of Hebrew words contain a root, that is a set of mostly three consonants, which is felt to have a meaning, though this meaning may be diversified by semantic shifts beyond recognition, or there may be roots homonymous from the outset, due to sound changes or to borrowing. All words also contain vowels, and some contain consonantal prefixes, infixes, and suffixes. These, and especially the words or parts of words without the consonantal affixes, are called 'patterns.' Since the reconstructed Proto-Semitic language had three short vowels and three long ones, and since certain combinations were excluded, the number of such patterns is limited. The theory developed by Jewish medieval grammarians and modern philologists is that in the noun some or all of these patterns had meaning. Inspection of the Biblical nouns does not support this theory, neither does early Classical Arabic. Similar derivational meaning is in no way prominent in nouns of the same pattern; moreover, many nouns are attested in several patterns without change of meaning. However, in late Biblical and Mishnaic Hebrew, a few meaningful patterns turn up, probably due to borrowing from Assyro-Babylonian, for example $C_1aC_2C_2\hat{a}C_3$ for 'professions.' Also the meanings of consonantal affixes in Biblical Hebrew are rather vague. The theory that vowel patterns have meaning may have arisen through generalizing from participles and verbal nouns, where in many cases the function is marked by vowel patterns, for example, $C_1\hat{o}C_2\hat{e}C_3$ 'active participle,' $C_1\hat{a}C_2\hat{u}C_3$[6] 'passive participle,' $C_1\hat{a}C_2\hat{o}C_3$ 'infinitive'. Once accepted, it was a self-fulfilling prophecy: large numbers of new nouns were created for meanings assumed to be those of the pattern, and old nouns and adjectives were sometimes reinterpreted to fit the theory. In Modern Hebrew this theory works like an automaton: $C_1\hat{a}C_2\hat{o}C_3(C_3)$ 'having the color of X,' $C_1aC_2C_2eC_3et$ (with fem, suffix) 'a disease with symptom X,' also 'an assembly of Xes,' $maC_1C_2eC_3$ 'a tool for purpose X,' $miC_1C_2\hat{a}C_3\hat{a}h$ 'a place or building where X is attended to,' $CaCC\hat{\imath}C$ 'X-able,' etc. Such derivations are freely made by Hebrew speakers, and immediately understood. A similar mechanism exists in the verb. Vowel patterns, doubling and affixes create new verbs with added meanings, mainly of a syntactic character: past form $C\hat{a}CaC$ 'he did X,' 'passive' $niC_1C_2aC_3$; $hiC_1C_2\hat{\imath}C_3$ 'he caused someone to do X,' 'passive' $huC_1C_2aC_3$; $hitCaCC\hat{e}C$ 'reflexive or mutual action.' A further derivation, with doubling of the second root letter, has no clear meaning in Modern Hebrew, and is used as a general means of denominative derivation; in Biblical Hebrew it seems to have indicated repeated action, though the theory taught in schools is that it denotes intensive action, a claim notoriously difficult to prove or, for that matter, to disprove.

As we stated above, the number of pure vowel patterns, even including consonant doubling (which is not pronounced in contemporary Hebrew, except for /f/, /v/, and /kh/ which become /p/, /b/, and /k/, respectively, when doubled) is severely limited. Also, the number of prefixes and suffixes inherited from older Hebrew is very small. Meanings are given in present-day word formation to certain suffixes, but they are so few that the same suffix has to represent multiple meanings, for instance -*ôn* denotes diminutive, a periodical appearing at X intervals, a printed collection of Xes, for example *shîr-ôn* 'song book,' and a small building made of X, for example *pax-ôn* 'a hut made of corrugated iron sheets.'

As did many European languages, Modern Hebrew is borrowing suffixes from other languages, such as -*ar* (already in Mishnaic Hebrew) from the Latin -*arius*, which came into English as -*er*; -*åtsyah* from Russian or Polish (cf. English -*ation*), originally Latin; -*ist* from some European language, originally Greek -*istês* (preserved in some Mishnaic Hebrew borrowings as -*istôs*); and from the Russian -*nik* (written -*nîq*, fem. -*nîqît*) 'adherent of X,' 'marked by characteristic X'; and -*tshik* (written -*cîq*) diminutive. It also happens that parts of words are separated as suffixes, the standard instance being -*trôn* as a suffix marking different kinds of theaters, abstracted from *teatron*, borrowed into Mishnaic Hebrew from the Greek *théatron*. Similar processes also exist in the verb. Mishnaic Hebrew has a few obviously derived verbs with the prefix *sh-*, the mark of the causative verb in Assyro-Babylonian and some other Semitic languages. At the beginning of the revival this prefix was occasionally used in this meaning to differentiate one causative from another of the same root. One of the instances was *shixzêr* 'he reconstructed,' as opposed to the normal Hebrew *hexzîr* 'he gave back,' 'he drove back.' The need to translate into Hebrew numerous verbs with the prefix *re-* caused this compound to be treated as a calque of 're-construct' (although *xâzar* does not mean 'to construct,' but 'to return'). Many *re-* verbs were translated in this way, which has become an additional verbal derivation, gradually ousting the older way of rendering *re-* verbs by adding after the verb the abverb *mê-xâdâsh,* 'anew.' No such possibilities were present in the existing grammar for translating other verbal prefixes from European languages, and the addition of adverbs is the only way they can be rendered.

Traditional Hebrew has a number of four-consonant roots, and these are handled in the verb by assimilating them to the above-mentioned 'intensive' derivation $C_1 iC_2 C_2 êC_3$, called *Piel*. The verbs with the *shi-* prefix were already conjugated that way in Mishnaic Hebrew. In principle, a denominative verb can be derived from any noun containing four or five consonants, whether these are a root or a form derived by affixes from a triconsonantal root. This provides us with further instances of the birth of new prefixes to verbs. Mishnaic Hebrew borrowed from Aramaic the formation of verbal nouns from the *Piel* derivation of the form $taC_1 C_2 ûC_3$. Such forms are now created for differentiation. From *shâ'al* 'to ask' the verbal noun is *she'êlâh*, in the meaning 'to borrow' it is *she'îlâh*, and in the meaning of 'police interrogation' it is *tish'ûl*. From this specialized term a new verb, *tish'êl*, is derived, and now the *ti-* derivation is also sometimes used where no *t-* noun existed previously. Following the Aramaic form of the Hebrew $hiC_1 C_2 îC_3$ causative derivation, a form with *i-* instead of *hi-* is employed for differentiation, but conjugated like a quadriconsonantal root, for example *hizkîr* 'he mentioned' and *izkêr* 'he referred to.'

European adjectives with Latin and Greek prefixes or vernacular equivalents are rendered in contemporary Hebrew by using Hebrew prepositions and other words, sometimes Aramaic, as prefixes, for instance *'al* 'super-,' *tat-* 'sub,' *qedam-* 'pre-,' and *bâtâr-* 'post-.' This is an innovation in Hebrew, since older Hebrew, like Arabic until today, could prefix only negations. Not all prefixes of this kind can as yet be rendered by prefixes in Hebrew, but on the other hand Hebrew has prefixes of its own, for example *kol-* 'all-,' as in *kol-artsî* 'countrywide.' These prefixes can also be used in abstract nouns.

Traditional Hebrew did not allow nominal compounds, although medieval Jewish exegesis employed the concept of compounds of two roots in order to provide ideological or mystical explanations of Biblical words. Already Ben-

Yehuda suggested compound nouns, such as *sax-râxôq* as a calque for 'telephone', where *sax-* is a minimum-vowel form of the root *syx* 'to talk,' plus *raxoq* 'far.' The word was not accepted, be it because of the novelty of its formation or because of its ugly sound. Today words of this kind are frequent, and their number increases constantly, using wherever possible minimum-vowel forms (the origin of which I have not yet discovered). Some examples are: from the root *mdd* 'to measure' *mad-xôm* 'thermometer' (later on, *mad* 'meter' came to be used as an independent noun); *shlat-râxôq* 'remote control'; *ramz-ôr* 'traffic light' (lit.: 'indicate [by] light'); *qôl-nôa'* 'sound film' (lit.: 'voice move,' cf. 'cinema' from Greek *kine-* 'to move,' and 'motion picture'). In some cases where elements at the end of the first word are the same as those at the beginning of the second, they appear only once, as in *daxpôr* 'bulldozer' (*daxôf* 'push' plus *x(a)fôr* 'dig,' with /f/ becoming /p/ after a consonant); and *midrâxôv* 'walking street' (*midrâkhâh* 'pavement' plus *rexôv* 'street').

Compound words that are not too long can serve as a basis for denominative verbs. Thus from *ramzôr* 'traffic light' is formed the transitive verb *rimzêr* 'he installed traffic lights in. ...'

This incorporation of an Indo-European language process into a Semitic language is but one example of the influence of vocabulary extension upon a language. In a way, the influx of foreign words is less likely to disturb the balance in the growing process of a language than is an insistence on reproducing all new concepts by native language material. Purism, by stretching the capabilities of a language beyond that which is customary, may lead to imbalance and to the gradual establishment of a new balance. The answer to the question whether this constitutes progress or irreparable damage depends upon the view one holds of the nature of language.

Besides vocabulary extension, the adaptation of a language to a new or enlarged world of thought also brings with it an extension of syntax, and new ways of expressing logical connections, of grading claims of the truth of assertions (hedging), and of assessing the truth or probability of assertions made by others. It is at present not possible to describe the innovations Westernization and modernization have introduced into written Hebrew. Not only do we lack synchronic descriptions of these matters in Hebrew texts, but even if we had them, we could only decide whether a given construction is an innovation if we had detailed syntactic descriptions of the Hebrew prose language of the centuries before the revival. However, the language of Hebrew non-literary prose of the Middle Ages and of the early modern period has largely remained outside the field of research, except for vocabulary.[7] Since the innovations are likely to concern discourse analysis as much as sentence syntax, existing partial research may be of little use. Certain studies have shown that minor syntactic phenomena of contemporary written, or even colloquial, Hebrew appear already in medieval and early modern texts, and it is quite likely that we shall find the same also for the features mentioned above.

It seems to me that languages which have at previous times in their history gone through a process of adapting themselves to another, wider culture are more likely to be successful in adapting themselves today to Western technical civilization. This may well be worth exploring.

Notes

1 On the implications of Ben-Yehuda's article, see Silberschlag (1981) and Mandel's article in that volume; see also Rabin 1983.
2 These words were first listed in Krauss (1899); however, since Krauss's time many more borrowings have been identified.
3 For this view of Mendele's type of Hebrew, see Rabin (1985). The generally accepted view is that he 'synthesized' Biblical and Mishnaic Hebrew; see the standard work by Kutscher (1982: 190).
4 See Rabin (1977) and Weinberg (1985). The Hebrew alphabet consists of consonants only. The letters ⟨h⟩, ⟨w⟩, and ⟨y⟩ also represent vowels in a vague and inconsistent manner. There is a set of signs above and below the letters which provide complete vowel representation, but it is used only for the Bible, prayer books, poetry, books for children, and for the needs of language learners. The spelling reform of 1968 merely standardized and somewhat amplified the use of ⟨w⟩ and ⟨y⟩ for vowels.
5 The Academy has now almost completed a computerized index of all of its vocabulary decisions.
6 Here C_1, C_2, etc. represent consonants, whichever they are, while the vowels are to be read as such. The distinction between short and long (ˆ) vowels corresponds to the orthography of the vowel system (see note 4) and is of grammatical importance, but there is no such differentiation in speech.
7 This highly productive and adaptable *état de langue* was described by an outstanding Hebraist and Semitist, Gotthelf Bergsträsser (1886–1933) in the following way: 'Mittelalterliches Hebräisch gehört zu den verwahrlosesten Sprachen' (Medieval Hebrew is one of the most degenerated languages) (1928: 47). The reason for this judgment was probably that the unstandardized Medieval Hebrew had neither grammar nor syntax according to Biblical or Mishnaic Hebrew norms.

References

Ben-Yehuda, Eliezer 1981. A Weighty Question. In E. Silberschlag (ed.) *Eliezer Ben-Yehuda. A Symposium in Oxford*. Oxford. Originally published in Hebrew 1879.
Bergsträsser, Gotthelf 1928. *Einführung in die semitischen Sprachen*. Munich.
Even-Shoshan, Abraham 1966–1983. *Ha-millon he-xadash*, 8 vols. Jerusalem.
Fellman, J. 1977. The Hebrew Academy: Orientation and Operation. In Joan Rubin *et al.* (eds.), *Language Planning Processes*. The Hague.
Krauss, Samuel 1899. *Griechische und lateinische Lehnwörter im Talmud, Midrasch und Targum*. Berlin. Reprinted Hildesheim 1964.
Kutscher, Eduard Y. 1982. *A History of the Hebrew Language*. Jerusalem, Leiden.
Medan, M. 1969. The Academy of the Hebrew Language. *Ariel*, 25.
Parfitt, T. 1972. The Use of Hebrew in Palestine, 1800–1882. *Journal of Semitic Studies*, 17: 237–252.

Rabin, Chaim 1977. Spelling Reform – Israel 1968. In J. A. Fishman (ed.), *Advances in the Creation and Revision of Writing Systems*. The Hague.
   1983. The National Idea and the Revival of Hebrew. *Studies in Zionism*, 7: 31–48.
   1985. The Origins of Present-Day Hebrew. *Ariel*, 59: 4–13.
Sarfatti, G.B. 1968. *Mathematical Terminology in Hebrew Scientific Literature of the Middle Ages*. Jerusalem. In Hebrew.
Silberschlag, E. (ed.) 1981. *Eliezer Ben-Yehuda. A Symposium in Oxford*. Oxford.
Weinberg, Werner 1985. *The History of Hebrew Plene Spelling*. Cincinnati.

3 Communicating in Arabic: problems and prospects[1]

MUHAMMAD H. IBRAHIM

Summary

In this chapter I discuss two major problem areas of communicating in Arabic today and one of their corollaries. The two major problems are diglossia and the Arabicization of higher education, and the corollary is the problem of scientific and technical terminology in Arabic. I shall make no mention of what others see as problems, and what I consider to be pseudo-problems, such as the claimed difficulties of the spelling system or the grammar (see Ibrahim 1983: 512–513). To me, these are pseudo-problems because they are in some ways consequences of the two major problems discussed in this paper, and because these pseudo-problems are often used, consciously or unconsciously, to dodge critical issues or sweep them under the carpet.

Arabic diglossia

The basic problem of communicating in Arabic today, which is by no means a recent phenomenon, lies in the existence of two language varieties, one spoken and one written. It is even questionable whether vernacular spoken Arabic and written Arabic may be called varieties of the same language rather than different languages. In a publication sponsored and published by one of the Arab League organizations, Ma'mouri *et al.*(1983: 12–13) argue that the widespread belief in the oneness of Arabic throughout the Arab region is a sign of the lack of an objective linguistic awareness in the Arab countries. They add that objectively and scientifically speaking it must be concluded that standard and spoken Arabic are two separate language systems.

The two varieties/languages have existed side by side for as long as we know. A widely held view among educated Arabs is that what is today written Arabic was once the mother tongue of the Arab tribes in Arabia and that it remained so until the first period of the Arab conquests (seventh and eighth centuries A.D.). These conquests took the Arabs to strange lands and brought them into contact with various non-Arabic-speaking peoples. The consequence of all this to language was the rise of the spoken dialects and the

39

beginning of a long history of linguistic normativism in written Arabic manifested in the production of a vast number of grammars, dictionaries, collections of texts, and other language books.

However, there is increasing evidence that written or Classical Arabic was never the native language of any particular tribe or group of Arabs, but that it arose as a common literary and commercial language of inter-tribal communication in pre-Islamic Arabia (Bateson 1967: 76), that is as a koine which made communication possible among the numerous Arab tribes scattered over a wide area (see Duri 1983: 1). Thus, at least 'as far back as the late sixth century, Classical Arabic was, apparently, a super-tribal language, absorbing lexical and at this time presumably also phonetic, morphological, and syntactic features of various tribal dialects' (Blau 1965: 2). The position of this super-tribal Arabic koine was enhanced when, in addition to its literary and business functions, it acquired a religious function with the rise of Islam and the revelation of the Koran in the koine. This religious function has always been the most powerful factor in the preservation of written Arabic. The codification of the language, which culminated in the eighth century A.D. in Sibawaihi's grammar, the first extant grammar of Arabic, was initiated with the specific aim of preserving the Koranic text from corruption after millions of non-Arab Muslims had converted to Islam and needed to read and understand the Koran and other religious texts.

The codification of what came to be called Classical Arabic in this manner was an act of language fossilization. This was inescapable since Arabic grammar was written and continued to develop as a closed system independently of living usage and continuous linguistic change. The texts which were used as a basis for codification were foreign to the age and the individuals who codified them. Modest attempts at codification were apparently made in the seventh century. But the first serious attempts began only at the beginning of the eighth century A.D. By the end of the eighth and the beginning of the ninth centuries, Arabic grammar, along with a number of other language and religious sciences, had been firmly established. The texts used as a basis in all of this activity were (1) pre-Islamic poetry, which spans a century, from the early sixth to the rise of Islam in the first decade of the seventh century, and (2) the Koran, revealed in the first half of the seventh century. Thus the earliest grammarians were separated from the texts they codified by a period of 150–250 years. The length of the period separating the grammarians from their texts would not be that significant were it not for the fact that it was also a period of many upheavals in the lives of Arabic speakers brought about by conquest and its many linguistic, cultural, social, and other consequences. These factors served only to widen the already existing gap between spoken and written Arabic and prompted the rise of Arabic grammar and normativism with regard to the codified variety of Arabic. Thus the grammarians came to codify a language which did not even belong to their age for the purpose of preventing any changes in the language of their chosen texts. It is in this sense that their work was an act of language fossilization (see Haas 1982b: 24–25).

Moreover, grammatical progress itself was checked and no significant advances were made beyond the eighth century. There is general agreement among historians of Arabic grammar that, after the eighth century, the development of Arabic grammar 'continued in the direction mapped out by Sibawaihi. The number and quality of facts that could be cited were limited. The colloquial language, the dialects, the literature of the day were all excluded from consideration' (Glazer 1974: xli). Language fossilization thus bred grammatical fossilization.

Other workers in the field of language, such as lexicographers, adopted the same philosophy and followed a similar policy. In this way, the old Arabic grammars, lexicons, and other language sources, which are still the basis of all language and grammar books produced and used in the Arab countries today, recognize as legitimate and correct only that variety of Arabic which was codified by the grammarians and recorded by the lexicographers. Naturally, at the same time, the spoken language has continued to change and to remove itself further from the written language.

Written Arabic today is the only variety of Arabic through which education of any sort may be acquired anywhere in the Arab countries. Since this variety is not acquired as a native language by any speaker of Arabic, it has to be acquired through formal instruction. When two language varieties, one of which is highly stable, exist side by side for such a long period of time, it is easy to imagine some of the consequences and problems inherent in such a situation. The gap between the varieties can only grow wider and become more and more unbridgeable, especially in view of the fact that education and the consequent access to written Arabic were, until quite recently, the privilege of only a tiny minority. In this way competence in written Arabic has come to be a sure mark of scholarship and elitism (see De Silva [1982: 99] on Sinhalese). Even today, with thousands of schools and scores of universities throughout the Arab countries, it is still the case that one of the highest compliments one can pay to an Arab is to praise the quality of his/her Arabic (i.e. the written variety). The fact that successful acquisition remains extremely limited, in spite of the tremendous time and effort spent on teaching this institutionalized form of the language, illustrates better than anything else the crisis of written Arabic. Standard written Arabic today is still the monopoly of a very small minority of educated Arabs. This state of affairs has not been achieved through any particular design, but through the total failure of all Arab educational systems, which have failed, individually and collectively, in making standard Arabic the common language of all social classes for all purposes and needs. One manifestation of this colossal failure is that most Arab university professors and graduates seem to be unable to comply with the rules and norms of literary Arabic. In fact, I very much suspect that the insecurity and anxiety caused by some Arab university professors' insufficient knowledge of, and inadequate proficiency in, standard Arabic must be one of the major reasons for these professors' opposition to the Arabicization of education in Arab universities.

To recapitulate thus far, the problem of diglossia is compounded and intensified by the fact that even modern written Arabic (also called M.S.A., Modern Standard Arabic) is not considered a valid source of grammatical rules. The thousands of new lexical items which have entered the language in the last hundred years are not recorded in our dictionaries. The grammar books teach a lot which long ago ceased to be of any relevance to standard Arabic as it is practiced today. There does not exist yet any Arabic dicitionary or grammar book derived from, or based on, an actual corpus of modern Arabic texts. In other words, the standard language has been developing rapidly, but the tools and means which should make it easily accessible to the masses have remained almost without change for the last twelve centuries.

In view of this situation, it is not surprising to find spoken Arabic competing with standard Arabic in every respect. The spoken language affects standard Arabic in the area which is dearest to the purists and which is least useful in communication, namely inflectional morphology. Thus, instead of acquiring a new language system, which is that of standard Arabic, the Arab schoolchild modifies the target system in such a way as to approximate to that of his/her spoken language. The standard language has little relevance to his life, and its existence is scarcely felt since it is confined to the school-books. Even teachers of Arabic use the local variety in most of their teaching. The local variety also rules supreme at home, among peers and playmates, in the school, and on radio and television, the programs of which are mostly in non-standard Arabic. And what little M.S.A. the child is exposed to through the mass media, children's books, and modern literature deviates in many ways from the rules of standard written Arabic and, not infrequently, even clashes with those rules. Since the rules of Arabic grammar are based on prescriptive rules instead of actual usage, they will remain hopeless and unattainable goals for the vast majority of Arab learners.

The failure to teach and learn Arabic adequately is a constant topic of debate and discussion in Arab educational and academic circles and in the Arab press and other mass media. The fact that the language question is discussed so frequently on such a massive level is another sure sign of the existence of an acute problem.

Mistakes in the use of standard Arabic (i.e. deviations from the prescribed norms) abound on all levels and in various media: in the language heard on radio and television, in formal speeches and oral renditions of scripted texts, in newspapers and magazines, in official documents and publications, in notices and signs, and in all sorts of books published in all Arab countries, including works of creative literature.[2] I have argued elsewhere that the only plausible explanation of this state of affairs lies in the linguistic distance which separates the formally learned standard written Arabic from the spoken and natively acquired varieties of Arabic (Ibrahim 1983: 510–513).

The situation just described also had a positive aspect to it. It is a situation fraught with indications and unmistakable signs that a 'new language' is in the making. It is, or rather *will be,* a language which is anathema to the purists since it violates a great many of the traditional rules, but it is or will be a much more realistic language born out of the interplay between spoken and written Arabic. The new language will no doubt become a supra-regional standard 'in touch with varieties of the living, orally developed and developing language,' and 'not artificial, unintelligible or unusable by all save the initiated few' (Mitchell 1986: 8).

There seems to be general agreement that the most powerful factor in the development of this new language variety is 'the increasing contact of Classical Arabic and the local dialects' (Palva 1969: 3) brought about by mass education and 'the unparalleled intensity of modern communication' (Haas 1982b: 14) which has been made possible by the mass media (e.g. Palva 1982: 17; Moussa 1955: 42–43; Ṣayyādī 1982a: 40). The emerging language variety of Arabic which will probably develop into a new 'supra koine' (Haas 1982b: 29) cannot be characterized with enough precision at this stage of its development. However, some general trends already at work may be discerned. It is clear that hybridization at both ends of the diglossia scale has taken, and is still taking, place, although it is impossible to measure the contribution of each variety to this hybrid with any degree of precision. Hybridization at the lower end of the scale is usually called 'classicization,' as opposed to 'colloquialization' at the higher end (Palva 1982: 15). In addition to classicization and colloquialization, a third tendency is at work, namely koineization or dialect levelling, 'a development that eliminates specific isoglosses and thus melts down local dialects into greater linguistic units' (*ibid.*: 16). Taken together, these three processes will undoubtedly result in greater linguistic unification of the Arab countries. It is doubtful whether diglossia in its classical formulation will disappear from the Arabic-speaking communities, but the gap will be greatly reduced thanks to the development of a hybrid or intermediate variety. On the basis of my own observations of spoken and written Arabic, and on the basis of my experience and knowledge of the use of Arabic at Arab universities and other private and public institutions, this 'intermediate' variety will have the following general characteristics, once it has developed fully:

1   The phonology and syntax of the new common variety will be primarily those of standard Arabic (see Chaieb 1976: 50–55).

2   In morphology, especially grammatical inflections, the new common variety will be fundamentally that of spoken Arabic (see al-Sayyid 1980: 289–290).

3   The vocabulary will be mixed. Although thousands of Classical roots will be preserved and continue to be used, a generous admixture of items from the

spoken dialects, as well as thousands of new terms, will be added to the
lexicon of the new variety (see Valdman [1968: 323] for similar developments
in Haitian Creole, and De Silva [1982: 98, 108] on Sinhalese).

In this way the spoken and written language varieties will come closer to
each other, and the extreme variation-cum-polarization which characterizes
the language use of educated Arabs will disappear. Naturally, variation will
continue to exist, but the polarization of functions characteristic of the
polarized language varieties will disappear from educated general use. There
will be a small group of diehards and purists left who will continue to preach
and perhaps use Classical Arabic, but their influence will be as limited and
inconsequential as that of the Catholic Church on the preservation of Latin.

Significantly enough, a contemporary Arab historian recognizes this 'intermediate' and 'common' Arabic language as a distinguishing feature of the
Arab nation. He goes on to define this 'intermediate common language' as
that which is read and understood instantly by any Arab reader in any part
of the Arab region, regardless of social class or educational level. Furthermore, it is the language in which modern Arabic books, newspapers, and
magazines are written; and it is the language of Arab theater, television,
cinema, and radio throughout the Arab countries. It is a language which has
developed and is still developing in the course of the struggle between 'the
language of lexicons' and the spoken dialects ('Amāra 1981: 101).

Brief mention in this section should be made of a 'theory' on the interplay
between Classical and colloquial Arabic put forward by the Tunisian scholar
and cabinet minister, Al-Bashīr bin Salāma, who maintains that each and
every Arab poet or prose writer who made an original contribution to Arabic
literature did so by consciously grafting the rhythms of his spoken dialect onto
his poetry or prose (Bin Salāma 1984: 11, 94). Unfortunately, the writer does
not elaborate on this basic claim, but the theory is interesting for us here since
it attributes all originality in Classical Arabic to its interaction with spoken
Arabic.

The developments which are currently taking place in standard Arabic can
be viewed positively since they will result in bringing the spoken and written
varieties closer to each other, thereby making the learning and acquisition of
the written form easily accessible to a much larger segment of the Arab
population than is the case at present. There is one inherent danger in this
situation, however, which can result in the fragmentation of written Arabic
into a number of unintelligible varieties. Because of present Arab disunity and
poor communication channels among Arab countries, written Arabic seems
to be developing and changing in each Arab country independently of the
other countries. This is particularly noticeable in the introduction of new
vocabulary items and the translation of foreign expressions and idioms, most
of which are taken from English and French. Even school-books contain a
fair number of local or regional words which would not be understandable in

other Arab countries or regions. The situation is especially serious in newspaper language, which sometimes employs such a large number of local and regional words in their local news stories and advertisements as to make these incomprehensible to Arab readers from other areas (see Ibrahim 1986; see also below on variations in technical terminology). If the present trend continues, more and more regional and local words will enter the written Arabic of various Arab regions, which, in addition to other aspects of variation, will lead to less uniformity and more variety in the developing standard Arabic.

Arabicization of higher education

If diglossia and its concomitant problems in Arabic have been the result of largely historical developments over which individuals have little or no control, the exclusion of Arabic from most Arab universities as a medium of instruction in scientific and technological fields has been essentially a matter of choice. This situation makes the language problem in higher education three-dimensional, with spoken Arabic, written Arabic, and the foreign language (English or French) each representing one dimension of the problem.

The major arguments which are usually put forward by those who are opposed to Arabicization may be summarized as follows:

1   Arabic is not yet sufficiently developed to be the language of science and technology, mainly because it lacks the required scientific terminology.
2   Scientific and technological publications in Arabic are very few and inadequate.
3   A language of wider communication, such as English or French, used as a medium of instruction will help our scholars in maintaining international scholarly ties and worldwide intellectual contacts.

The first and second arguments are in fact a judgment on the language users rather than on the language itself. A language can only be as developed or underdeveloped as its speakers. In this connection, it is safe to generalize by saying that there cannot exist a modern or developed language apart from a modern or developed society. The opposite must also be true: a modern and developed society is not possible without a modern and developed language. Since all Arabic countries belong to the category of developing countries, Arabic must necessarily be a developing or underdeveloped language. Time alone is no cure for underdevelopment, whether linguistic or otherwise. A language can be modernized only through utilization. As long as Arabic remains underutilized as a language of science it will continue to be hard to write on scientific topics in Arabic, because a less used language will have more gaps in concepts and terminology than a used one:

Assez souvent, on met en évidence le degré insuffisant de modernization des langues des pays en développement, c.-à-d. l'absence de terminologie scientifique, la quantité et la qualité limitées du discours scientifique. C'est oublier que ce qui importe, ce n'est pas la disponibilité immédiate et préalable des termes scientifiques et techniques mais l'utilisation de la langue pour créer, transmettre, 'faire' la science et la technologie qui engendre le discours scientifique et technique qui modernise la langue.

(Zachariev 1981: 170)

This was the course of action which the Japanese followed and which resulted in changing the status of Japanese from a pre- modern language into a modern one. Thus, since the Meiji era and during a period of less than a century, nearly every relevant book from any language was translated into Japanese: 'After World War II alone, more than 150,000 books were translated into Japanese' (Alisjahbana 1984: 50).

The third argument used by the opponents of Arabicization is hardly relevant for the great majority of Arab university students since the number of graduates who become scholars with international ties is extremely small. This means that the interests of the majority are being sacrificed for the sake of a tiny minority. The use of a foreign language as a medium of instruction to a certain extent resembles the use of Classical Arabic to the exclusion of other varieties, in that both are the product of an elitist mentality. Apart from elitism, this situation is also very odd for two reasons. The first one is because students come to the university poorly prepared for studying in a foreign language since Arabic is the only medium of instruction in all pre-university years.[3] The second reason is related to the linguistic practice of the vast majority of Arab university graduates in their post-university years. Arabic is virtually the only language they will need and/or use after graduation. Those who are science or mathematics teachers will have to instruct their students in Arabic, and those who are physicians, pharmacists, dentists, engineers, architects, or specialists in agriculture must revert to Arabic in their respective professions since they deal with Arabic-speaking individuals all the time. But perhaps the most serious consequence of using a foreign language as a medium of instruction is the alienation of an important and sizeable segment of society from its own language, culture, values, and society (Zachariev 1981: 160).

If the foreign language is the vehicle for modern science and technology, whereas Arabic is good only for 'the humanities,' the Arab students' conclusion is inevitable: Arabic is an inferior language and what is written in Arabic must be inferior to what is written in the foreign language (Ma'mouri *et al.* 1983: 30). A study of 500 sociology students at Oran University, Algeria, is worth quoting here. Half of the students investigated studied sociology in Arabic, whereas the other half studied it through the medium of French. Table 3.1 summarizes the responses of the two groups of students to some key questions.[4]

Moreover, instruction through a foreign language often results in the students suffering from two interrelated handicaps: a low self-image and unsatisfactory performance 'compounded by a low expectation of learning capacity on the part of the student himself, his parents, teachers and adminis-

Table 3.1

	Arabic students	French students
Arabic is adequate for our age	80%	47%
Arabicization in higher education is a must	95%	54%
Use only Arabic in daily life	36%	23%
Rarely use Arabic in daily life	17%	36%

Source: Ma'mouri *et al.* 1983: 46.

trators' (Saville and Troike, quoted in Fox [1974: 12]). Ideas like these are not romantic speculations with no roots in reality, but have been supported by empirical field research. The author of one such study conducted at the University of Khartoum in the Sudan came to the conclusion that the main problem which students faced at the university was language, and that 'upon being faced with the necessity of achieving success through a foreign language, students applied the well-tried methods of school life: carefully copied texts, rote memorization and "spotting"' (Douglas, 1986: 97f). Once this is known, we cannot help wondering with the same author:

Of what value is the enormous body of published material in English if students have not the linguistic competence to make use of it? Of what value are the impressive qualifications and experience of the teaching staff if their lectures and tutorials are incomprehensible to most of their students? To what extent does intellectual contact or international business depend upon the medium of instruction in an educational system? (*ibid.*)

Two other studies, one from Jordan and the other from Saudi Arabia, of the effects of Arabicization on university undergraduates, found, among other things, that the use of Arabic as a medium of instruction instead of English reduced the drop-out and failure rates very significantly. In addition, subjects in the Saudi study (a sample of students and staff members from two Saudi universities) expressed their belief that

The use of English has become a solid barrier against the participation of a large segment of the population in the development process. It has perpetuated elitism and an unequal class structure, and has weakened the link between the population and the center that is in charge of national development. (al-Qurashi 1982: 237)

The proponents of Arabicization in the Arab countries, whether individuals or institutions, constitute a majority. But it has been largely an impotent and ineffectual majority which, in most cases, has been the victim of its own short-sightedness and ignorance of even the most basic requirements for successful language planning. The efforts of this majority in the field of Arabicization have been confined for the most part to one of two activities which, although not entirely useless, are far from making Arabicization an actuality:

1   Defending the Arabic language and its glorious past, and asserting in the strongest terms its ability to be a vehicle for science and technology in the modern age.
2   Making modest attempts at suggesting Arabic equivalents for a limited number of technical terms in various fields and compiling glossaries and bilingual dictionaries of such terms.

Because of the impotence of the proponents of Arabicization and the inadequacy of their strategies, they are almost unanimous in their call for a 'political solution,' that is a decree or an order from the highest political authority in each Arab country for universities to Arabicize instruction in all fields. But confidence in the efficacy of such action is misfounded for more than one reason. Firstly, there is the fact that conservatism tends to be innate within establishments. Several Arab countries inherited their present language policy from colonial times. The natural inertia of establishments has kept things the way they were before independence. In fact, there is clear evidence that the position of the major foreign languages in the Arab region, English and French, has been greatly enhanced after independence. In addition to their omnipresence in all Arab educational systems, English and French have made sweeping gains in the Arab mass media and the Arab system of values. Most Arab countries have English and/or French newspapers, radio stations, and/or television channels. Knowledge of French or English has become a pre-requisite to social mobility, professional advancement, and psychological security. Secondly, most Arab regimes are by their very nature undemocratic and, therefore, would not do anything to rectify the inequity and injustice caused by the use of a foreign language as a vehicle for education. Because of their very nature, those regimes encourage elitism and are unaware of the dangers of their present language policies. Thirdly, most Arab leaders are foreign-educated and probably share the beliefs of the opponents of Arabicization. In spite of some public statements in which they exalt Arabic and sing its glory, most Arab leaders' allegiance to their national language is not genuine. The best support for this claim lies in the fact that many of these leaders educate their children from an early age in foreign countries where no Arabic is taught at all. Not only would these leaders do nothing to help Arabicization, but some of them stand actively against it, as the following quotation from a speech by King Hassan II of Morocco illustrates:

We must organize our culture and our instruction as seems necessary, and reform what must be reformed, in order to turn into an instrument capable of shaping our children, who hope thanks to it, to become citizens of their country, and of their continent which does not speak Arabic. We live in a continent which speaks English and French.

(Quoted in Gallagher 1968: 149)

Similar ideas were expressed in 1979 by the then Tunisian Prime Minister, Al-Hadi Nweira, in an inaugural speech to the Arab League Educational, Cultural, and Scientific Organization (A.L.E.C.S.O.). The golden rule, he said, which Arab universities must follow, is to give utmost attention to foreign languages so that our students and researchers can read science in its original language. Translating into Arabic, he added, is neither enough nor very useful. 'Therefore,' he concluded, 'to save time and effort, and in order to guarantee success, sciences must be taught in the language of science' – that is, in English or French (quoted in Ma'mouri *et al.* 1983: 73, note 14).

Finally, cases where Arabicization failed, despite its attempted imposition by the political leadership, also demonstrate the futility of the political solution. This happened in Egypt under Nasser when the total Arabicization of Egyptian universities was ordered, but has not yet been implemented, in Algeria after independence in the 1960s and the 1970s, and in Iraq at the beginning of the 1980s. Arabicization in these, and possibly other, cases failed because the universities themselves did not favor it. Although Arabicization and politics are doubtless interrelated, politics need not be the key to a solution. The constitutions of all Arab countries and the by-laws of all Arab universities include articles and clauses to the effect that Arabic is the official language of instruction in these universities. If these universities and their staff wanted to Arabicize, they would only be acting in accordance with their legal status as granted to them by their respective governments. The truth of the matter is that most Arab university administrators, like Arab political leaders, are at best tepid in their attitude to Arabicization, and their belief in it rarely goes beyond lip service. What Arabicization needs is action on the part of those who believe in it, not reaction, which has characterized most attempts thus far.

What we have called 'the futility of the political solution' should not be construed as a denial of any connection between Arabicization and politics. Arabicization *is*, in fact, primarily a political issue. A brief historical review of the issue will clarify this matter.

Arabic became firmly established as a language of science and other branches of knowledge as early as the first decades of the ninth century A.D., when translation into Arabic from Greek, Persian and Sanskrit reached its zenith under the Abbasid caliph al-Ma'mun (A.D. 813–833). Sure of themselves and confident of their language, the Arabs of those days had none of the sensitivities and inferiority complexes which many modern Arabs suffer from. Soon Arabic was to become an international language of science and knowledge, and it continued in that capacity throughout the Middle Ages. A series of political and military developments and disasters led eventually to the disintegration of the state and the decline of learning and knowledge. Baghdad was devastated by the Mongols in 1258, Spain was lost forever in 1492, and the Mamluks – the last medieval dynasty of the Arab world, who were 'on the whole uncultured and blood-thirsty' (Hitti 1943: 239) – ruled much of the Arab region from 1250 until 1517, when the Ottomans took over and ruled the entire Arab region for the next four centuries – a period which witnessed the total neglect of, and not infrequently the waging of war against, Arabic. Ottoman rule ended with World War I and a new era began, namely the domination of the Arab region by European powers and the political fragmentation of the Arab countries, from which they have not yet recovered. Thus the recession of Arabic coincided with the European Renaissance.

For more than seven centuries, during which knowledge had been expanding at an increasing rate, Arabic remained virtually stagnant and was excluded from use as an instrument in the creation and transmission of new sciences and knowledge.

At about the same time that attempts began to be made to modernize Japanese, a similar but abortive attempt was made for Arabic when the first modern schools of medicine and translation in the Arab countries were founded in Cairo, in 1826 and 1835 respectively, by Muhammad Ali, the viceroy of Egypt and the founder of its royal family, which survived until 1952. The language of instruction in the medical school, which is now the Cairo University School of Medicine, was Arabic from the beginning until 1887, when the British, who had occupied Egypt in 1882, ordered Arabic to be replaced by English. The translation school was also closed and not re-opened until Nasser came to power in 1952. Similarly, the American University of Beirut, founded in 1866, began by teaching all subjects, including medicine and pharmacy, in Arabic and continued to do so until the Turks were driven out of the area (Khūrī 1984: 138), when the university switched to English as a medium of instruction.

The latter case illustrates the politics of language use clearly. Apparently, the Vatican and other European religious institutions in those days used Arabic as a weapon to fight Ottoman influence in the Arab region, and their missionaries in the area were very busy studying and teaching it. They also edited and published a large number of old Arabic manuscripts, opened schools, and generally spread the use of Arabic as a modern language. With the departure of the Turks from the area, the political services of Arabic were automatically rendered useless (Ḍāher 1978: 83–84).

It is interesting to speculate that, had these attempts at modernizing Arabic not been interrupted, Arabic might today be in a much more favorable position. The sad fact, however, is that the gap between Arabic and modern life has been widening all the time. The longer Arabic remains excluded from education, the more serious the problem will become. Time will only help complicate matters for Arabic, and the only solution is to put the language immediately to practice in all fields on all levels. The Syrian experience of teaching medicine through Arabic, which dates back to 1919, and which was later extended to other fields of scientific study, proves that 'an Arab country can function using Arabic almost exclusively in all fields of endeavor without running up against insurmountable problems' (Gallagher 1968: 140).

Technical and scientific terminology

In an otherwise insightful and well-written paper, Gallagher (1968: 140) summarizes the problems of modern written Arabic in the following manner:

Objectively viewed, Arabic faces some grave problems if it is to adapt itself to the efficient transmission of technical information. It is burdened with an inadequate and ossified script which needs overhauling and simplification. The present-day hesitancy of the language (which has not been true at all times in the past) to borrow directly is a sign of weakness. The inability to prefix and suffix easily and to build combining forms is a serious handicap in a world whose vocabulary is being enlarged every day with compound constructs. But above all ... the fundamental question is that of setting up a unified scientific and technological terminology.

In spite of its claim to objectivity, the above inventory of problems can be easily contested. The orthography or morphology of a language can never seriously hinder its development. Arabic still has the same script and derivational morphology it had centuries ago when it was an international language of science and knowledge. To invoke the example of Japanese yet again, the script and morphology of Arabic are much more 'adequate' than those of Japanese, although Japanese is the more developed of the two languages. Gallagher's remarks on Arabic script and morphology should be classified with those accusations that are 'based more on casual observations and impressionistic evidence than on empirical research' (Mahmoud, 1979: 131). Again, Gallagher is unfair to Arabic when he talks of its 'hestitancy ... to borrow,' as this is the fault of the purists, not the language. One has only to look into any spoken dialect of Arabic to realize that Arabic is capable of extensive borrowing when it is left to do so freely. And standard Arabic did not seem to be hesitant to borrow words extensively in the Middle Ages and earlier from Greek and Persian, among other languages.

The last problem cited by Gallagher, namely the unification of scientific terminology, is real and serious. Variation in the technical terms adopted in different Arab countries is today one of the more serious problems facing Arabicization and the adaptation of Arabic for modern communication needs. One of the major factors behind this problem is the lack of co-ordination among individual Arab countries and among individuals and agencies within the same country in the fields of Arabicization and terminology work. The problem is so serious that one often finds different Arabic equivalents for the same English or French term in glossaries and dictionaries printed by the same publisher. In fact, this linguistic anarchy is no longer confined to the field of technical terms, but today extends to other non-technical aspects of modern Arabic vocabulary.

Lexical variation is quite extensive in all Arab newspapers, magazines, and other mass media. This is a disturbing realization in view of the fact that, by their very nature, the mass media are the most widely read or heard sources of written Arabic. Textbooks, including Arabic school-books, abound with instances of lexical variation. A study of the first-grade Arabic textbooks in Egypt, Morocco, Tunisia, and Yemen revealed a long list of lexical items in each book which would not be understood by Jordanian first-graders. Quite a few words in each book were unknown to me (see Ibrahim 1986). This situation has created the need for certain words which are used in one part of the Arab region to be glossed for the benefit of readers in other countries. In a 1984 article written by a Moroccan professor and published in one of the most respectable Arab journals, the editor found it necessary to explain to his readers that *qārra* in the Arab countries of North Africa means *thābita* or *dā'ima* (stable, permanent) (al-Jābirī 1984: 55). Maʿmouri *et al.* find it necessary to gloss a large number of words in their book, but a larger number of variant items remain unglossed. One extreme example of glossing is the provision of four different terms for 'school supervisors,' namely *muwajjihīn*, *mufattishīn*, *murshidīn* and *matafaqqidīn* (Maʿmouri *et al.* 1983: 134). Examples of unglossed items in the same book include the following:

> munāḍhara – 'test' (p. 42);
> taḥaṣṣala ʿala – 'achieved, attained' (p. 43);
> muwāliya – 'following' (p. 63); and
> waḍhīf – 'job' (p. 126).

The first book in what is to be a series of books published by A.L.E.C.S.O. for teaching Arabic to speakers of other languages contains at least three dozen words which betray a specific regional origin and which would have been replaced by other words had the book been produced in, say, Jordan.[5] These variable items include words for 'yoghurt,' 'police station,' 'wardrobe,' 'to study,' and others (Badawī *et al.* 1983). When the word for 'bus' is introduced in the same book, *ḥāfila* is used as the basic term, with *bāṣ* given in brackets. Next to the word in the margin is reproduced an Egyptian bus ticket on which the word *utubīs* is used for 'bus' (*ibid.*: 189).

Another disturbing example of serious variation in written Arabic comes from the 'functional linguistic corpus' of the Maghrib, that is Algeria, Libya, Morocco, and Tunisia. In a study of this list of 4,800 words, Benabdi (1986) has found that 3.5% of the words differ from Modern Standard Arabic words, which automatically renders them incomprehensible in other Arab countries.

Examples of much more serious instances of variation in technical terminology are numerous. In a 1982 study, one investigator surveyed 33 bilingual Arabic dictionaries and a number of technical glossaries and specialized vocabulary lists – all of which except two were compiled between 1955 and 1975. The aim of the study was to find the extent of agreement among these sources on technical vocabulary. The results were astounding, for he found a total of 11 different Arabic equivalents for 'mineralogy', 18 for 'metallurgy' and 23 for 'geology' (al-Faḍlī 1982). In the introduction to his French–Arabic dictionary of linguistics, Mseddi (1984: 72) lists 23 Arabic equivalents for 'linguistics,' all of which are currently in use throughout the Arab countries. If so much variation and disagreement can exist with regard to such relatively simple and general terms, one can imagine what the situation would be like for other more specific and less-known or understood terms (see al-Shihābī 1965: 128ff). The seriousness of lexical and terminological variation in Arabic becomes clear in the light of Mitchell's remark that 'as far as Arabic is concerned, it is especially in the lexical area that misunderstanding or failure to understand can arise' (Mitchell 1986: 27).

Apart from variation in terminology work, Arabic suffers from another problem, which is the belief that once the needed lists of terms have been compiled the problems of using Arabic as a scientific language will be solved automatically. It goes without saying that this is a naive and far from realistic view. Since terminology lists consist of individual words, most of this type of work is carried out in a vacuum. Finding an equivalent for a word in isolation and for the same word when used in an appropriate context (a scientific article or book) are not the same thing and at times are even two different matters. Thus authors and translators often discover that many of the words suggested by the academies or the dictionary compilers are unusable. The situation would be different if the new terms resulted from translating or writing scientific and technical books.

Work on terminology lists will remain of very limited value and largely ineffectual unless the proposed terms are put to the test immediately, as is the case with terms suggested by the Damascus language academy, which find their way almost immediately into everyday use in oral and written scientific discourse at the university level, where all subjects are taught in Arabic. The implication of this argument is that the Arabicization of education should not wait until the terms needed have been compiled. If anything, the process should be reversed. Arabicization should be implemented as soon as possible since this is the most reasonable process for generating the needed terms. There can also be little doubt that Arabicization will contribute significantly to the standardization of scientific and technical terminology in Arabic. Arabicization will cause Arabic to be extensively utilized by members of the scientific community, and through this utilization the language will produce and incorporate viable terms, which, for the most part, are bound to be uniform and fit for survival.

Conclusions: Arabicization vs Aribization

Throughout this chapter I have deliberately used the term 'Arabicization' to the exclusion of 'Arabization.' Although the two terms are used interchangeably by some, the difference between them is not insignificant. 'Arabicization' refers to and involves the use of the Arabic language in place of some other language. The term 'Arabization,' however, has a much wider application as well as a more profound implication for modern Arab society. Thus, whereas 'Arabicization' is a linguistic process whereby a foreign language is replaced by Arabic, 'Arabization' is cultural as well as linguistic. When 'Arabicization' is discussed, it is usually seen as an isolated problem having little or nothing to do with the other problems from which modern Arab societies are suffering. In this concluding section of the chapter, I shall briefly explore the connection between 'Arabization' and 'Arabicization' and argue that the latter, if it is to be meaningful, depends heavily on the former.

A number of Arab writers have pointed out that the problem of Arabicization cannot and should not be considered in isolation from the wider linguistic, social, and cultural context prevailing in all Arab countries without exception (see, for example, al-Jinḥānī 1982a, 1982b; Juʿaiṭ 1982; and Sharīṭ 1984). Arabicization, they add, will remain extremely superficial and confined to the verbal level unless due attention is paid to the human element and unless it is part of a more comprehensive cultural ideology which seeks to revolutionize the Arabic language and, with it, the contemporary Arab culture and mentality. The real problem of Arabic is not linguistic, but lies in the largely uncreative modern Arab culture (Juʿaiṭ 1982: 59). A language can develop and mature only to the extent that its users are developed and mature.

Any person who is capable of original ideas and theories in science and thought and of new inventions and discoveries in technology will also be capable of presenting his contributions and naming his inventions in his own language. All attempts at developing Arab societies and modernizing them will have a limited outcome and remain restricted to a small elite unless the tool used in such modernization and development programs is the language of the people. The language of the people is neither the English or French nor the Medieval Arabic which language academies, Arabic departments in Arab universities, and other conservative forces have been trying unsuccessfully to impose on their societies. Seen in this light, the use of a foreign language and the use of an outmoded and fettered variety of the national language are two sides of the same coin. Both are the distinguishing marks of a small elitist and privileged class, and both can be and are used, consciously or unconsciously, as effective means by a minority to control and exclude the majority. In this way, Arabization, in the sense of modernizing Arabic in such a way as to make it accessible to the overwhelming majority of Arabs, must go hand in hand with Arabicization. Thus we are in a position to understand why an Arab writer should call for a ban on the teaching of Arabic by Arab universities and academics, who are far less advanced in their understanding of the Arabic language than the early Arab grammarians of more than one thousand years ago (al-Yousef 1978: 40; see also Muṣṭafā 1982: 215). Arabization, however, encompasses more than modernizing Arabic. Among other things, it also means Arabicizing the humanities, which, although taught in Arabic in almost all Arab universities, are still foreign in their content, methods, and the problems with which they deal. In sociology, economics, and psychology, to name only three fields, the problems, cases, and models dealt with belong to other societies. In other words, these fields have been Arabicized, but not Arabized.

To conclude on a more optimistic note, let me briefly indicate some encouraging signs of change in the right direction. In the first place, there is evey reason to believe that the grip of Medieval Arabic is weakening and that a new variety which is much more accessible to the Arab masses is being born. Arabicization has also been gaining ground in the 1980s. The fact that the Syrian universities have withstood the test is significant. Today, the Syrian example is often invoked as a strong argument in favor of Arabicization. There is hardly any Arab country now in which Arabicization is not making some progress, slow as this may be. By 1990, Iraq is scheduled to complete the Arabicization of its universities in all fields. The Arabicization of the first two years of instruction in the basic sciences at Jordanian universities will be completed in the early 1990s. The Sudan government has resolved that university education in all fields shall be Arabicized by 1988. And Sana'a University has decided to Arabicize its medical school.

Interest in scientific translation and publishing and the compilation of bilingual technical dictionaries has also been mounting in the 1980s to the extent that a number of major publishers in the U.K., the U.S.A., and the U.S.S.R. regularly publish scientific books in Arabic. Arabicization of university instruction is always accompanied by the writing or translation of some books to be used as textbooks. Thus in Jordan, the Arabic Language Academy has published more than a dozen volumes in all of the basic sciences and plans to commission the translation of more such books. As a result of the Arabicization of university education in Iraq, the percentage of scientific books published in that country increased from 3.7% in 1979 to 12.3% in 1983. The total number of scientific titles published in Iraq during these five years was 306, of which only 100 were translations. Mention should also be made of Algeria, which on the eve of its independence in 1962, faced a more difficult situation than any other Arab country with regard to Arabicization. In view of this fact, we consider it no mean achievement for Algeria to have completed the Arabicization of practically all fields of education in non-scientific subjects at the school and university levels.

The problem of diversity in Arabic terminology has for long been the subject of numerous articles and several publications. Recently, a pan-Arab conference, the first of its kind, was convened in Tunis to study the problem and to suggest solutions. Attended by about a hundred participants from most Arab countries, as well as by representatives of a number of Arab League, U.N. and other international organizations, the Conference on Arab Co-operation in Terminology (Tunis, July 7–10, 1986) resolved that an Arab terminology network be created immediately with temporary headquarters in Tunis. If set up, the proposed network would no doubt be instrumental in co-ordinating, and consequently helping to standardize, the diverse and disparate terminological projects in the Arab countries.

Despite these efforts, the general feeling is that not enough is being done to speed up the process of Arabicization and bring about Arabization. The majority of the Arab states do not seem to be concerned with the issue, and those that do show some concern are not doing enough. With one or two exceptions, the Arab states, individually and collectively, have no comprehensive strategy or plan for the implementation of Arabicization. It would be even more desirable for the Arab countries to adopt a comprehensive language policy. The envisaged policy would address the major language issues in the Arab countries and how to deal with them. Because of their immediate relevance to the topic of this paper, the following issues, among others, would be part of the proposed policy:

1   The old norms of written Arabic must be reconsidered. The new norms must be based on contemporary usage. In general, the present and the future should be heeded much more than the past.

2   The teaching of Arabic must be improved and modernized in such a way as to achieve universal literacy in the entire Arab region by the year 2000.

3   Whereas variation in spoken Arabic and in the oral rendition of written Arabic is acceptable and should be tolerated, standardization of written Arabic must be the goal if all Arab countries are to remain one language community, whose members can communicate with each other. The standardization of written Arabic has also become a necessity in view of the international status accorded to Arabic during the 1970s and 1980s, since internationalism is incompatible with diversity and regionalism.

4   Each country must set a target date, not to exceed ten years, when full Arabicization at all levels of education will have been completed.

The implementation of the above policy points would be enough to make Arabic completely adaptable to the needs of modern communication.

Notes

1 In preparing this revised version of the paper originally presented at the Symposium on Adapting Vernacular Languages to the Demands of Modern Communication (Bad Homburg, June 12–15, 1985), I have benefited from comments made by H. Abdel-Jawad, J. Calbert, T. Crocker, B. Harris, M. Matthews, and S. Suliman. Their comments have led to substantial improvements in the paper. Needless to say, I remain solely responsible for any shortcomings which the paper may still have.

2 In 1983, a Jordanian columnist called for a summit conference to deal with the problems of the Arabic language. What prompted him to make this facetious suggestion, he says, is the incredibly low standard of Arabic used in the press and other media, as well as that used by well-known writers. Were it not for interventions by editors and proofreaders, he adds, the country would witness some high-level literary scandals (Fakhrī Qaʿwār in *Al-Raʾi* [Amman], no. 4934, December 15, 1983: 12).

3 Morocco and Tunisia are exceptions to this statement. In these two countries, French is still the language of instruction in the majority of school subjects.

4 The study summarized here was made by M. A. Zuʿbi and is reported in Maʿmouri *et al.* (1983: 46). I have not been able to consult the original study.

5 It must be added, though, that the differences among several of these items are minor. But even if we disregard such minor differences, the number of truly different terms would still exceed a dozen.

References

Alisjahbana, S. Takdir 1984. The Problem of Minority Languages in the Overall Linguistic Problems of Our Time. In Florian Coulmas, (ed.), *Linguistic Minorities and Literacy. Language Policy Issues in Developing Countries*. Berlin.

'Amāra, Muhammad 1981. *Al-'Arab Yastaygiḍhūn* [The Arabs Awaken], part 3, *Al-Umma 1-'Arabiyya wa Qaḍiyyatu 1-waḥda* [The Arab Nation and the Question of Unity], 3rd edn. Beirut.

Badawī, al-Sa'īd M. *et al.* 1983. *Al-Kitābu 1-asāsiyy fī ta'līmi 1-'Arabiyya li ghayri 1-Nāṭigīna bihā* [The Basic Book for Teaching Arabic to Speakers of Other Languages]. Tunis.

Bateson, Mary C. 1967. *Arabic Language Handbook*. Washington, D.C.

Benabdi, Linda 1986. Lexical Expansion in the Maghrib: The 'Functional Linguistic Corpus.' *International Journal of the Sociology of Language*, 61: 65–78.

Bin Salāma, Al-Bashīr 1984. *Naḍhariyyatu al-Tat'īmi 1-iqā'iyyi fī 1-fushā* [The Theory of Rhythmic Grafting in Classical Arabic]. Tunis.

Blau, Joshua 1965. *The Emergence and Linguistic Background of Judaeo-Arabic. A Study of the Origins of Middle Arabic*. Oxford.

Chaieb, Mohamed 1976. al-'Arabiyya al-wusṭā wa mā nasha'a fīhā min tadāxul bayn al-fuṣhā wa al-dārija [Middle Arabic and Interference into it from Standard and Spoken Arabic]. *Revue tunisienne de sciences sociales*, 13, 46: 47–66.

Ḍāher, Mas'ūd 1978. Al-ṭā'ifiyya wa 1-manhaj fī dirāsat ṭārīkh lubnān al-ḥadīth wa 1-mu'āṣir [Sectarianism and the Approach to the Study of the Modern and Contemporary History of Lebanon]. *Al-Fikr Al-'Arabī*, 1, 2: 70–102.

De Silva, M. W. S. 1982. Some Consequences of Diglossia. In W. Haas (ed.), *Standard Languages. Spoken and Written*. Manchester.

Douglas, Dan 1986. From School to University: Language Policy and Performance at the University of Khartoum. *International Journal of the Sociology of Language*, 61: 89–112.

Duri, Abdel Aziz 1983. *The Historical Formation of the Arab Nation*. Occasional Papers Series, Centre for Contemporary Arab Studies, Georgetown University. Washington. D.C.

al-Faḍlī, Ibrāhīm Jawād 1982. Al-tarjama bayna 1-ta'sīli 1-'ilmiyy wa 1-'amali 1-i'tibatiyy [Scientific Foundations vs Arbitrary Action]. Paper presented at the Conference on the Arabicization of Higher Education, Damascus University, May 1982.

Fishman, Joshua A. *et al.* (eds.) 1968. *Language Problems of Developing Nations*. New York.

Fox, Melvin 1974. *Language Education in Developing Countries. The Changing Role of the Ford Foundation*. New York.

Gallagher, Charles F. 1968. North African problems and prospects: Language and Identity. In Joshua A. Fishman *et al.* (eds.), *Language Problems of Developing Nations*. New York.

Glazer, Sidney 1974. 'Introduction' to his edition of *Abu Hayyan's Commentary to the Alfiyya of Ibn Malik*. American Oriental Series 31. New Haven, Conn.

Haas, W. (ed.) 1982a. *Standard Languages. Spoken and Written*. Manchester.

Hass, W. 1982b. On the Normative Character of Language. In W. Haas (ed.), *Standard Languages. Spoken and Written*. Manchester.

58   *Muhammad H. Ibrahim*

Hitti, Philip K. 1943. *The Arabs. A Short History.* Chicago.

Ibrahim, Muhammad H. 1983. Linguistic Distance and Literacy in Arabic. *Journal of Pragmatics,* 7: 507–515.

Ibrahim, Mudammad H. 1986. Wāqiʻal-Muṣṭalaḥāt al-ʻArabiyya wa mushkilātuhā [The State and Probelms of Arabic Terminology]. Paper presented to the Conference on Arab Co-operation in Terminology, Tunis, July, 7–10.

al-Jābirī, Muhammad ʻĀbid 1984. Ishkāliyyatu 1-assālti wa 1-muʻāṣara [The problem of Traditionalism vs Modernism]. *Al-Mustagbal al-ʻArabī,* 69: 54–80.

al-Jalīlī, Maḥmūd 1984. Tajārib fī 1-taʻrīb (Experiments in Arabicization). In *Muḥāḍarāt al-Mawsim al-Thaqāfī al-Thānī* [Lectures of the Second Cultural Season]. Amman.

al-Jinhānī, al-Ḥabīb 1982a. Taʻrīb al-taʻlīm al-jāmiʻī wa 1-mashrūʻal-ḥaḍārī al-ʻarabī [The Arabicization of University Education and the Arab Cultural Project]. Paper presented at the Conference on the Arabicization of Higher Education, Damascus University, 1982.

al-Jinhanī, al-Ḥabīb 1982b. Al-taʻrīb wa 1-aṣāla al-thaqāfiyya wa 1-muʻāṣara [Arabicization, cultural traditionalism, and modernism]. In M. M. Ṣayyādī, *et al., Al-Taʻrīb wa dawruhu fi tadʻīmi l-wujūdi l-ʻarabiyy wa l-wihda l-ʻarabiyya.* Beirut.

Juʻait, Hishām 1982. Comment on Sayyādī (1982a) (in Arabic) In M. M. Ṣayyādī *et al., Al-Taʻrīb wa dawruhu fi tadʻīmi l-wujūdi l-ʻarabiyy wa l-wihda l-ʻarabiyya.* Beirut.

Khūrī, Sheḥādeh 1984. Taʻrib al-taʻlīm al-ʻālī wa ṣilatuhu bi al-tarjamah [Arabicization of Higher Education and its Relation to Translation]. *Al-Lisan Al-ʻArabī,* 21: 137–156.

Mahmoud, Youssef 1979. The Arabic Writing System and the Sociolinguistics of Orthography Reform. Unpublished Ph.D. dissertation, Georgetown University.

Maʻmouri, M., ʻAbīd A. and al-Ghazālī, S. 1983. *Taʼthīr Taʻlīm al-Lughāt al-Ajnabiyya fī Taʼallum al-Lugha al-ʻArabiyya* [The Influence of Teaching Foreign Languages on the Learning of Arabic]. Tunis.

Mitchell, T. F. 1986. What is Educated Spoken Arabic? *International Journal of the Sociology of Language,* 61: 7–32.

Moussa, Salama 1955. Arabic Language Problems. *Middle Eastern Affairs,* February: 41–44.

Mseddi, Abdessalem 1984. *Dictionnaire de linguistique.* Tunis.

Muṣṭafā, Shākir 1982. Taʻqīb [Rejoinder]. In M. M. Ṣayyādī, *et al., Al-Taʻrīb wa dawruhu fi tadʻīmi l-wujūdi l-ʻarabiyy wa l-wihda l-ʻarabiyya.* Beirut.

Palva, Heikki 1969. Notes on Classicization in Modern Colloquial Arabic. *Studia Orientalia,* 40, 3: 1–41.

Palva, Heikki 1982. Patterns of Koineization in Modern Colloquial Arabic. *Acta Orientalia,* 43, 13: 13–32.

al-Qurashi, Khedir O. A. 1982. The Feasibility of the Arabic Language as Medium of Instruction in Sciences. Unpublished Ph.D. dissertation, Indiana University.

Ṣayyādī, M. M. 1982a. Al-taʻrīb fi l-waṭani l-ʻarabiyy [Arabicization in the Arab countries]. In M. M. Ṣayyādī, *et al., Al-Taʻrīb wa dawruhu fi tadʻīmi l-wujūdi l-ʻarabiyy wa l-wihda l-ʻarabiyya.* Beirut.

Ṣayyādī, M. M. 1982b. *Al-Taʻrīb wa dawruhu fi tadʻīmi l-wujūdi l-ʻarabiyy wa l-wihda l-ʻarabiyya* [Arabicization and its Role in Enhancing the Arab Identity and Arab Unity]. Beirut.

al-Sayyid, Maḥmūd A. 1980. *Al-isti'mālāt al-Lughawiyya al-Naḥwiyya fi al-Ta'bīr* [The Use of Grammatical Structures in (Oral and Written) Expression]. Damascus.

Sharīt, 'Abullah 1984. *Naḍhariyya Ḥawla Siyāsat al-ta'līm wa l-ta'rīb* [A Theory Concerning the Policy of Education and Arabicization]. Algiers.

al-Shihābī, Muṣṭafā 1965. *Al-Muṣṭalaḥāt al-'Ilmiyya fi l-Lugha al-'Arabiyya fi l-Qadīm wa l-Ḥadīth* [Scientific Terms in Arabic: Past and Present], 2nd edn. Damascus.

Valdman, Albert 1968. Language Standardization in a Diglossia Situation. In Joshua A. Fishman, *et al.* (eds.), *Language Problems of Developing Nations.* New York.

al-Yousef, Yousef 1978. Naḥwa falsafa li al-lugha al-'arabiyya [Towards a Philosophy of the Arabic Language]. *Al-Ma'rifa,* 178: 17–40.

Zachariev, Zachari 1981. Coexistence de langues écrites et problèmes socioculturels dans les pays en développement. In *La Traduction et la coopération culturelle internationale.* Sofia.

4 An assessment of the development and modernization of the Kiswahili language in Tanzania

DAVID P. B. MASSAMBA

The spread of Kiswahili

Kiswahili is one of the more than 120 languages[1] of Tanzania. Like the great majority of them (i.e. 102), it is a Bantu language (Batibo 1984; Whiteley 1969; Chiraggdin and Mnyampala 1977; Knappert 1979; Nurse and Spear 1985). Since the speakers of every language regard their language as being as good as the others, it would be difficult for any one language to dominate the others. Yet, for a variety of reasons, the status of Kiswahili has for a long time been different from that of other African languages in Tanzania.

Of course, in its early stages of development Kiswahili did not play the role it has assumed today. It was used by its native speakers only, who lived along the East African coast.[2] In this respect its status was not different from that of other African languages, but with the establishment of trade relations along the coast, Kiswahili became gradually more important as a language of wider communication.

The Arab slave traders realized the importance of Kiswahili and contributed to its spread along the East African coast and to the interior. Small slave-trading centers which were established in the interior developed into small towns in which Kiswahili became the major language of communication. After the abolition of the slave trade it continued to be used in this capacity. Trade between rural and urban areas as well as intermarriage further accelerated the spread of Kiswahili.

Religion was another factor which enhanced the spread of Kiswahili in Tanzania. The Muslims used it in preaching the Islamic faith. Christian missionaries first favored local languages over Kiswahili, since the latter was associated with Islam, but later they adopted Kiswahili both as a means of communication and as a medium of instruction.

When the Germans came to East Africa in the 1880s, Kiswahili had already acquired the status of an important African language. They therefore found it worthwhile to use the language. Under German administration the acquisition of Kiswahili was a first step towards participating in government through membership in the junior civil service (Whiteley 1969). The British administration, too, could not do without Kiswahili, using it as a medium of instruction in primary schools and as a means of communication for the district administration. Kiswahili was considered to be the only 'neutral' indigenous language. The colonialists used it as a language of power.

Despite the seemingly negative intentions that motivated the colonialists' use of Kiswahili, there was a positive effect. The requirement to know Kiswahili as a condition to be able to work for the junior civil service and the district administration prompted many Tanganyikans to learn the language, which thus continued to spread.

It is important to point out that during the struggles for independence Kiswahili was associated with nationalism, patriotism, and liberation – a kind of driving force that made everyone involved in the struggle, either directly or indirectly, strive to learn the language.

The development of Kiswahili

The development of Kiswahili in Tanzania has a long history, beginning before independence when a number of steps were taken for its promotion and development. After independence the government of Tanzania actively promoted the development of the language.

Pre-independence development

Some of the steps towards the development of Kiswahili taken before independence were coincidental, others were planned. In the 1860s missionaries began to use Kiswahili for their purposes. The Holy Ghost Fathers, the United Methodist Church, and, somewhat later, the German Protestant Mission, produced textbooks and newspapers (Whiteley 1969). Further, the colonial administration felt the need to have one African language which could be used throughout East Africa (i.e. Kenya, Uganda, Tanganyika, and Zanzibar). As a first step towards this goal, an education commission met in Dar es Salaam in 1925 in order to discuss which language should be used as the lingua franca.[3] The choice of Kiswahili was obvious. On the basis of the recommendations made by the education commission, the Inter-Territorial Language Committee was founded in 1930. It was this committee that defined standard Kiswahili as being based on the Zanzibar dialect.

Work on the standardization of Kiswahili began immediately after the 1925 education commission conference. A central publishing committee was set up charged with monitoring all projected textbooks for secular schools in order to avoid duplication of effort and to ascertain the standard. The standardization and development of Kiswahili was the responsibility of the Inter-Territorial Language Committee. In order to achieve this, the following strategies had to be pursued:

1   standardizing the orthography and obtaining complete inter-territorial agreement;

2   securing as much uniformity as possible in the use of existing and new words;

3   securing uniformity of grammar and syntax through the publication of standard books on the subject;

4   encouraging and assisting authors whose native tongue was Kiswahili;

5   giving advice to all prospective authors on books which they proposed to write;

6   procuring the revision where necessary of approved Kiswahili textbooks and books of a general nature already published;

7   drawing up an annual program of Kiswahili textbooks required under the headings of (a) textbooks and (b) general literature;

8   making arrangements for translating textbooks into Kiswahili or for writing such books in Kiswahili;

9   examining and where necessary correcting the Kiswahili of such textbooks and general literature before publication;

10   revising and giving advice on all Kiswahili books dealt with by the Committee;

11   supplying authors with information on teaching methods;

12   answering general inquiries concerning the Kiswahili language and literature;

13   undertaking such activities as may have been deemed instrumental and conducive to attaining the above objectives.

After the founding of the East African High Commission in 1948, the East African Inter-Territorial Language Committee was placed under its jurisdiction. A few years later another committee was established, known as the East African Literature Bureau. Its main objective was to assume the role of controlling publishing matters. However, the Inter-Territorial Language Committee remained the authority in matters of Kiswahili research and orthography.

Initially the Committee consisted of 17 members, the director of education, one official and two non-officials from each country, together with the organizing secretary. These members were whites, and it was not until 1946 that Africans participated in the meetings.

As long as it existed the Committee dealt with a number of issues pertaining to the development of the Kiswahili language, including the standardization of grammar and vocabulary, the production of textbooks, the creation of new words, and research on the various dialects of Kiswahili. Its involvement in the promotion of Kiswahili was tremendous and remains unparalleled. Whether or not the colonialists' endeavor to develop the language was in their own best interests need not concern us here; rather, what is important to note is the seriousness with which the colonialists attended to the development of Kiswahili. With Whiteley (1969: 82) it can be said that the work of the Committee laid the foundations for the development of Kiswahili as a modern African language.

Post-independence development

During the struggle for independence Kiswahili played an important role in uniting the people. Immediately after independence, in 1962, the then Tanganyika government therefore designated Kiswahili as the national language. Prime Minister Rashid Mfaume Kawawa declared: 'In the future Kiswahili will normally be used at State and Public functions when ministers and other members of Government are the speakers. In addition it is proposed, after Tanganyika becomes a republic, to permit Members of Parliament to use either English or Kiswahili in the National Assembly.'[4] In keeping with this statement President Julius Nyerere became the first African head of state to address a parliament in an indigenous African language.[5] From then on Kiswahili became the major language of parliament.

The use of Kiswahili in parliament was followed by introducing Kiswahili as a medium of instruction in all public primary schools. Government followed suit. On January 4, 1967, an official directive was issued prescribing the use of Kiswahili in all government and official business.

In Zanzibar Kiswahili was declared the official language shortly after the revolution in 1964 (Khatib 1983). A council was established which was charged with the responsibility of selecting Kiswahili books to be used in primary and secondary schools.[6] A number of institutions were established for the promotion of the Kiswahili language.

The Institute of Kiswahili Research. In 1963 the East African Swahili Committee moved to Dar es Salaam, where in 1964 it became the Institute of Kiswahili Research (I.K.R.). In 1970 it was integrated into the University of Dar es Salaam, where it was charged with the following responsibilities:

1   to study and promote the development of the Kiswahili language in all its aspects, with special reference to the support of current and long-term development plans in the United Republic of Tanzania, in East Africa and elsewhere, and in the University of Dar es Salaam;

2   to maintain the publication of the journal *Swahili* with articles of academic and general interest, and such other supplementary studies as might appear desirable from time to time;

3   to issue any other useful publications;

4   to collect up-to-date information on a world scale about the Kiswahili language and its use, about relevant policies, about materials available in archives and elsewhere, and about teaching and research in progress at all levels;

5   to disseminate and make available such information as widely as possible and to encourage relevant research, including the collection and publication of oral and written texts;

6   to carry out long-term research projects such as the preparation and updating of a standard dictionary and other types of dictionaries;

7   to organize short-term intensive research projects at all levels, from academic
          conferences to workshops, for the production of primary school materials in
          Kiswahili.

In order to carry out its responsibilities in a more effective way, the Institute
was divided into four sections. (1) the Lexicography Section was given the
task of compiling dictionaries, for example the monolingual Kiswahili dictionary and the English–Kiswahili dictionary. It was also entrusted with the
development of terminologies for the school subjects. (2) The Linguistics
Section was established to undertake research on Kiswahili phonology, morphology, syntax, sociolinguistics, and dialectology. (3) The Literature Section
was established to do research on written and oral literature in Kiswahili
within Tanzania. (4) Finally there was the Administration Section.

The National Swahili Council. From a political point of view, it was deemed
necessary to have a national body that would ensure that Kiswahili was being
developed in accordance with the goals and aspirations of the Tanzanian
nation. Hence the establishment of the National Swahili Council, commonly
known as 'BAKITA' (*Baraza la Kiswahili la Taifa*), in 1967 by an Act of
Parliament. The aims and objectives of BAKITA were stipulated as follows:

1   to create a healthy atmosphere for the development and use of Kiswahili in
          Tanzania;
2   to co-operate with other institutions involved in the development of Ki-
          swahili and co-ordinate their activities;
3   to encourage the use of Kiswahili in government functions and all other
          business in general;
4   to emphasize and encourage correct and standard Kiswahili usage;
5   to co-operate with relevant sectors and/or institutions in providing simple
          translations of technical terminology;
6   to publish a pamphlet or journal on Kiswahili language and literature;
7   to provide services for the development of Kiswahili to the government,
          public meetings, and writers who write in Kiswahili. (My translation)

By an amendment Act of Parliament in 1983, the activities of BAKITA
were expanded to include the following:

8   as regards co-operation with other institutions, organs, or individuals, advise
          on, co-ordinate, and follow up all activities that pertain to the promotion of
          the Kiswahili language;
9   to establish a variety of national institutions and organs to co-ordinate
          research on Kiswahili in the United Republic;
10   to examine, if requested by authors and translators, all new material written
          and translated into Kiswahili in order to ascertain the standard nature of the
          language;
11   to co-operate with publishers in helping authors to write standard Kiswahili;
12   to conduct Kiswahili essay competitions;
13   to co-operate with the Ministry of Education in examining and approving
          Kiswahili textbooks before they are actually printed. (My translation)

Comparing the two organs – the I.K.R. and BAKITA, – one realizes that their objectives are rather different. The I.K.R. is an academic institution, while BAKITA is a politically oriented organ. Whereas the I.K.R. strives for academic excellence, BAKITA's purpose is to make sure that Kiswahili is developed in the best interests of the Tanzanian nation. It is BAKITA which has been entrusted with the seal of approval with regard to usage and standardization.

Department of Kiswahili, University of Dar es Salaam. The University of Dar es Salaam Act of 1970 provided for the establishment of the Department of Swahili. Its main objective was to train students interested in Kiswahili linguistics, literature, and theater. Most of the students are enrolled in a teacher education program for secondary schools and colleges of education.

The Institute of Education. The Institute of Education was not designed primarily to promote Kiswahili; however, one of its duties is curriculum development. As far as Kiswahili is concerned, the Institute prepares syllabuses for primary and secondary schools and teachers' colleges. It has a special unit for the preparation of seminars on teaching methodology for Kiswahili addressed to language and literature teachers. It is also engaged in the preparation of Kiswahili textbooks for primary schools.

Ministry of Youth and Culture. Since Kiswahili is part of Tanzanian culture, it was deemed appropriate to charge the Ministry of Youth and Culture with some responsibility for the language. A Directorate of Kiswahili Language Promotion and Development was set up, and a cultural office was established in each region and district of Tanzania. Each of the cultural offices had a language officer who was responsible for the development of Kiswahili in his own area.

The Kiswahili language situation

Given the steps that have been taken, so far, in order to foster the development and promotion of Kiswahili as surveyed in the previous section, one might wish at this juncture to examine the present language situation in Tanzania.

In non-technical domains the development of Kiswahili has been quite encouraging. It is used in almost all social gatherings as well as in public and government business. In Tanzania Kiswahili is the medium of instruction in all public and some private primary schools. There is much more popular literature written in Kiswahili today than there was thirty years ago. Also Kiswahili is an effective tool of political propaganda.

In technical domains, however, Kiswahili seems to have a long way to go. The medium of instruction in secondary schools, colleges, and universities is English, even though there was speculation that perhaps by the year 1990 Kiswahili would be the medium of instruction in all secondary schools and higher institutions of learning. In any discussion with technical aspects speakers often switch to English. Moreover, not all technical subjects have been written about in Kiswahili, and translations of textbooks are scarce. It is clear, therefore, that in the domain of modern technology Kiswahili is still far from adequate. In the following we examine the reasons for this situation.

Inadequacies in language planning

We saw earlier that a number of formal steps were taken to foster the development of Kiswahili after independence. However, language planning has more implications than setting up some institutions.

Before we delve into the problems of language planning in Tanzania in more detail, it is important to clarify our stand on the concept of 'language planning.' Daswani (see chapter 5) correctly points out that 'terms such as "language standardization" (Ray 1963), "language development" (Ferguson 1971), "language modernization" (Krishnamurti and Mukherjee 1984), and "language planning" (Haugen 1971) are used almost interchangeably.' In our opinion, this cannot be regarded as terminological confusion. Rather, there is a legitimacy in using these terms interchangeably because the concepts represented by them overlap. It is precisely this difficulty that creates disagreement among scholars regarding the definition and scope of language planning. Our own concept of 'language planning' is similar to Haugen's (1971). The only difference is that we allow it to include both language development and language modernization, while Haugen's definition does not include these concepts.

Language planning cannot be equated with mere pronouncements with regard to what the language situation ought to be. In other words, it does not suffice to merely declare that language L is a national or offical language of a people P. Nor does it suffice to simply establish an institute for language development or language research. Quite a number of questions have to be addressed first.

To begin with, it is necessary to identify the problems involved in the language-planning process. For instance, we need to know who the people are that should be involved in the planning exercise itself. It should not be the task of politicians alone; the relevant technical experts also need to be involved, for they have much to contribute. Unfortunately, most of the pronouncements on language policy in Tanzania so far have been made by politicians with no technical expertise.

Next, we need to assess the social implications of a given language-planning decision. We need to know, for example, whether the people will readily accept the suggested language or dialect, and, if not, what is to be done to alleviate the situation. Further, we need to know what kind of organs should be established and for what specific purposes, how those organs should be run, and what kind of training is needed for their personnel. We also need to know what problems are likely to arise and how to go about them. Above all, we need to have a clear picture of the financial implications of all this.

Notice that at this stage we are only concerned with identifying problems. The 'fact-finding stage,' as Rubin (1972) calls it, is crucial in the sense that it enables us to see exactly what we are going into before the planning itself takes off. To the best of our knowledge this never took place in Tanzania. Moreover, in its strictest sense the second stage, that is the actual planning, was never realized either. In order to have 'actual planning,' we need to be clear about the goals, the strategies to be used, and what the expected outcomes are.

It is true that institutions such as the I.K.R. at the University of Dar es Salaam, the Institute of Kiswahili and Foreign Languages in Zanzibar, BAKITA, and the Department of Kiswahili of the University of Dar es Salaam are all geared towards the development of the Kiswahili language. It is also true that the government has been financing these institutions. This has not been done, however, with a perspective of language planning similar to the one sketched above.

Unlike its predecessor – the East African Swahili Committee – the I.K.R. is not directly under the surveillance of the government. Since its integration into the University of Dar es Salaam, it has pursued academic purposes. Of course, this is not a negative quality as far as language development is concerned. As will become more obvious below, its role for the promotion of Kiswahili cannot be overemphasized. Also, it is precisely this quality that has promoted the I.K.R. from national to international recognition. What is to be noted here, though, is that the I.K.R. has reached its present status out of its own initiative as an academic institution of a university and not on the basis of a language-planning policy in Tanzania.

On the other hand, BAKITA which is the national organ entrusted with the promotion and development of the Kiswahili language in Tanzania has not fared quite as well. Since its inception in 1967, BAKITA has not gained the recognition a body of its kind should have. Considering the conditions under which BAKITA has been operating, this could have been expected. While the aims and objectives of BAKITA seem reasonable, a closer examination reveals certain weaknesses. Consider, for example, the first three aims and objectives. The first one is 'to create a healthy atmosphere for the development and usage of Kiswahili in Tanzania.' It is not said how this is to be achieved. The second one is 'to co-operate with other institutions involved in the development of Kiswahili and co-ordinate their activities.' Again, this is extremely vague. What would the parameters be for such co-operation? Which institutions are to be involved, and at what level? The third one is 'to encourage the use of Kiswahili in government functions and all other business in general.' Here too it does not say how this is to be carried out. This points back to the problem we touched upon earlier – the failure to know exactly what one is going into before the actual planning takes off. Yet another problem of BAKITA is its financial difficulties. Because of them it has failed to carry out its activities as effectively as it should have. It is clear that the government of Tanzania has not given BAKITA the status it deserves. To create an organ entrusted with the responsibility for language standard-ization, terminology development, and imprimatur, and then fail to give it the required financial support, is to make it futile.

Furthermore, the above mentioned language officers under the direction of the Ministry of Youth and Culture are mere figure-heads. They have no clearly defined programs adopted uniformly throughout the country; instead, every language officer tends to define his/her own program. Most of them are not even university graduates. Hence it is difficult for them to draw up any language program at all.

If we compare institutions for the promotion and development of Kiswahili established before and after independence, we notice a significant contrast. Clearly there were fewer organs involved in the promotion of Kiswahili before independence than there are now. Surprisingly, however, more seriousness seems to have been attached to the development of the language before independence than after independence. The reasons for this state of affairs are examined in the section that follows.

Lack of systematic follow-ups and evaluations

The 'actual planning' stage is followed by the implementation stage which, among other things, includes follow-ups. Systematic follow-ups are necessary in order to ensure that the planning is not only implemented, but that it is implemented in the way intended.

Language planning is a long-term process. Therefore follow-ups have to be carried out in a systematic manner, allowing enough time for every stage of implementation. Each of these stages has to be evaluated separately, and the evaluation should contain recommendations as to how the following stage should proceed.

Since no systematic language-planning procedures were followed in Tan-zania, the absence of follow-ups and evaluations of the activities of the various institutions and bodies established by the Tanzanian government for the development of Kiswahili is only an expected consequence. It is mainly due to these deficiencies that the Tanzanian government has found it difficult to achieve the anticipated goals with regard to the promotion and development of the Kiswahili language.

As suggested above, follow-ups and evaluations of the individual stages of implementation help to monitor and co-ordinate the development of the language in question, which can then be expected to proceed in a systematic and uniform manner.[7] Since this has not been done in Tanzania, the develop-ment of the Kiswahili language has been neither 'systematic' nor 'uniform.'

For example, radio broadcasts often diverge from so-called 'standard'

Kiswahili.[8] Vocabulary and terminology are used rather inconsistently and incorrectly. The same situation obtains in the press. There are no clearly established norms of usage. As a consequence, there have been a number of debates both on the radio and in the newspapers about what ought to be regarded as 'correct' usage. This situation is mainly due to the fact that there is, in practice, no organ that controls the imprimatur of Kiswahili books and other printed material. In the past this was not a big problem because the Inter-Territorial Language Committee controlled the imprimatur of almost every Kiswahili publication. In Tanzania it is BAKITA which was empowered with the seal of approval with regard to language usage. BAKITA has, however, proved to be ineffective. The problem is becoming ever more serious because of the increasing number of publications in Kiswahili.

Problems of the sort described above are not really peculiar to the language situation in Tanzania. Mistakes in the use of the standard language have also been evident in Arabic (see chapter 3). Comparing the situation of Arabic with that of Kiswahili, two important points come to mind. First, it is clear that the two languages have one thing in common, namely that in both cases one finds incorrect usage of the standard language. Once this has become the usual practice, a 'new language,' as Ibrahim calls it, will emerge. Secondly, in spite of this commonality, there is also a big difference between the two languages. While in Arabic there is a great distance separating the formally learned written standard language from the natively acquired spoken varieties, in Kiswahili the situation is not quite the same. Although there are many dialects, the disparity between the spoken and the written forms is reduced since Kiswahili is mostly written as it is spoken. Moreover, native speakers of Kiswahili along the Tanzanian coast speak a dialect which is more or less the same as standard Kiswahili. Most native speakers of Kiswahili in Tanzania speak better standard Kiswahili than educated speakers who studied it at school. Indeed, most of the incorrect usage in the standard language in the mass media is attributable to people who speak Kiswahili as their second or third language. As regards books and other printed material, incorrect usage is more evident in those written by non-native speakers than in those written by native speakers. This is not to say, however, that all native speakers of Kiswahili in Tanzania have a better command of the standard language than all educated people who speak it as their second language.

To sum up, we might say, therefore, that if BAKITA had effectively assumed its role of approval on published material in Kiswahili, the language situation in Tanzania would be very different from what it is now. For a language which is just beginning to emerge as one of the world's most important languages, imprimatur on books and other published materials is a necessary requirement. To leave the written language in a state of *laissez-faire* is to do the language more harm than good.

Lack of systematic terminology development

One of the most important tasks in developing a language which is under-developed in the spheres of science and technology is the deliberate effort of forming neologisms (see, for example, Tumbo 1982). No language is truly modern unless it can cope with modern technology.

In Tanzania the development of scientific and technical terminology in the Kiswahili language has been realized in two forms, formally and informally. Formally the work has been the responsibility of BAKITA. Informally it has been dealt with by institutions and individuals who are interested in developing terminologies for use in their day-to-day activities. Although BAKITA has been entrusted with this work, it does not itself have any trained and qualified terminologists. It does have a terminology committee, but most of its members have no background in linguistics or terminology formation. Thus BAKITA cannot seriously engage in terminology development. It depends largely on terminologies submitted to it by institutions and individuals, who may well not be experts in terminology work either. Once terminologies have been received by BAKITA, they are discussed by the terminology committee and sent back to the institutions and individuals who submitted them for revision. Such decisions are made on the basis of guidelines drawn up for terminology work. Approved terminology lists are published in small booklets.

For two reasons BAKITA's efforts in terminology development have not been very encouraging. The first has to do with the whole set-up of BAKITA as a politically oriented organ. Its constitution requires that the chairman of the council be appointed by the President of the United Republic. The council must have between fifty and sixty members appointed by the Minister of Youth and Culture. The council members must come from Tanzania mainland and Zanzibar in a ratio of two to one. The constitution also provides that there be members from organizations and institutions which are involved in language promotion, and that every region must be represented. However, there is no provision for academic qualifications of council members which could guarantee that BAKITA has the expertise it requires. Hence its ineffectiveness.

The second reason that accounts for BAKITA's shortcomings has to do with financial problems; because of these BAKITA is unable to convene its meetings regularly. Furthermore, terminologies that have been approved cannot be disseminated properly because of a lack of funds.

The institutions and individuals who urgently need Kiswahili terminologies for use in their everyday activities cannot wait for BAKITA's lists to appear. They therefore often develop their own terminologies and use them without BAKITA's approval. The danger here is that most of these terminologies are developed without any terminography expertise or co-ordination. This gives rise to what one might call 'terminology chaos.'

The terminology chaos which is already emerging in Kiswahili should not be underrated; its implications are far-reaching. Once it has been allowed to continue unchecked for some time, there will be no system to Kiswahili terminology development. After all, the main reason for having to submit all terminologies to BAKITA for approval is to ensure that the forms are uniformly standardized.

The seriousness of terminology chaos has been witnessed elsewhere. In Arabic, for example, extensive variation in technical terms has taken its toll. According to Ibrahim (see chapter 3), one of the more serious problems facing Arabicization and the adaptation of Arabic for modern communication needs is variability in usage of technical terms. Ibrahim argues that this is due to the fact that there is no co-ordination among the Arab countries and among individuals and agencies within any one country in the field of Arabicization and terminology work. This situation, according to Ibrahim, is so serious that it is common to find different Arabic equivalents of English terms even in dictionaries and glossaries printed by the same publisher.

The danger with such a situation is that if it continues for a long time, then the terminology chaos will invade the non-technical vocabulary too. And if this happens and is allowed to persist for some time, it will result in the formation of sub-dialects, which in turn will ultimately develop into distinct dialects whose appearance will then have defeated the whole purpose of having a standard language.

The need for a more effective composition of BAKITA

In the preceding section we saw that BAKITA's set-up is for the most part political. Most of the members appointed to the council are representatives of the various regions rather than technical experts with the necessary know-how. For an organ that is designed to operate from a political perspective this may not be a problem, but with the kind of activities that BAKITA is charged with the members of the council should be selected on the basis of their technical know-how and not on political grounds. The author's own experience in this council is that many of its members, while attending the sessions, never contribute anything to the discussions.

A related problem is the question of the number of council members. In view of BAKITA's persistent financial problems a minimum of 50 councillors seems too many. The number could be reduced in order to save money and to serve the council better. Experience elsewhere has shown that where technical know-how is required, the smaller the number of participants the better. Let us take a practical example. During the 1983–1986 triennium BAKITA had five committees, namely the Executive Committee, the Standardization Committee, the Committee on Grammar and Imprimatur, the Translation Committee, and the Committee for Journals and Writing. The members of these committees numbered 7, 25, 15, 15, and 15, respectively. Given the financial constraints under which the council has to operate, the numbers could have been reduced to something like 7, 8, 8, 8, and 8. This would have cut the expenses and made the discussions more lively and effective. The snag here, however, is that the set-up of the council does not allow for this kind of reduction, which could easily be realized if technical expertise were the criterion for the selection of council members.

In any case, if BAKITA is to be effective in its work, its composition will have to be restructured. As a model of how this could be achieved one might consider the terminology work done in Israel as described by Rabin (see chapter 2). Its most interesting feature for our present discussion is that in Israel those who will have to use the new terminologies are involved in the process of their development. In other words, we are suggesting that the composition of a terminology committee should be based on technical know-how and not on political inclinations. If new terminologies are worked out by practitioners, the future users will not find them strange once they are published with official approval.

Terminology development is a technical field which should be handled by technical experts, that is practitioners in the various fields of application, and linguists. If BAKITA's activities are academic the choice of its members ought to reflect this. Only if its activities are not academic is there a case for a more broadly based body to take over the responsibilities of terminology formation.

The question of attitudes

That language planning and language development at the national level depend upon the attitudes and aspirations of the 'the powers that be' is a foregone conclusion. Since they are the decision makers they have great influence on language planning and language policy. After all, the colonialists became interested in developing Kiswahili because to them it was a language of power; the Tanzanian nationalists who were at the forefront in the struggles for independence stressed the importance of, and need for, Kiswahili because to them it was a language of liberation. What this means is that politicians, be they colonialists or nationalists, will strive to promote and develop a language only when it serves their interests.

As Coulmas argues (see chapter 13): 'Language cultivation requires certain language attitudes, such as the willingness of an elite to use language as a means of social control and unification, as a barrier to outsiders, and as a symbol of national identity.' That is to say, if the elites are not willing to use their language as a means of social control, then that language is likely to face adaptation problems. On the other hand, if the elites are willing and determined to develop the language, there is no doubt the language will eventually reach a high level of development.

Attitudes in Tanzania

Most of the decision makers and the educated elite in Tanzania attended schools whose medium of instruction was English, from the then middle schools to colleges and universities. Many of them do not regard Kiswahili as an 'academic language,' maintaining that one cannot argue academically in Kiswahili. Some even go so far as to say that the falling standards in education are attributable to the use of Kiswahili in schools. Clearly this is a problem of attitude, since their arguments cannot be substantiated by any clear facts. After all, Kiswahili is used as a medium of instruction in primary schools only. Moreover, studies like those by Mlama and Matteru (1979) have demonstrated that the English medium in many secondary schools and colleges is an obstacle to the learning process. Their study shows that students have problems not only in expressing themselves in English but also in understanding it. Furthermore, even the teachers of these institutions have problems in expressing themselves in English. Thus it is the falling standard of English which has affected the education standard in Tanzania. The falling standard of English is understandable considering the relatively minor role that English has in Tanzania as a means of communication since Kiswahili took over as the official language.

It would be absurd to underrate the importance of English as a commercial language. The emphasis, however, should be put on teaching English as a subject rather than insisting on its being used as a medium of instruction.

Experience elsewhere

Proponents of using English as a medium of instruction in Tanzania argue that Kiswahili is not capable of handling modern technology. It is true that up till now Kiswahili has been inadequate in this regard, but this does not mean that it is by its very nature incapable of handling modern technology. The problem that Kiswahili faces is one of time more than anything else. It needs to be developed and modernized before it can do what can be expected of it. Language adaptation is not an overnight phenomenon. It takes place gradually and can take many years before the expected results are realized.

The difficulties that Kiswahili faces are not peculiar to this language alone. Even the most highly developed languages of today, like English, French, and German, had similar problems when they first emerged as modern standard languages. Coulmas (see chapter 13) observes, for example, that up till the turn of the seventeenth century German was regarded as a boorish language unfit not only for modern technology but even for the demands of educated discourse. Indeed, the situation in which Kiswahili is now, one might say with confidence, is characteristic of all developing languages in the world.

Reasons for slow progress in Tanzania

While, clearly, Kiswahili needs time to adapt to new functions, it should not be taken for granted that, as time goes by, the language *will* adapt. In order to achieve this there must be deliberate efforts to develop the language. Arguably the slow progress in the development of Kiswahili is due to the fact that the government has not given it the attention it requires. The government expected the language to develop into a language of modern technology, but no serious steps were taken to bring this about. Among the necessary steps are, for example, (1) to commission people to write Kiswahili textbooks for secondary schools and higher institutions of learning; (2) to commission people to translate important textbooks into Kiswahili; (3) to form serious and effective terminology commissions. However, because no such efforts were undertaken, it is not surprising that the development has been slow.

Positive indications

In the preceding sections we have discussed in some detail the nature of the development of Kiswahili and tried to pinpoint the problems and obstacles. This does not mean that no achievements have been made so far. Despite the many problems there are some encouraging signs of success.

The Institute of Kiswahili Research

Since the I.K.R. became an integral part of the University of Dar es Salaam in 1970, its contribution to the development of Kiswahili has been tremendous. We cannot enumerate all the activities in which the I.K.R. has been involved. For the purpose of our discussion we will only point out what we consider the major achievements.

One of the responsibilities that the I.K.R. was charged with when it took over from the East African Swahili Committee was to maintain the publication of the journal *Swahili*, which was renamed *Kiswahili* in 1970. This journal, which deals with linguistic, lexicographic, terminological, literary, and theatrical aspects of the Kiswahili language has since then been maintained and has become more academically oriented than it was before. The journal has claimed international status; it is ordered and read in almost every part of the academic world. In this way it has helped to expand the academic boundaries of Kiswahili.

The Institute also publishes another journal known as *Mulika* which deals mainly with critiques and book reviews concerning all aspects of the Kiswahili language. In addition, it also publishes articles in the fields of Kiswahili linguistics, literature, theater, and terminology. However, unlike *Kiswahili* this journal is aimed at secondary schools and colleges as a guide to both students and teachers.

The Institute has also published quite a few books on the Kiswahili language. One of the most remarkable achievements of the I.K.R. is the mono-lingual Kiswahili dictionary published in 1981.[9] The Institute is now working on an English–Kiswahili dictionary and a Kiswahili syntax. In 1984 the first book on Kiswahili morphology written entirely in Kiswahili appeared.

Another achievement of the Institute is the technical terminology for litera-ture and theater arts which was approved by BAKITA in 1984. Also, articles on terminology have been published regularly in *Kiswahili*. The Institute is now working on technical terminologies in the fields of chemistry, physics, linguistics, and biology.

Further, under the auspices of Unesco and the S.I.D.A. (Swedish Inter-national Development), the I.K.R. has organized four international confer-ences involving delegates from all Kiswahili-speaking areas, that is Kenya, Zaire, Burundi, Rwanda, Comoro, Tanzania, and Uganda. Three volumes of proceedings have been published. These conferences have not only helped to expand the boundaries of Kiswahili, but they have also provided people from different Kiswahili-speaking areas an opportunity to exchange views and learn from each other's experiences. The Institute intends to continue to hold similar conferences at least once a year.

As far as Kiswahili literature is concerned, the I.K.R. has done a great deal of research, especially in the area of oral literature. Proverbs, narratives, and riddles have been collected from different parts of the country and published. Materials relevant to Kiswahili literature which were first redacted in the Arabic script were transliterated. Most of them are poems. The Institute intends to do more research on the history and development of Kiswahili poetry.

BAKITA (National Kiswahili Council)

In spite of its many difficulties, the National Kiswahili Council can boast of some achievements. One of its major activities is to approve Kiswahili tech-nical terms which have been suggested either by institutions, by its own mem-bers, or by individuals who are interested in terminology development. Up till now quite a number of technical terms have been approved by BAKITA in such fields as economics, mathematics, history, biology, physics, chemistry, geography, political science, finance, and business.

BAKITA also has a weekly radio program, *Lugha ya taifa* (The national language), which discusses a variety of aspects of the Kiswahili language, ranging from linguistics to literature. In the past BAKITA used to publish small pamphlets such as *Lugha yetu* (Our language) and *Jifunze Kiswahili uwafunze na wengine* (Learn Kiswahili so that you may teach others), but because of financial difficulties publication has been discontinued. Other activities include the editing of manuscripts and documents from government offices, and translation work.

The Kiswahili Department

The contribution of the Kiswahili Department at the University of Dar es Salaam to the development of Kiswahili has also been tremendous. It should be remembered that the Department was established for the purpose of training students interested in Kiswahili linguistics, literature, and theater arts. Since most of these students also take teacher education courses after completion of their degree studies, they become teachers of Kiswahili in secondary schools and colleges of education. During the last five years a total of 96 students graduated in Kiswahili: 68 of them majored in Kiswahili, while the rest took it as their minor subject. Although these figures may look small, it must be realized that the impact of these graduates has been considerable. This is because if we examine all institutions in Tanzania which are concerned with the teaching, development, or promotion of Kiswahili we find that more than 75% of the personnel are graduates from the Kiswahili Department. For example, more than 90% of the academic staff of the I.K.R. graduated from the Kiswahili Department. It would be fair, therefore, to say that since in every institution which has to do with the teaching, development, or promotion of Kiswahili, more than half of the academic staff graduated from the Kiswahili Department, it has made a greater contribution to the development and promotion of Kiswahili than any other institution.

In addition to training teachers and researchers, the Department also issues the journal *Kioo cha Lugha* (Language mirror) of the Chama cha Kiswahili (Kiswahili Society). The journal publishes academic articles concerning linguistic, literary, and theatrical aspects of the Kiswahili language.

Individual efforts

During the past fifteen years the number of writers in Kiswahili has increased steadily, especially in popular literature. The many new books pose a certain problem because, since there is no imprimatur, the language used is not always standard. In most of them the spoken language is not differentiated from the written language.

Of late some writers have made attempts to write technical books in such fields as physics, chemistry, biology, and secretarial courses at an elementary level. The government's policy to emphasize English as a medium of instruction has, however, discouraged such potentially prolific writers in Kiswahili.

Concluding remarks

In this chapter we have discussed in some detail the spread, development, and promotion of Kiswahili in East Africa, especially in Tanzania. We have observed the various steps that have been taken towards the development of this language before and after independence. Our discussion has revealed that there are a number of problems that have slowed down the development of Kiswahili in Tanzania which, as we have argued, can be attributed among other things to the unclear language-planning policy. In view of this we have tried to pinpoint the main weaknesses and have put forward some suggestions for their correction.

We have also noted that, notwithstanding the various problems, there have been some encouraging achievements. We have seen that institutions such as the I.K.R., BAKITA, and the Kiswahili Department have contributed much to the spread, development, and promotion of the Kiswahili language in Tanzania, which, as a result, is far ahead of other Kiswahili-speaking countries in this regard.

Given this state of affairs we can say that although the development of Kiswahili in Tanzania has had a number of obstacles to overcome, the language is slowly developing into a language of modern technology. The boundaries of Kiswahili have been expanded greatly during the last twenty years. More and more people are learning and teaching Kiswahili in their respective countries. Almost every reputable radio station has a Kiswahili program. Many countries are taking a keen interest in the language because it is one of the major lingua francas of Africa; optimists have it that it will eventually be *the* major lingua franca of Africa.

In order to ensure the steady and accelerated development of Kiswahili in Tanzania the whole question of language planning and language policy needs to be re-examined. Such an exercise should involve experts; it should not be left in the hands of platform politicians who merely sing songs of praise without having the grasp of what those songs mean!

Notes

1 Note that we are using the term 'language' in a rather loose sense. Although each of the 120 'languages' claims its own linguistic identity, from a linguistic point of view some would not qualify as languages. For example, I have shown elsewhere (Massamba 1977: 138) that, although Ci-Ruri, Ci-Jita, and Ki-Kwaya are claimed to be different languages, they are actually dialects of the same language.
2 Although it is now widely accepted that Kiswahili is a Bantu language, the question as to where exactly along the East African coast it originated remains in dispute.
3 The commission was known as the Phelp-Stokes Commission. The 1925 meeting was followed by a meeting of representatives of the four countries held in Mombasa in 1928, where the possibility was deliberated of using one of the Kiswahili dialects as the standard form.
4 As reported in Tanganyika newspapers of September 7, 1962.
5 This also took place in 1962, immediately after President Nyerere took office.
6 The main purpose of this exercise was to make sure that the textbooks had no 'colonial hangover.'
7 Here by 'language' we mean the standard language and not necessarily all the dialects of the particular language.

8 It must be noted, however, that the question of what exactly should be regarded as standard Kiswahili remains controversial.

9 We are aware of the problems involved in this work. Nevertheless, we are convinced that this dictionary is quite a breakthrough.

References

Batibo, H. M. 1984. Language Policy and Research Priorities in Tanzania. Unpublished documentary paper for Linguistics Conference of the S.A.D.C.C. Universities, Zomba, Malawi.

Chiraggdin, S. and Mnyampala, M. 1977. *Historia ya Kiswahili.* Nairobi.

Ferguson, C. A. (1971). Language Development. In Anwar S. Dil (ed.), *Language Structure and Language Use.* Stanford.

Haugen, Einar 1971. Instrumentalism in Language Planning. In J. Rubin and Björn H. Jernudd (eds.), *Can Language be Planned?* Honolulu.

Khatib, M. S. 1983. Historia na maendelo ya Kiswahili Zanzibar. In *Proceedings of the International Seminar for Kiswahili Writers. The Kiswahili Language.* Dar es Salaam.

Knappert, J. 1979. *Four Centuries of Swahili Verse.* London.

Krishnamurti, B. and Mukherjee, A. (eds.) 1984. *Modernization of Indian Languages in News Media.* Hyderabad.

Massamba, D. P. B. 1977. A Comparative Study of the Ruri, Jita and Kwaya 'Languages' of the Eastern Shores of Lake Nyanza (Victoria). M.A. thesis, University of Dar es Salaam.

Mlama, Penina O. and Matteru, M. B. 1979. Haja ya Kutumia Kiswahili Kufundishia katika Elimu ya Juu. *Lugha Yetu,* 35/36: 1–31.

Nurse, D. and Spear, T. 1985. *The Swahili. Reconstructing the History and Language of an African Society, 800–1500.*

Ray, P. S. 1963. *Language Standardization.* The Hague.

Rubin, J. 1972. Evaluation and Language Planning. In J. A. Fishman (ed.) *Advances in the Sociology of Language,* vol. 2. The Hague.

Tumbo, Z. N. 1982. The Coining of Scientific Terms in Kiswahili. *Kiswahili, Journal of the Institute of Kiswahili Research* 49, 1: 403–407.

Whiteley, W. H. 1969. *Swahili. The Rise of a National Language.* London.

5 Aspects of modernization in Indian languages

C. J. DASWANI

Language planning

Any consideration of the strategies for adaptation of a language belongs, probably, to the relatively recent field of language planning. Even a superficial survey of some of the available literature on language planning reveals a remarkable variety of opinion on what forms the subject matter of language planning. Indeed, one encounters conflicting viewpoints and contradictions in the basic assumptions underlying the various attempts at formulation of a theoretical framework for the study of language-planning goals and processes. There is also a great deal of ambiguity and overlap in the terminology employed by the various scholars. Terms such as 'language standardization' (Ray 1963), 'language development' (Ferguson 1971), 'language modernization' (Krishnamurti and Mukherjee 1984), and 'language planning' (Haugen 1966a, 1971; Rubin and Jernudd 1971; Southworth and Daswani 1974; and many others) are used almost interchangeably. For Ferguson (1971) modernization is only one of the three components of language development, the other two being graphization and standardization. Haugen (1971: 281) uses 'language planning' and 'language standardization' in roughly identical meanings.

There is also no consensus on the definition and scope of language planning. In 1959, Haugen defined language planning as 'the activity of preparing a normative orthography, grammar and dictionary for the guidance of writers and speakers in a non-homogeneous speech community ... Planning implies an attempt to guide the development of a language in a direction desired by the planners' (Haugen 1968: 673f). In 1966, Haugen defined language planning thus: 'LP (language planning) is called for wherever there are language problems ... The heart of LP is rather what I referred to as the "exercise of judgment in the form of choices among available linguistic forms." Even more concisely, I think we can define LP as *the evaluation of linguistic change*' (Haugen 1966a: 52). Elsewhere in this paper, Haugen suggests that the problems that give rise to language planning may be considered special cases of the problems of non-communication. According to Rubin and Jernudd

(1971: xvi), 'language planning is *deliberate* language change, that is, changes in the systems of language code or speaking or both that are planned by organizations that are established for such purposes or given a mandate to fulfill such purposes.' Rubin (1971: 218) states: 'Language planning focusses upon the solutions to language problems through decisions about alternative goals, means, and outcomes to solve these problems.'

While the foregoing definitions of language planning are externally oriented in the sense of there being an external agency that plans a language, the notion 'language development' as used by Ferguson (1971) focusses on the process of development within a language. Ferguson is aware that structurally no language (or dialect) can be legitimately called 'backward' or 'primitive.' He therefore sets up 'three dimensions relevant for measuring language development: graphization – reduction to writing; standardization – the development of a norm which overrides regional and social dialects; and, for want of a better term, modernization – the development of intertranslatability with other languages in a range of topics and forms of discourse characteristic of industrialized, secularized, structurally differentiated "modern" societies' (Ferguson 1971: 221). Ferguson's formulation is both more specific and value-loaded. According to this formulation, languages can be at various stages – at least three – of development. By implication a language has to pass through the stages of graphization and standardization before it can become intertranslatable with other languages and meet the communicative needs of modern society. This formulation also implies that only industrialized, secularized, and structurally differentiated societies are 'modern.' There is a danger of circularity here.

Ferguson equates his formulation with several other approaches, particularly that of Haugen (1966b), which sets up a four-way matrix for language development:

1   selection of norm;
2   codification of form;
3   elaboration of function;
4   acceptance by the community.

Ferguson equates Haugen's elaboration of function with his own modernization feature, and the other three points in Haugen's model with aspects of standardization. Presumably both Ferguson (1971) and Haugen (1966b) are still dealing with external or extra-linguistic factors in language development as distinct from natural linguistic change. If that assumption can be made, then Haugen is talking of the development of a dialect into a standard language through elaborated communicative functions, while Ferguson is essentially concerned with the development in an underdeveloped country which faces the problem of national multilingualism. In fact, the major slant in language-planning theory seems to be that 'a country that is linguistically highly heterogeneous is always underdeveloped' (Pool 1972: 222).

The view that economic development and monolingualism go together is put forward on the basis of what has happened in Europe and the Western hemisphere in the wake of industrialization. The emergence of the standard languages in Europe is seen at least as a necessary (if not also a sufficient) condition for economic development in these countries.

While the Western viewpoint of language planning is generally accepted, linguists in the developing countries are now raising questions about the validity of this viewpoint in a stable grassroots multilingual society. The issue that is being raised is whether a political and economic model can be found to sustain multilingualism without sacrificing national development (see Pattanayak 1981).

Language modernization

Let us return to Ferguson's concept of modernization. The process of modernization is seen to have 'two aspects: (a) the expansion of the lexicon of the language by new words and expressions and, (b) the development of new styles and forms of discourse.' (Ferguson 1971: 227). Ferguson states that the second aspect has been less studied than the first. He is clear that lexical expansion, in order to be effective, must not be too fast. Lexical expansion can be effected both from within the language as well as by borrowing from other languages.

Strictly speaking, when reduced to these two aspects, modernization in the development of a language need not be a modern phenomenon. Surely, all languages go through a process of modernization at various periods in their history. In addition to the natural growth of the lexicon through semantic change, speech communities need to consciously add to their vocabularies in order to cope with new concepts and objects which result from accelerated activity both at the real-world (instrumental) level and at the philosophical (expressive) level. As Ferguson points out, the English language went through a process of modernization in the fifteenth century. Similarly, there is historical evidence to show that most Indian languages, particularly the languages of the Indo-Aryan family, have borrowed words from Sanskrit at various stages in their development (Emeneau 1964; Pandit 1972). It is important to emphasize that lexical expansion does not necessarily take place in areas such as science and technology alone. Languages have depended on their neighbors or other contact languages for borrowing words in the domains of culture and social organization. As Sapir (1921) points out, languages like Chinese, Sanskrit, Arabic, Greek, and Latin have been outstanding carriers of culture.

In one sense, therefore, Ferguson's definition of the feature of modernization is fairly general, although it is value-loaded in that it projects as models the modern industrialized Western nation states. Alisjahbana (1967) rejects the Western approach to modernization as value-loaded and dominating. Kelkar (1984) makes a distinction between technical use and poetic use which may be seen as two extremes in specialized language use, both making special demands on the structural and contextual resources of a language.

Vernacular and language

Haugen (1966b) equates a dialect with a vernacular. Language for him is superordinate, and dialect subordinate; language is developed, and dialect undeveloped (or underdeveloped). A dialect is, in a sense, an underdeveloped language. Having set up this equation, Haugen (1966b: 927) goes on to assert that 'all the great languages of today were once undeveloped.' He also suggests that the term 'vernacular' may be used for an undeveloped language.

According to Haugen's definition, most Indian languages would be considered vernaculars. Perhaps Sanskrit alone, of all the Indian languages recognized by the Indian constitution, would qualify as a language that once fulfilled the four aspects of language development discussed above; but now even Sanskrit, in its present function, would not be considered a developed language in terms of Haugen's (1966b) matrix.

The Unesco monograph entitled *The Use of Vernacular Languages in Education* (1953) defines 'vernacular language' as 'a language which is the mother tongue of a group which is socially or politically dominated by another group speaking a different language. We do not consider the language of a minority in one country as a vernacular if it is an official language in another country' (Unesco 1953: 46).

If the Unesco definition of 'vernacular language' were to be applied to the Indian languages, not one of them would qualify. No language group in India can be said to be under the social or political domination of another language group. One might, perhaps, argue that since Hindi is the stated official language of the Indian Union, all other regional languages may be termed 'vernaculars.' But all the major regional languages are 'official' languages at the regional level, which would disqualify them as vernaculars. Of course, since there is no strictly monolingual region in India, speakers of other regional languages resident in a particular state would have been termed as speakers of vernaculars except for the rider in the Unesco definition which does not consider as a minority language a vernacular if it is an official language elsewhere.

Of course, according to this definition Sanskrit might qualify for the status of vernacular, since it is not the official language of any Indian state or another country. Also scores of 'mother tongues' spoken by large numbers of people might qualify for the status of vernacular under the Unesco dispensation. And within the Haugen definition these mother tongues would be mere dialects (regional or social varieties) of languages irrespective of development status.

The Indian situation

Linguistic diversity in India is both phenomenal and astounding. According to the 1961 census about 520 million people in India claimed to be speakers of 1,652 mother tongues. And yet the Indian constitution recognizes only 14 major languages in addition to the official languages, Hindi and English.

Every Indian adult is a bi- or multilingual speaker. Even an illiterate rural Indian is able to manipulate several dialects or languages. An educated urbanized Indian controls several languages and uses two or more languages in his day-to-day communicative existence.

Every school-going Indian formally learns three languages: (1) his mother tongue or regional language, (2) Hindi, and (3) English. Where Hindi is the mother tongue or the regional language, he learns another Indian language in addition to English. A parent has the choice of sending his child to a school that imparts instruction in the mother tongue or English (or in Hindi in some non-Hindi-speaking areas). At college and university levels, technical and science subjects are invariably taught through the medium of English. Other subjects are taught through the regional language and English.

In the professions and trades there is an implicit gradation, the regional language being preferred at the local level, and English or Hindi being used in the larger urban centers and in more structured and formal contexts. Over the last three decades, however, the regional languages have tended to spread to contexts once controlled through English.

In the judiciary, for instance, the regional language is used in the local law courts and English in the High Courts and the Supreme Court of India. The language of governance can be the regional language, Hindi or English. The Indian government communicates with the states in English and Hindi and the state governments communicate with the government of India likewise in English or Hindi. At the state level, the government uses the regional language.

It can perhaps be said with some justification that although there is a stated language policy, language use all over the country follows the simple rule of efficiency. That is not to say that there are no problems or conflicts. The Indian language situation is often held up as an example of inefficient and unsuccessful language planning. Admittedly, the situation outlined here oversimplifies the reality in India. There are innumerable complications that have socio-politico-economic implications and repercussions. For instance, the availability of choice of the language of instruction has resulted in a continued prestige status for English. The perception of different languages and dialects as superior or inferior has helped maintain a language hierarchy characteristic of a traditionally multilingual society.

The language situation in India is dynamic, often volatile. Yet there are indicators that the nation is capable of working towards a multilingual solution to the problem of language choice at various levels of communication.

Language modernization in India

The constitution of India in article 351 (part xvii, chapter iv) provides that:

It shall be the duty of the Union to promote the spread of the Hindi language, to develop it so that it may serve as a medium of expression for all the elements of the composite culture of India and to secure its enrichment by assimilating without interfering with its genius, the forms, style and expressions used in Hindustani and in the other languages of India specified in the eighth Schedule, and by drawing, wherever necessary or desirable, for its vocabulary, primarily on Sanskrit and secondarily on other languages.

This statement, formulated by the makers of the Indian constitution in 1949, could very easily become a part of a treatise on language planning or language modernization. It was the official blueprint to be followed for the development of the official language of India.

Soon after the adoption of the constitution, in 1950, the government of India took steps to evolve technical terminology in Hindi. The task was assigned to the Commission for Scientific and Technical Terminology set up for this purpose. Concurrently with the evolution of terminology, the task of translating technical and scientific textbooks and reference books into Hindi, and also the task of producing dictionaries and encyclopedias in Hindi, were taken up by various groups of experts. The National Council of Educational Research and Teaching was established to produce curricula and textbooks to replace the older texts produced in English, often outside India.

What was attempted for Hindi by way of modernization and standardization by the Union government, the state governments replicated for the modernization and standardization of the regional languages, particularly those listed in the Eighth Schedule of the constitution as 'major' languages of India. Government efforts were reinforced by the individual efforts of scholars, academicians and voluntary social-service and educational institutions both at national and state level.

National institutes were established to research on the various languages and to evolve methodologies for the modernization and standardization of these languages. The starting of national and regional radio broadcasts in all the languages, the creation of literary academies, the encouraging of film and drama in the various languages, and the institution of prizes and rewards in all the languages formed some of the planned activities initiated by the Union and state governments to bring about the modernization of Indian languages.

Nationalism, language identity and language modernization in India

Throughout its political and social history, India has been a bi- or multilingual entity. No one standardized or unified language has held sway over all the communicative domains and needs of the multilingual people of India. There have always existed a number of languages that have lived and developed together. Indeed, it is not difficult to believe that there must always have been language tensions and language clashes in India. In its multilingual ethos, before 1947, India had always had a foreign language as the language of political authority and national administration. Sanskrit, Persian, and

English have each successively held sway over the political and administrative fortunes of the people.

Almost all the Indian languages (Indo-Aryan, Dravidian, Tibeto-Burman, and Austro-Asiatic) have borrowed freely from the dominant languages either directly or through neighboring languages. Nor has the borrowing of vocabulary (and structures) been restricted to words from foreign languages. Inter-regional borrowing of vocabulary among various languages has been attested too (Emeneau 1964).

However, in addition to acceptance of the superposed language of their political rulers or conquerors, the people have always retained strong emotional links with the local or regional languages. While there has been intimate borrowing across languages and language families, national identity or political allegiance has not led to the acceptance of a single language as the sole vehicle of communication of all people.

It might be profitable to study the phenomena of modernization and multilingualism as dynamic aspects of Indian nationalism, although this may militate against the theoretical assumptions of scholars who study nationalism and language development. The question of the relationship between language diversity and economic underdevelopment is a serious question and cannot be ignored. But this question too must be re-examined in the context of the realities in India, where every ethnic and cultural group wants its own identity and at the same time wants the umbrella of the nation, that is both the comfort of unity and the pleasure of identity. No one has any answers at present, but the questions are of great significance for a clear understanding of the relationship between nationalism and language development on the one hand, and between nationalism and multilingualism on the other.

Dynamics of language modernization in India

Urbanization, industrialization, and education are major factors in the processes of modernization of Indian languages. While education has brought formal language within the reach of many people, industrialization and urbanization have helped to liberate the people from traditional roles within a hierarchical social structure requiring pre-determined communicative behavior patterns. Formal language is now common property. More and more people are reading in their languages and, as the demand for information increases, the regional languages have to evolve strategies for acquiring, processing and transmitting information. The two areas where there has been tremendous and spontaneous language modernization in India are (1) the news media, particularly the newspapers, and (2) the school textbooks.

In a recent publication (Krishnamurti and Mukherjee 1984) of papers presented at a national seminar on the Modernization of Indian Languages in News Media held in Osmania University in 1978, thirteen papers on different aspects of modernization of the news media in six languages attest to the development of the registers and styles of newspaper and other media in Bengali, Hindi, Kannada, Marathi, Oriya, Tamil, and Telugu.

In an overview article, Krishnamurti (1984) provides a very cogent account of the processes of lexical innovation in Indian languages, particularly in the South Indian (Dravidian) languages. He draws on several other papers in the volume and demonstrates that almost all the languages represented in the volume employ common mechanisms of modernization. Krishnamurti claims that, despite their individual development independently of each other, these languages have a common socio-political history and share a common reliance on Sanskrit as a source of lexical expansion. Additionally, the mechanisms employed by these languages fall within the known universal patterns followed by languages in a contact situation. It is found that these languages rely heavily on English, and Sanskrit and Persian, for lexical expansion in addition to exploiting internal resources.

Krishnamurti attests eight mechanisms employed by these languages:

1   Straight borrowing from English with phonetic and orthographic adjustments. This is a common strategy, though not a favored one (e.g. '*bank*,' '*hotel*,' '*police*,' '*bonus*,' '*license*').

2   Hybrids or loan blends with English, Sanskrit or Perso-Arabic constituents compounded with native words or with each other. For instance:

World Bank

Telugu: *prapancha byaanku*
           (Sanskrit + English)
Kannada: *wiswa byaanku*
           (Sanskrit + English)
Tamil: *ulaka vanki*
           (Tamil + English)

3   Loan translations or calquing. For instance:

black market

Telugu: *nella bajaaru*
Kannada: *KaaLa sante*
Oriya: *KaaLa bajaara*

black money

Telegu: *nalla dhanam*
Tamil: *karuppu paaNam*
Kannada: *kappu haaNa*
Oriya: *KaaLa dhana*
Bengali: *Kaalo Taka*
Marathi: *kaalaa paisaa*

4   Adaptive coining, that is adapting the existing native meaning of an existing native or non-native word to indicate a meaning not originally indicated by the word. In this class of lexical innovation different Indian languages have developed different meanings for the same non-native words. For instance:

	state	republic	nation	caste
Telugu:	*raaStram*	*raajyaangam*	*jaati*	–
Hindi:	*raajya*	*raaStra*	–	*jaati*

5   Paraphrasing, where, in the absence of an equivalent, a phrase is used to replace the borrowed lexical item.
6   Semantic re-interpretation of Sanskrit words. For instance:
        Telugu: radio
                    aakaaSwaaNi (lit. 'sky-voice')
7   Expanding the semantic range of native words.
8   Total assimilation of the non-native concept into the native vocabulary. For instance:

	Telugu
smuggled goods	*donga saruku*
smuggling, black market	*donga wyaapaaram*
illicit liquor	*donga saaraayi*
black money	*donga sommu*
illegal license	*donga laysensu*

What is significant is that several of the authors writing in *Modernization of Indian Languages in News Media* assert that while some years ago the vernacular newspapers tended to translate their news copy from the English original, now they write the news originally in the vernaculars. In several languages newspapers have created and popularized a colloquial style of writing. Many lexical items first introduced by newspapers have become part of the native lexicon.

In the field of textbook writing, regional language textbooks were translated from English until a few years ago. Currently many textbooks are first written in the regional language and subsequently translated into English for use in English-medium schools. This is particularly true of textbooks in the social sciences, where the textbook writer has to have knowledge of local social structures and terminology.

In the area of script reform there has been less success (Daswani 1976). An attempt was made to introduce a uniform Devanagari-based script for all Indian languages. The major reason why the single script was not accepted by all the other languages is perhaps the long written traditions in several of the non-Hindi languages, each with a script tradition of its own. Arguments in favor of the Romanization of Indian languages (Ray 1963; Daswani 1975) have also not been accepted. It is likely that with the advent of computer technology the question of a common script will become more real and urgent.

Conclusion

Indian languages seem to have come out of the phase of total dependence on English for receiving new information. After passing through the phase of literal translation, several Indian languages have now evolved vocabularies and structural nuances to handle the several new registers and styles necessary for receiving, processing and transmitting information essential for the forming and maintenance of modern societies.

Language adaptation is a process that can be continuous or abrupt: there are languages that seem to adapt continuously and others that adapt at particular points of time in their development. Moreover, as regards modernization, languages differ in yet another respect. There are speech communities that adapt their languages unabashedly without really feeling conscious of their borrowing and their bringing-in of new concepts and lexical items, and there are others that are extremely reluctant in borrowing or adapting, hanging on to what is known rather than calling for something from the outside. Further, there is natural adaptation, and there is artificial or induced adaptation. Artificial adaptation, of course, can be managed or legislated or monitored, but natural adaptation is normally not managed or legislated or monitored. Both aspects of adaptation interact. While there may be a tendency either to remain within one's resources or to rely on external agencies and languages, one cannot compel a language to adapt in ways different from its own genius. Adaptation means taking in foreign or new material and adjusting it within one's own system. Thus adaptation is the naturalization of material within the system of the language rather than superficial borrowing or infusion. The genius of the language is something that has to be understood, and adaptation processes that are at play are subject to these constraints. The mechanisms discussed above seem to indicate that such processes are fruitfully at work in several Indian languages at the present time. Therefore, it is possible that in the future Indian languages will achieve total inter-translatability with languages like English, German, French, and Russian.

References

Alisjahbana, S. Takdir 1967. The Modernization of Languages in Asia in Historical and Socio-cultural Perspective. In S. Takdir Alisjahbana (ed.), *The Modernization of Languages in Asia*. Kuala Lumpur.
    (ed.) 1967. *The Modernization of Languages in Asia*. Kuala Lumpur.
Daswani, C. J. 1975. The Question of One Script for Indian Languages; Devanagari or Roman. *Indian Linguistics*, 36, 3: 182–185.
    1976. A Common National Script for Indian Languages: Augmented Devanagari. *Journal of the School of Languages* (New Delhi), Winter 1975/1976: 36–42.
Emeneau, Murray B. 1964. India as a Linguistic Area. In Dell Hymes (ed.), *Language in Culture and Society*. The Hague.
Ferguson, Charles A. 1971. Language Development. In Anwar S. Dil (ed.), *Language Structure and Language Use*. Stanford.
Fishman, Joshua A. (ed.) 1968. *Readings in the Sociology of Language*. The Hague.
    (ed.) 1972. *Advances in the Sociology of Language*, vol. 2. The Hague.
Fishman, Joshua A., Das Gupta J. and Ferguson C. A., (eds.) 1968. *Language Problems of Developing Nations*. New York.
Haugen, Einar 1966a. Linguistics and Language Planning. In William Bright (ed.), *Sociolinguistics*. The Hague.
    1966b. Dialect, Language, Nation. *American Anthropologist*, 68: 922–935.
    1968. Language Planning in Modern Norway. In J. A. Fishman (ed.) *Readings in*

the Sociology of Language. The Hague. First published in *Anthropological Linguistics*, 1, 3 (1959).

1971. Instrumentalism in Language Planning. In J. Rubin and B. Jernudd (eds.) *Can Language Be Planned?* Honolulu.

Hymes, Dell (ed.) 1964. *Language in Culture and Society. A Reader in Linguistics and Anthropology.* New York.

Kelkar, Ashok R. 1984. Language in Action in a Developing Country. *India International Centre Quarterly*, 11, 2: 145–154.

Krishnamurti, Bh. 1984. Modernization of South Indian Languages: Lexical Innovations in Newspaper Language. In Bh. Krishnamurti and Aditi Mukherjee (eds.), *Modernization of Indian Languages in News Media*. Hyderabad.

Krishnamurti, Bh. and Mukherjee, Aditi (eds.) 1984. *Modernization of Indian Languages in News Media*. Hyderabad.

Pandit, P.B. 1972. *India as a Sociolinguistic Area.* Poona.

Pattanayak, P. D. 1981. *Multilingualism and Mother Tongue Education.* New Delhi.

Pool, Jonathan. 1972. National Development and Language Diversity. In J. A. Fishman (ed.) *Advances in the Sociology of Language*, vol. 2, 213–330. The Hague.

Pride, John B. and Holmes J., (eds.) 1972. *Sociolinguistics.* Harmondsworth.

Ray, Punya Sloka 1963. *Language Standardization.* The Hague.

Rubin, Joan 1971. Evaluation and Language Planning. In J. Rubin and B. Jernudd (eds.) *Can Language Be Planned?* Honolulu.

Rubin, Joan and Jernudd, Björn 1971. Language Planning as an Element in Modernization. In J. Rubin and B. Jernudd (eds.) *Can Language Be Planned?* Honolulu.

(eds.) 1971. *Can Language Be Planned? Sociolinguistic Theory and Practice for Developing Nations.* Honolulu.

Sapir, Edward 1921. *Language.* New York.

Southworth, F. C. and Daswani C. J., 1974. *Foundations of Linguistics.* New York.

Unesco 1953. *The Use of Vernacular Languages in Education.* Unesco Monographs on Fundamental Education 8. Paris.

6 Adaptation processes in Chinese: word formation

FRITZ PASIERBSKY

The Chinese are lenders, not borrowers. With the notable exceptions of Buddhism and Marxism, their civilization has remained remarkably free of foreign influence, while Chinese civilization has had a marked impact on that of its neighbors. The traditional Chinese reaction to altered circumstances is to adapt what already exists rather than to borrow from elsewhere. For example, beginning with the Opium War, China suffered one heavy defeat after another at the hands of the Western powers. The Chinese response to these defeats was to undertake a self-strengthening movement the essence of which, as formulated in the 1890s by the reform politician Zhang Zhidong, was this:

中	学	为	体	西	学
zhōng	xué	wéi	tǐ	xī	xué
Chinese	learning	be	body, essentials	Western	learning

为	用。
wéi	yòng
be	use, apply

Chinese learning for the essential principles, Western learning for the practical application.

This capacity of the Chinese to not essentially change their own behavior and attitudes, their own system of values, and their own ways of communication by borrowing from abroad, but rather to adapt, to modify the already existing aspects of their own life to make them more suitable to new circumstances and new social needs, is also to be seen in the Chinese language. Not being borrowers, the Chinese, compared to other peoples, have only very few loan words in their language. There are Buddhist terms such as

菩	萨
pú	sà

short for

菩	提	萨	埵
pú	tí	sà	duǒ

90

which is the Bôdhisattva – he whose essence is intelligence. There are also some Western words like

鸦　　片
yā　　piàn　　(opium),

a drug that was forced by the British upon the Chinese. Then, under the influence of the October Revolution another set of words were introduced. Two examples are:

苏　　维　　埃
sū　　wéi　　āi　　　(Soviet)

and

布　　尔　　什　　维　　克
bù　　ěr　　shí　　wéi　　kè　　(Bolshevik).

Only a few loanwords that came into Chinese from Western languages in this century have survived, such as, for instance,

盘　　尼　　西　　林
pán　　ní　　xī　　lín　　(penicillin),

which was recently replaced, however, by a genuine Chinese expression

青　　霉素
qīng　　dúsù　　(blue toxin),

and

坦　　克
tǎn　　kè　　(tank, armored carrier).

Consultation of the *English–Chinese Dictionary of Technology*, which has about 75,000 entries, shows that there are only very few loanwords like *tǎnkè*. The large amount of 'international loanwords' that we have in the Western world were all adapted to a Chinese pattern:

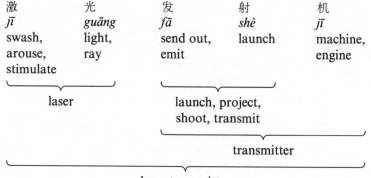

适	应	过	程
shì	*yìng*	*guò*	*chéng*
fit,	answer,	cross,	rule,
suitable	respond to	pass	procedure

suit, adapt, fit   process, course

adaptation process

When looking at a translation of a text from a Western language we shall find almost no loanwords in it, all the foreign contents being reformulated in a typically Chinese way. Compare, for example, the following definition of *Arbeitskraft* (labour power) that Karl Marx gave in his *Das Kapital*, where in the English version we find a lot of loanwords of Latin/French origin, while the Chinese text exclusively uses its own word roots:

Unter Arbeitskraft oder Arbeitsvermögen verstehen wir den Inbegriff der physischen und geistigen Fähigkeiten, die in der Leiblichkeit, der lebendigen Persönlichkeit eines Menschen existieren und die er in Bewegung setzt, sooft er Gebrauchswerte irgendeiner Art produziert.   (Marx 1962: 181)

By labour-power or capacity for labour is to be understood the aggregate of those mental and physical capabilities existing in a human being, which he exercises whenever he produces a use-value of any description.   (Marx 1962/1954: 164)

We can make a test of how extensive the borrowed lexical stock of English is by leaving out all the loanwords in the English text. What remains is a skeleton of grammatical function words, the only exception being the word 'understood':

By ...... or ... for ... is to be understood the ... of those ... and .... in a ... being, which he ... whenever he ... a .... of any ...

This demonstrates that even all the decisive concepts in this text are represented by loanwords. Now compare this to the Chinese version, where all the word-building material is Chinese:

我	们	把		劳	动	力
wǒ	*men*	*bǎ*		*láo*	*dòng*	*lì*
	we	(particle for object)		labor		power

或	劳	动	能	力,
huò	*láo*	*dòng*	*néng*	*lì*
or	labor		capacity	

理	解	为	人	的
lǐ	*jiě*	*wéi*	*rén*	*de*
understand	be		man	(particle for attribute)

身	体	即	活		的	人
shēn	*tǐ*	*jí*	*huó*		*de*	*rén*
body		namely	living, lively		(...)	man(s)

体	中	存	在	的
tǐ	*zhōng*	*cún*	*zài*	*de*
body	within	exist		(...)

每	当	人	生	产
měi	*dāng*	*rén*	*shēng*	*chǎn*
whenever		man	produce	

某	种	使	用	价	值
mǒu	*zhǒng*	*shǐ*	*yòng*	*jià*	*zhí*
certain	kind of,	use		value	

'of any
description'

时	就	运	用	的	体
shí	*jiù*	*yùn*	*yòng*	*de*	*tǐ*
time,	then	utilize, apply,		(...)	bodily,
when ...		'exercise'			physical

力	和	智	力		的
lì	*hé*	*zhì*	*lì*		*de*
strength,	and	mental	strength,		(...)
power,			power,		
'capabilities'			'capabilities'		

总	和。
zǒng	*hé*
sum, total, 'aggregate'	

(Marx 1962/1972)

How is it that the Chinese rendition of a Western text can do without loanwords? Modern Chinese is no longer a monosyllabic language as ancient Chinese largely was. More than 80% of the words in a contemporary text of public language use consist of compound words having two or more morphemes, almost always represented by as many syllables and characters. In general, the equation of one morpheme – one syllable – one character is valid in Chinese. Moreover, there is a tendency to keep the outer structure of the lexical units, namely of the Chinese characters. They are individual entities with graphemic, morphological phonological and semantic peculiarities of their own, which are put into new contexts to make them suitable for new communication needs. In modern written Chinese the character is the basic building block of larger entities, that is compounds, syntagmas, phrases, sentences, and texts.

To describe some of the most important morphological and semantic features let us consider the key words of the final sentence of the above quote:

劳动力
láodòng lì (labor-power)

劳动能力
láodòng nénglì (capacity for labor)

体力
tǐlì (physical capabilities)

智力
zhìlì (mental capabilities)

In these key words we find a building block in the character 力, *lì*, which today, means 'strength, power, force.' From the times of the first written documents we find this character in the most varied of contexts. In the 书经, *Shujing*, for example, which is the first Chinese work on history, parts of which date back to a time before Confucius, we find:

今	商	王	受	力	行
jīn	*Shāng*	*wáng*	*Shòu*	*lì*	*xíng*
now	Shang	king	Shou	strength	pursue

无	度。	[书经]
wú	*dù*	
without	law	

Now Show, the king of Shang, with strength pursues his lawless way.

(Legge 1983, vol. 3: 290)

One of the modern uses of 力, *lì*, is as a technical term in physics:

荷	载	作	用	在	梁
hè	*zài*	*zuò*	*yong*	*zài*	*liáng*
load		act on, affect, effect	act on, affect,	on	beam

上	的	力
shang	*de*	*lì*
upon	(...)	strength,
(post-		power,
position)		force

the force of the load of the beam

In both examples the character 力, *lì*, is used as a single word, but it is put into two very different contexts. A second feature is the integration of characters into other characters as semantic radicals. We find in our key words the integrative force of the character 力, *lì*, within the two complex characters:

勞 (simplified 劳) *láo* (work, labor; to toil, to fatigue)

動 (simplified 动) *dòng* (to move, to take action, exercise).

According to the *Morohashi Dai Kan-Wa Ji-ten* (the 13-volume Chinese–Japanese dictionary) the character 力, *lì*, is the semantic radical of more than 200 compound characters, many of which are very productive in modern word formation processes. Chinese has 214 semantic radicals like 力, *lì*, from which more than 60,000 compound characters (or root words) are formed. The 60,000 single-character words like 劳, *láo*, are used to form hundreds of thousands of compound words, such as 劳动, *láodòng* (labor). To express the modern term 'labor-power' 力, *lì*, is used in combination with the compound word 劳动, *láodòng*, which itself contains 力, *lì*, as a semantic radical in both of its constituents.

Now, many of the compound words which we find in the modern language have a very long history. The combination 劳动, *láodòng*, for instance, has been in existence since the fourth century B.C. In the Taoist text of *Zhuangzi* (chapter 让王 'Giving away a Throne') we read:

春	耕	种	形	足	以
chūn	*gēng*	*zhòng*	*xíng*	*zú*	*yǐ*
spring	plow	plant	body	enough	so that

劳	动。	[庄子 · 让王]
láo	*dòng*	
labor,	move,	
work	exercise	

In spring I plow and plant – this gives my body the labor and exercise it needs.

(Watson 1968: 310)

In the Middle Ages the Japanese borrowed the compound word from the Chinese, where, under the influence of modern Western science, it got its final use as 'manual labor, work.' (In modern Japanese writing it is 労働, pronounced /rōdō/.) Then, at the end of the nineteenth and at the beginning of the twentieth century, the Chinese integrated the modern Japanese word into their own system, as they did with a lot of other words such as

革命
gémìng (revolution)

文化
wénhuà (culture)

文学
wénxué (literature)

社会
shèhuì (society)

all of which were old Chinese words that were re-integrated into the Chinese language system after they had been modernized by the Japanese. This is another example of the Chinese attitude of 'Chinese learning for the essential principles, Western learning for the practical application' – for the Chinese 'the West' includes Japan, even though it is located to the east of China.

From what I have said so far, one might get the impression that all these adaptation processes in Chinese take place on the level of the learned or literary language, and that it has little to do with the vernacular language. But there is a very important and very effective pattern in the Chinese way of adapting the 'essential principles' of the Chinese language to fulfill the growing and changing needs of society. Instead of borrowing foreign words, the typical adaptation pattern of the Chinese is to use lexical metaphors.

Metaphors in a general sense are names applied to objects to which they literally are not applicable, thus implying a comparison (see *The Concise Oxford Dictionary*: 763). We have to distinguish between two kinds of metaphors – 'stylistic metaphors,' which are used to intensify the meaning in figurative speech, for example when we speak of 'a glaring error,' or when we find in a sentence of Shakespeare, 'There is a tide in the affairs of men, / Which, taken at the flood, leads on to fortune,' (*Julius Caesar*, IV, iii, 217–218). In contradistinction to stylistic metaphors we speak of 'lexical metaphors' when in the course of history the figurative use of a linguistic unit has reached a certain steadiness and has become an integrated part of the lexical system. Thus talking about 'a farm hand' or 'the foot of a mountain' is no longer figurative in the sense of stylistics, but is a normal way of designating a farm laborer or the lower part of a mountain.

When adapting vernacular languages to the communicative needs of modern societies, lexical metaphors play a major role by transferring expressions of the vernacular language into a nomenclature, that is into a system of names used in a particular science or art. Here the lexical metaphor is not the result of a dying stylistic metaphor, but the outcome of a transfer in language use. Take, for example, the English word 'wave,' a noun derived from the verb 'to wave' meaning 'to move up and down or back and forth in a curving or undulating motion' (*Webster's New Twentieth Century Dictionary*: 2070). As a lexical metaphor the noun 'wave' has become a technical term in physics, where it designates 'any of the series of advancing impulses set up by a vibration, pulsation, or disturbance in air or some other medium, as in the transmission of heat, light, sound, etc' (*ibid.*). In the following I will discuss, from a historical point of view, an example of how Chinese lexical metaphors work to fulfill the needs of a developing society and the developing communicative needs of a changing society.

As has been pointed out above, the simple Chinese character 力, *lì*, today means 'strength, power, force.' Its ancient phonetic form has been reconstructed as */ljək/, comparable to the Cantonese *lik*, the Japanese *riki, ryoku*, the Korean *ryŏk*, and the Vietnamese *lúc*. According to Karlgren (1972: no. 928), the character as found on an early Zhou inscription from almost 3,000 years ago seems to depict an arm with a hand, its early form being ⅃ . It is also suggested that the variant form 𝔰 shows a hand with a sinew (Karlgren 1923: 172). It is evident that already in the earliest times the originally concrete meaning of 'muscular arm, powerful hand' was transferred to designate persons having such hands and then to describe the qualities of such persons as having 'strength.' This transfer of meaning was due to a developing communicative need in early Chinese society to have names not only for concrete objects and persons but also for their qualities and features. The progressive division of labour developed the need for an increasing differentiation in world outlook and in the system of designations. In the *Book of Odes*, a collection of about 300 songs, some of which might be more than 3,000 years old, we already find a differentiated use of the character 力, *lì*, the concrete meaning of the 'muscular arm, powerful hand' being transferred to at least three different entities.

First, 力, *lì*, as a quality of man, as, for example, in the ode 简分, *Jian fen*, which is probably the song of a young lady admiring a man with the words:

有	力	如	虎。	［诗经 · 简分］
yǒu	*lì*	*rú*	*hǔ*	
have	strength	like	tiger	

He has strength like a tiger.   (Karlgren 1974: no. 38)

The beginning of the ode which contains our sentence, reads:

> Oh great, great! They are just going to perform the great dance;
> when the sun is just at the zenith, he is at the uppermost place at the front.
> The tall man is very great, he performs the great dance in the prince's
>   courtyard;
> he has strength like a tiger, he holds [chariot] reins as if they were silk
>   strings ...

Here it would still make sense to refer to the earliest concrete meaning of the word as 'he has muscular limbs like a tiger.'

Second, 力, *lì*, as the action of man. The ode 正月, *Zheng yue*, begins with an outcry:

> In the first month there is ample hoar-frost;
>   my heart is grieved and pained; the false speeches
>   of the people also greatly ... make it worse;
> I think of how I am lone,
>   the grief of my heart is very great;
> alas for my cares, I am painfully grieved so that
>   I am sick ...   (Karlgren 1974: no. 192)

Verse seven continues thus:

> Look at that field on the slope,
>   luxuriant is its straight rising [grain],
> Heaven shakes me, but it does not crush me,

they ... try to emulate me, but they do not attain to me ...;
they have seized me, enemy-fashion, and yet they cannot force me ...

In this last sentence

亦	不	我	力。	［诗经・正月］
yì	*bù*	*wǒ*	*lì*	
and, yet	not	I, me	force	

and yet they cannot force me   (Karlgren 1974: no. 192)

we find the verbal use of 力, *lì*, describing the action of using force.

Third, 力, *lì*, as an abstract entity, as in the ode 荡, *Dang*. King Wen, the founder of the Zhou dynasty, is cited here as having said:

> Alas! Alas, you Yin-Shang! Those [men] are refractory,
> they are [crushing and subduing] oppressive,
> but they are in official positions, they are in the services;
> Heaven [sent down] gave them a reckless disposition,
> but you raise them and give them power ...

(Karlgren 1984: no. 255)

In the phrase

如	兴	是	力。	［诗经・荡］
rú	*xīng*	*shì*	*lì*	
you	raise	this	(give) power	

You raise them and give them power.   (Karlgren 1974: 255)

the meaning of 力, *lì*, is 'to give power to somebody.'

These three modifications the word 力, *lì*, underwent have something in common. In all three cases the transfer did not go beyond the limits of the vernacular language. The language of the *Book of Odes* as handed down to our days was the everyday language of the people, or at least very close to it. Lexical metaphors were in principle understood by everybody; they were not yet integrated into a nomenclature and were therefore not connected with the specified knowledge of a science or an art.

Things in China changed fundamentally with the rise of feudalism. By the beginning of the Chun–Qiu–Zhanguo period (eighth to third centuries B.C.), the division of labor had reached a very high form of development which was reflected in the division of highly specified language usages. If we look, for example, at the text by 孟子, Mengzi, a Confucian philosopher of the early third century B.C., we see a split in the meaning of individual words such as 力, *lì*. On the one hand, the vernacular meaning was kept or developed within the realm of the language of everyday life; on the other hand, new lexical metaphors were used to fulfill the higher communicative needs of specified new activities of human beings, like economics and the art of war.

In the book 孟子, *Mengzi*, we find, for example, the vernacular meaning of 力, *lì*, (strength), as in

吾	力	足	以	举	百
wú	*lì*	*zú*	*yǐ*	*jǔ*	*bǎi*
my	strength	enough	so that	lift	hundred

钧	而	不	足	以	举
jūn	*ér*	*bù*	*zú*	*yǐ*	*jǔ*
30 catties	but	not	enough	so that	lift

一	羽。	［孟子］
yī	*yǔ*	
one	feather	

My strength is sufficient to lift three thousand catties, but it is not sufficient to lift one feather.   (Legge 1983, vol. 2: 454)

One of the modifications 力, *lì*, acquired in the book 孟子, *Mengzi*, was the development of the opposition between

力
lì (physical strength)

and

心
xīn (heart, regarded in ancient China as the center of thoughts, feelings, wishes).

Consider the following example:

以	力	服	人	者	非
yǐ	*lì*	*fú*	*rén*	*zhě*	*fēi*
take	force	subdue	man	(particle for nouns)	be not

心	服	也。	［孟子］
xīn	*fú*	*yě*	
heart	subdue	(final particle)	

When one by [physical] force subdues men, they do not submit to him in heart.
(Legge 1983, vol. 2: 540)

This opposition of 力, *lì*, and 心, *xīn*, was then applied to the field of economics. As lexical metaphors they expressed the division of labor into physical (*lì*) and mental (*xīn*) labour:

或	劳	心	或	劳	力	［孟子］
huò	*láo*	*xīn*	*huò*	*laó*	*lì*	
some	labor	heart	some	labor	strength	

Some labor with their minds, some labor with their strength.
(Legge 1983, vol. 2: 627)

Mengzi quotes from an economic treatise which states: 'Those who labor with their minds govern others; those tho labor with their strength are governed by others. Those who are governed by others support them; those who govern others are supported by them.' 'This,' concludes Mengzi, 'is a principle universally recognized' (Legge 1983, vol. 2: 627). As early as the fourth century B.C., we meet the word *lì* as an economic term. And there is still another lexical-metaphorical use of this word in the book of Mengzi. In the seventh chapter he deals with the different kinds of taxes that people had to pay: the tax on cloth and silk in the summer, that on grain after harvest, and that on personal service or corvée in the winter, called

力	役	之	征	[孟子]
lì	*yì*	*zhī*	*zhēng*	
strength	serve	(attrib.)	taxes	

the exactions of . . . personal service   (Legge 1983, vol. 2: 997)

The word *lì* as a lexical metaphor signifies here a special kind of surplus labor.

Around the beginning of the fourth century B.C. there was another transfer of the vernacular word *lì* to a nomenclature, namely to the technical terms of the art of war. In the *Sunzi bingfa* (*Sunzi on the Art of War*) the word *lì* means among other things the 'fighting strength,' the 'combat effectiveness' of an army, and is mentioned, together with 气, *qì*, here the 'fighting energy,' the 'fighting spirits' of the troops, for example, in the maxim:

併	气	积	力	[孙子兵法]
bìng	*qì*	*jī*	*lì*	
together,	spirit,	collect,	strength	
concentrate	energy	hoard		

Concentrate your energy and hoard your strength.   (*Sunzi bingfa*: 124)

The economic and military use of *lì* are only two examples of how, by using lexical metaphors, the vernacular language was adapted to new communicative needs in early Chinese society. More importantly, this pattern has been preserved. Today, too, the Chinese use lexical metaphors to fulfill new communicative needs that develop under the influence from abroad – a situation in which most languages of the world use loanwords.

To conclude, I would like to illustrate the modern usage of the word 力, *lì*, and its manifold adaptative capacity. In modern economics we have words like the above mentioned

劳动力
láodòng-lì (labor-power).

Others are:

脑力劳动
nǎolì-láodòng (mental work),

体力劳动
tǐlì-láodòng (physical work),

生产力
shēngchán-lì (productive forces),

土地肥力
tǔdì-féilì (fertility of soil – as a factor of productivity of labor).

In modern military sciences *lì* has gained a very large field of adaptation, for example:

兵力
bīnglì (military strength, military capability),

武力
wǔlì (military force, force of arms),

武装力量
wǔzhuāng-lìliàng (armed forces).

In physics a whole discipline (Chinese 学, *xué*) has acquired the name of *lì*:

力学
lìxué (mechanics).

Further, we find:

水力
shuǐlì (hydraulic power),

压力计
yālìjì (pressure meter),

电力
diànlì (electric power),

原子动力船
yuánzi-dònglì-chuán (atomic-powered ship).

In musicology

力度
lìdù

refers to dynamics, that is the variation and gradation of volume, as, for example, 'piano,' 'fortissimo,' and 'crescendo.' In linguistics, too the word *lì* helps to build up a terminology. In the Chinese translation of the *Dictionary of Language and Linguistics* by R. R. K. Hartmann and F. C. Stork we find several terms containing *lì*, as, for example,

听力图
tīnglìtú (audiogram).

Yet another example is:

激发力
jīfā-lì (evocative),

which is the power of a word or phrase to cause an emotional reaction in the hearer or reader by its ameliorative or pejorative connotations.

To describe the current state of affairs, one could say that China, for so long a lender but not a borrower, is now neither a lender nor a borrower in terms of language. The days of China's cultural and linguistic prestige or even domination of its neighbors (Korea, Japan, Vietnam) are over. However, the days when China was dominated by the imperialist powers are also past. This does not mean that China has returned to its state of 'splendid isolation.' On the contrary, much is changing in China as Chinese society has become more open to the rest of the world during 1980s. But the important point is that this changing and opening is taking place in a manner that is in perfect agreement with Chinese tradition. The pattern of word formation – namely to use native material to adapt to changed circumstances – may be seen as a part of a larger cultural pattern: to borrow if necessary, but to ensure that the act of borrowing does not bring with it other aspects of the foreign culture, like the name of the borrowed concept. And that means to make the word Chinese in form and content. The Chinese expression for this is

中国化
Zhōngguóhuà (to make something Chinese in form and character, to sinicize).

What the Chinese are doing today is borrowing Western concepts, but before a concept can enter the language system, its foreign name must be stripped away – it must be cleansed of all possible foreign influence and made Chinese in form and character (in the double sense of the word). The Chinese vernacular may thus be seen as a source of material for linguistic adaptation as a means of modernization.

References

The Concise Oxford Dictionary of Current English, 5th edn 1964, ed. H. W. Fowler and F. G. Fowler. Oxford.

De-Han dianzi jisuanji cihui [German–Chinese Dictionary] 1979. Beijing.

Duiwai Hanyu jiaoxue lunji [Comparative Encyclopedia of Foreign and Chinese Education] 1985. Beijing.

Frolova, O. P. 1981. *Slovoobrazovanie v terminologiceskoj leksike sovremennogo kitajskogo jazyka*. Novosibirsk.

Hartmann, R. R. K. and Stork, F. C. 1972. *Dictionary of Language and Linguistics*. London. Chinese translation: *Yuyan yu yuyanxue cidian*. Shanghai 1981.

Hermanová-Novotaná, Z. 1974. Coinage and Structure of Economic Terms in Modern Chinese. In V. Cerny *et al.* (eds.), *Asian and African Languages in Social Context*. Prague.

Karlgren, Bernard 1923. *Analytic Dictionary of Chinese and Sino-Japanese*. Paris.

1972. *Grammata Serica Recensa*. Stockholm.

1974. *The Book of Odes*. Stockholm.

Legge, J. 1966. *The Four Books. Confucian Analects, The Great Learning, The Doctrine of the Mean, and The Work of Mencius*. New York.

1983. *The Chinese Classics with a Translation, Critical and Exegetical Notes, Prolegomena, and Copious Indexes*, 7 vols. Oxford.

Li Dun J. 1969. *China in Transition: 1517–1911*. New York.

Lippert, W. 1979. *Entstehung und Funktion einiger chinesischer marxistischer Termini. Der lexikalisch-begriffliche Aspekt der Rezeption des Marxismus in Japan und China*. Wiesbaden.

Louven, E. 1983, 1984. Chinesische Wirtschaftsterminologie: Definitionen und Kompatibilitätsprobleme. *China Aktuell*, April, August 1983: 235–242, 503–508; January, April, September 1984: 31–39, 205–212, 523–527.

Marx, K. 1962. *Das Kapital. Kritik der politischen Ökonomie*, vol. 1. Berlin. (English translation: *Capital. A Critical Analysis of Capitalist Production*, vol. 1. Moscow 1954; Chinese translation: *Ziben lun. Zhengzhi jingjixue pipan*, vol. 1. Ma-ke-si En-ge-si quanji, di 23 juan. Beijing 1972.)

Mathew's Chinese–English Dictionary, revised American edn 1963. Cambridge, Mass.

Sunzi bingfa [Sun Tzu on the Art of War] 1910. Translated by L. Giles. Shanghai.

Wang Li 1958. *Hanyu shigao*, vol. 3. Beijing.

Watson, B. 1968. *The Complete Works of Chuang Tzu*. New York.

Webster's New Twentieth Century Dictionary of the English Language, 2nd edn 1970. Cleveland, New York.

Ying-Han jishu cidian. An English–Chinese Dictionary of Technology 1978. Beijing.

7 The development of Japanese society and the modernization of Japanese during the Meiji Restoration

MAKOTO TAKADA

Introduction

Japan experienced a period of great social change in the middle of the nineteenth century which is called the Meiji Restoration. After more than two hundred years of national seclusion, Japan opened her gates to foreign countries.

The Tokugawa Shogunate in Edo, the old name of Tokyo, had secluded the nation from the beginning of the seventeenth century to exclude Catholic missionaries and political invaders from Western Europe. Only the Dutch and the Chinese were permitted to have contacts – with a limited number of Japanese at Nagasaki, the only port open to them. The Dutch were given this privilege because they were judged to be interested in pursuing a commercial approach without religious objectives. And the Chinese were not Christian at all. The modernization of Japanese society was delayed by the national seclusion policy, but, on the other hand, Japan managed to avoid being swallowed up by the gigantic colonialization undertaken by the Western nations.

Towards the middle of the nineteenth century a series of conflicts between Western countries and China gave rise to the view that Japan should open her gates to the world in order to strengthen her economic and military power and to protect the country from colonialization by the Western powers. In this manner the Tokugawa Shogunate was compelled to abandon the national seclusion policy and to open several ports to foreign traders between 1854 and 1868. In the process, however, the Tokugawa Shogunate gradually lost control of the whole nation.

The Meiji Restoration occured in 1868, when the Tokugawa Shogunate returned political rule to the Emperor and his advisers. As a symbolic gesture of the effort to modernize Japan the young Emperor Meiji moved to Edo from Kyoto, where generations of emperors had resided for more than one thousand years. Edo was renamed Tokyo, which means 'eastern Kyo,' that is 'eastern capital.'

The new government of the Emperor Meiji began the modernization of the nation very rapidly. They introduced all sorts of modern Western civilization and culture within a very short period such as science, technology, medicine, literature, philology, laws, and so on. This social movement was called *Bunmei-kaika*, which literally means 'civilization opening,' that is civilization and enlightenment.

In the course of this modernization and Westernization, the Meiji leaders advanced significantly the modernization of the Japanese language and succeeded in adapting it to the needs of a modern society.

This modernization had two phases: one was the establishment of Modern Colloquial Japanese, especially Modern Written Colloquial Japanese, and the other was the establishment of a modern vocabulary with which the concepts and ideas introduced from the Western world could be expressed and understood.

A brief outline of the history of Japanese

Before beginning the description of the course of the modernization of the Japanese language, a short introduction to the history and the stylistic varieties of Japanese is in order.

The history of the Japanese language can be divided roughly into five stages: Old Japanese, Middle Japanese, Early Early Modern Japanese, Early Modern Japanese, and Modern Japanese.

Old Japanese

Old Japanese is divided into two stages: Early old Japanese and Late Old Japanese.

Early Old Japanese is the language which was used mainly in the Nara period, that is in the eighth century. The writing system used Chinese characters which had been borrowed in the fifth century. In this period the pronunciation of Chinese characters was adapted to Japanese. The characters were used by Japanese scribes to transcribe Japanese syllables irrespective of the original meaning of the characters. They thus obtained a tool for writing Japanese syllable by syllable. Characters used in this way are called *kana*. They were first used on a large scale in the *Man'yooshuu*, a 20-volume collection of 4,516 poems, and are therefore called *Man'yoogana*.

Another way of using Chinese characters was to adopt them together with their Chinese meaning while providing them with a Japanese word form. In this case, as opposed to the *kana* transcription, the original pronunciation of the Chinese characters was completely ignored.

In addition to these two ways of using Chinese characters for writing Japanese, the Japanese of the Nara (eighth century) and later periods borrowed Chinese words, that is characters with their respective meaning and pronunciation, which were of course read with a Japanese accent. In this way a great many words were borrowed, a process which began in the earliest stage of Old Japanese and continued until the most recent stage of Early Modern Japanese. These Japanese words were called *kango*, literally 'Chinese words.' The proportion of *kango* in the Japanese vocabulary was, and still is, very high. In Modern Japanese more than 50% of the vocabulary is *kango*. In Early Modern Japanese the word formation rules for *kango* became productive in Japanese, so that many *kango* words were first coined in Japan as terms for the new ideas which were being introduced to Japan from the West during the Edo period and, especially, in the time following the Meiji Restoration.

Thus the writing of Japanese was formed by using a mixture of these three ways of using Chinese characters. While it was possible to write Japanese with syllabic letters only, this was unusual, the combined use of *kana* and Chinese characters being the normal practice.

Japanese is an agglutinative language. It has suffixes, which have no semantic meaning but which stand for grammatical functions of nouns or pronouns such as cases or adnominal as well as adverbial modifications. The verbals and adjectivals are followed by many kinds of endings, which also indicate grammatical functions. Chinese, by contrast, is an isolating language. Chinese words have no morphological elements which stand for grammatical roles. For writing Japanese, *kana* syllabic letters were used for particles and endings, while Chinese characters were generally used to write word stems. Of course, a great many of the stems were also written with *kana* syllabic letters.

Later Old Japanese evolved during the Heian period, which lasted from the end of the eighth century to the end of the twelfth century. A new capital was constructed in Kyoto, where an aristocratic court culture came into existence.

During this period the Japanese developed the style and the writing system of Pure Classical Japanese, which was preferred by the ladies in waiting at the imperial court. Works of prose literature such as *Genji Monogatari*, a tale of a prince by the name of Genji, were written in this style by the ladies at the emperor's court. For this reason the literature of this period is called 'the women's literature of the Heian period.'

In this period the writing style of *kana* was developed in two ways: *hiragana* (commonly used *kana*) and *katakana* (*partial kana*). *Hiragana* was developed from one of the traditional writing styles of Chinese characters, a style which is cursive and well suited to rapid handwriting. Since *hiragana* letters have very cursive forms and are round and fluent, they were preferred by female writers of Pure Classical Japanese literature.

Middle Japanese

Middle Japanese is characterized by a Sino-Japanese style, which is briefly introduced below. In the periods of Kamakura, Muromachi and Azuchi-Momoyama, which covered roughly the period from the end of the twelfth century to the end of the sixteenth century, the warrior class assumed political power. They preferred the more masculine style of Sino-Japanese. The words of martial literature such as *Heike Monogatari*, a tale of the rise and fall of the Heike family, were written in this style.

Early Early Modern Japanese

Early Early Modern Japanese is the language which was used by the people under the feudal rule of theTokugawa Shogunate, which lasted from 1600 to 1868. It is the language of the theatrical works of *kabuki* drama and *bunraku* puppet theater as well as popular literature of various genres. This style was preferred by the people of the townfolk class. However, the warrior class still preferred the Sino-Japanese style.

Throughout this period Japanese scholars had kept contact with the Dutch through the trading port of Nagasaki. Through this contact they acquired all sorts of European knowledge; this was disseminated more widely in Japanese society during the second half of this period. In the process many new words were created to express new concepts. In this manner the introduction of Western knowledge, as well as the formation of new words to express it, functioned as a preparation for the explosive introduction of Western knowledge after the Meiji Restoration.

Early Modern Japanese

The term 'Early Modern Japanese' refers to the language used after the Meiji Restoration in 1868, which is essentially the same as Modern Colloquial Japanese. Simultaneously, until the end of World War II, the Sino-Japanese style also continued to be used, especially for official communications. This paralleled Colloquial Written Japanese, which was now taught in the modern public education system.

Modern Japanese

It was not until immediately after World War II that Modern Colloquial Japanese was used for official communications. Although Japanese of this last stage is nearly identical with that of the period before 1945, it is referred to as 'Modern Japanese' as opposed to 'Early Modern Japanese.'

A multiplicity of written styles

As should be clear from the preceding section, Japanese was written in several different styles. In this section, each of them will be introduced by way of preparing the ground for an explanation of the modernization process at the time of the Meiji Restoration.

Pure Classical Chinese

What is called 'Pure Classical Chinese' in the Japanese context is really no longer Chinese. The visual appearance of this language is similar to Chinese, but it is read in Classical Sino-Japanese. Official documents were often redacted in this style, especially in the period of Old Japanese.

Sino-Japanese

Sino-Japanese is a variety of Classical Japanese which consists of transforming a Chinese text into Japanese word order and adding Japanese morphological suffixes after Chinese content words. This style is called *kanbun kundokutai*, which literally means 'Chinese-in-Japanese reading style.' It makes use of a number of diacritic symbols indicating the order of reading the Chinese words according to the syntactic rules of Japanese. For example, the Chinese sentence (1) has the following word order, where 'S' stands for subject, 'Neg' for negation, 'V' for verb and 'N obj' for the objective noun:

(1)   Chinese: S   Neg V   N obj

The word order of the Japanese equivalent is given in (2):

(2)   Japanese: S N obj   V   Neg

Since the sequential order of the elements in Japanese was indicated by using diacritic symbols as in (1a), the Japanese reader could understand (1) without any knowledge of Chinese by tracking down the order of the symbols, for which *a*, *b* and *c* stand conventionally in (1a):

(1a)
$$S \quad Neg \quad V \quad N\,obj$$
$$c \qquad b \qquad a$$

An element without any symbol is to be read before all the others. It is followed by another element with a symbol which indicates the top of the sequence. Several sets of Chinese characters which imply the sequential order were used, such as 一 (one), 二 (two), 三 (three), 上 (upper), 中 (middle), 下 (down), and so on. レ is put between two characters to indicate that the former is to be read immediately after the latter. This symbol is called *kaeri-ten* (return(ing)-point), or *re-ten* (re-point) because it resembles the *kana* letter for [re].

Further, the particles and endings of Japanese were also attached to the Chinese words using small *katakana* syllabic letters, as schematized and illustrated in (1b):

	prt.	end.	end.		prt.
(1b)	S	Neg	V	N obj	
	c	b		a	

Figure 7.1. Five varieties of Japanese writing. (Editor's note: notice that all of the above representations are given the same pronunciation. They are all uniformly read as follows: Hyakubun wa ikken ni shikazu, 'Hearing it one hundred times is not the same thing as seeing it once.')

These secondary symbols and suffixes were written on both sides of the lines of the text, which were written from top to bottom (see Figure 7.1).

With the aid of these symbols one could read Chinese texts in Japanese without rewriting them. Experienced scholars and officials could often read them without the aid of the secondary symbols. The Chinese texts which are read in this way, with or without the aid of the diacritic symbols, are called Pure Classical Chinese. In Japanese it is called *kanbun*. *Kan* is the Japanese pronunciation of the Chinese *han*, that is 'Chinese,' and *bun* means 'sentence.'

A complete Japanese sentence can be produced when a Chinese sentence with such symbols as illustrated in (1b) is written down according to the order of the diacritic reading aids by adding the morphological elements with *kana* syllabic letters, as illustrated in (2a).

(2a)   Japanese: S prt N obj prt V end N end

This peculiar mixture of Chinese and Japanese elements is *kanbun-kundoku-tai*, that is Sino-Japanese. Pure Classical Japanese and Sino-Japanese are twin styles in the sense that they were used side by side. Competence in Sino-Japanese was cultivated through philological training, that is reading the Chinese classics in the manner illustrated above. The stylistic impression of Sino-Japanese is very masculine, that is square-built or angular, prompt and rhythmical. This style was, therefore, preferred by the warriors, who used it, for example, in martial literature.

Varieties of Sino-Japanese

The Sino-Japanese style has several varieties. *Hentaikanbun*, literally 'varied *kanbun*,' is among the most prominent. It is a style of the Old Japanese period modeled on Pure Classical Chinese. Nevertheless, most of the texts witness a certain influence of the structure of Japanese, containing as they do phrases which are inappropriate or outright wrong in Chinese, which, however, conveniently render certain frequently occurring Japanese expressions. This style could be considered to be a variety of Pure Classical Chinese. It is subsumed under Sino-Japanese in this chapter because it was meant to be used for the composition of 'Japanese sentences,' which were always read in Sino-Japanese. This style was often used both for official and private correspondence as well as diaries, poems, and the like.

Another variety of Sino-Japanese is the epistolary style, which itself covers a wide range of stylistic variation. The expressions most characteristic of *hentaikanbun* were also used in this style. Another characteristic feature is the honorific auxiliary *sooroo* (to be). It is therefore often called *sooroobun* (*sooroo* sentence). This style was the standard way of writing Japanese until the period of Early Early Modern Japanese. It is highly situation-bound because of the many suffixes indicating speaker–hearer relations. It is suitable for personal communication, but less appropriate for describing objective situations outside the speaker–hearer setting.

Pure Classical Japanese

The impression of this style is feminine, as it first came into existence in the literary works of ladies at the imperial court. During the Edo period some scholars tried to make this style the standard of written Japanese, but most writers did not accept it. Why this attempt failed is not entirely clear, but it may have been because in addition to being feminine it was slower than the Sino-Japanese style.

Written Colloquial Japanese

The creation of this style and its establishment after the Meiji Restoration is discussed by Sugito (see chapter 8).

Establishment of a new written language

Throughout the Shogunate era until the beginning of the Meiji Restoration, that is from the beginning of the seventeenth until the middle of the nineteenth century, the standard way of writing Japanese was Sino-Japanese. Writing the epistolary *sooroobun* and *hentaikanbun* was an indication of erudition which was especially cultivated by the warrior class. The samurai were the leading class of the Shogunate government, the regional governments, as well as of the new government after the Meiji Restoration.

The Sino-Japanese style, including its epistolary variety, differed greatly from the spoken language of the time. The differences were so substantial that these two styles could be regarded as two different languages.

The movement for the establishment of a modern written language had already begun in the final years of the Shogunate era. The first proposal for the innovation was made by Maejima Hisoka, an official translator of the Shogunate government, in 1866, two years before the Restoration. It was a proposal for the abolition of Chinese characters. Maejima expressed his opinion as follows:

The foundation of the nation is the education of the people. Education must be spread to all people, not to the warriors only. In order to achieve this we have to use simple letters and a simple style. We should not choose a way of teaching that is so difficult and involved that people can understand the basic content of learning only after having studied the complicated letters. (Maejima 1868/1978: 127f)

This proposal was, however, not accepted by the government.

After the Restoration, Maejima and some other politicians continued to make suggestions for simplifying the written language, but none were adopted by Emperor Meiji's new government. Some newspapers and periodicals tried to use a colloquial style for a few years immediately following the Restoration, but they abandoned it soon and continued to use the difficult Sino-Japanese style.

Proposals for the enlightenment of the people were made by politicians and scholars belonging to the highest social class. They must have felt that the new style they advocated and tried to put into practice was too pedestrian for themselves, not allowing them to maintain their dignity if they were to use it in their proposals. It is a remarkable fact that all of these proposals, like the one by Maejima cited above, were written in Sino-Japanese, the most difficult of written Japanese styles and the one they intended to replace.

Another movement for the establishment of a new written language was initiated after the failure of the above mentioned proposals inspired by the idea of enlightenment for the people. It was a movement for the unification of the spoken and the written language which was called *genbun itchi*. Literally, *gen* means 'speech,' *bun* 'written sentence,' and *itchi* 'unification.' This movement did not strive for the enlightenment of the people, but was concerned with developing a revolutionary way of giving expression to one's inner feelings which is known as 'naturalism' in literary history. Novelists and politicians who had studied European languages and translated European works into Japanese could not but notice the close relationship between the spoken and written language in Europe. They strongly advocated that the same should be achieved in Japanese.

First attempts at unifying spoken and the written language were made by novelists such as Futabatei Shimei, Yamada Bimyoo, and Ozaki Kooyoo between 1887 and 1889. The first novel written in colloquial Japanese was Futabatei's *Ukigumo*, or *Floating Clouds*. Yamada wrote not only novels in colloquial Japanese, but also introductions to theoretical discussions of the unification of the spoken and the written language. They both proposed several different styles of colloquial Japanese. The colloquial style of their novels was based on the 'high-city variety' of the Edo, or rather Tokyo, dialect. The Tokyo dialect had two varieties, the 'low-city variety,' that is the language of the common people, and the 'high-city variety,' which was spoken in those parts of the city where the warriors lived. They had come to Edo from all regions of Japan as part of their duty concerning the administration of the regional feudal governments. They were also vassal-warriors who were directly subordinate to the Shogunate. Thus the warrior class in Edo developed a new common language during the Shogunate era.

Futabatei first tried to use the style of the storyteller Enchoo, who was very creative and prolific in his genre, using the style of the low-city variety. His work was highly regarded in those days. For Futabatei, however, this style proved to be too close to the vernacular. He therefore abandoned it and adopted a style which was much closer to that of high-city speech. The creativity of the novelists in developing a new written style came to a peak at the end of the nineteenth century. They wrote all their novels in Modern Colloquial Japanese, and the unification of the spoken and the written language was largely accepted by the first decade of the twentieth century.

The Ministry of Education changed the language of textbooks for primary schools to Modern Colloquial Japanese in 1903 and at the same time standardized the forms of the *kana* syllabic letters, which used to have several different graphic varieties.

Newspapers were more conservative. Although they had for a short time experimented with a kind of colloquial style, they returned to the difficult style of Sino-Japanese, and it was not until the end of the second decade of the twentieth century that a colloquial style was eventually adopted by the newspapers, which, after all, were read by a large part of the population throughout the country. At this point the establishment of Modern Written Colloquial Japanese was complete.

Sino-Japanese and the epistolary style were, however, still often used for official documents, administration, law, and many kinds of political publications. Yet these were supposed to be read by the common people. This practice continued until the end of World War II. The bureaucrats, politicians, and the military seem to have thought that the Sino-Japanese style, which was too difficult for ordinary people to read, possessed more gravity and dignity than the colloquial style. It should thus be emphasized that the real unification of the spoken and the written language was achieved only after World War II when practically everything came to be written in Modern Written Colloquial Japanese and the Sino-Japanese style was finally relegated to classical literature.

The other phase of the modernization of Japanese besides the unification of the spoken and the written language was the formation of a modern vocabulary for the new concepts and ideas from the West. A particular aspect of the development of a modern vocabulary is discussed by Sugito (see chapter 8). The present chapter provides some background information for a better understanding of this development.

After the Meiji Restoration, the Japanese acquired all sorts of Western knowledge. Since the concepts they had to deal with in this connection were all new to them, the translators had to create new words, for which they employed the word formation rules of *kango*, that is Sino-Japanese words. In those days, Chinese philology was part of the education of every scholar. Intellectuals, therefore, possessed extensive knowledge of Chinese characters and words; these proved to be an important resource for terminology formation. Instead of creating new words, they often (re-)discovered ancient Chinese words approximating to the intended meaning, which they then associated with new concepts. During the early years of the Meiji period, the translators proposed several alternative words for the new concepts on the basis of their knowledge of Classical Chinese. More than a dozen words were sometimes produced for a single concept. Such lexical chaos continued for a couple of decades after the Restoration.

As yet, both lexicographical and lexicological explanations of the integration of modern vocabulary into the Japanese lexicon are quite inadequate, a fact which is due partly to the enormous number of items that were then created but did not survive in the modern vocabulary, and partly to the overwhelming amount of publications.

Prior to the introduction of so many Western concepts during the Meiji period, there was a long tradition in Japan of Western learning, especially Dutch learning. The Japanese experienced their first contact with Europeans in the sixteenth century, when Spanish and Portuguese missionaries came to Japan. They borrowed some words then, some of which are still in use today.

During the second half of the eighteenth century, the Japanese began to engage seriously in the study of Dutch learning, which was called *Rangaku*, *Ran* being the second syllable of 'Holland' and *gaku* meaning 'study.' *Rangaku* was pursued by scholars in Nagasaki and Edo who translated many Dutch publications. One of the most famous of such publications was the translation of a Dutch medical book, *Tafel Anatomia*, from 1774, entitled *Kaitai shinsho*. It contains a great many translations of Western medical terms.

During the final years of the Shogunate, gradual familiarization with European civilization was accomplished largely by official translators in Nagasaki and through scholars in Edo who studied Dutch and later also English and French publications. This background of study of Western civilization, however perfunctory, saved the Japanese from being completely overwhelmed at the beginning of the Meiji Restoration, in 1868, when contacts with Western civilization were established very suddenly at all levels.

Public education: a prerequisite of modernization

The early development of a system of public education during the Edo period (1600–1868) provided an important background for the success in adapting the Japanese language to the needs of modern society. The benefits of public education were not reserved to those who had actively supported and taken part in the modernization of Japanese society, but shared with a considerable part of the population at large. This educational background enabled the new government to establish a new educational system for primary and secondary schools shortly after the Restoration.

While during the Tokugawa period (1600–1868) children of the warrior class were normally educated in fief schools, elementary education for commoners as well as some warrior children was provided by private schools known as *terakoya*, *tera* meaning 'temple,' *ko* 'child,' and *ya* 'shop' or 'shop-keeper.' *Terakoya* were first managed by Buddhist priests, usually on the precincts of the local temple; later, however, they were taken over by teachers who had no connection with the temple.

The *terakoya* schools provided a solid training in the three fundamental skills of reading, writing, and calculating. The epistolary style was taught, usually with the aid of models called *oraimono*, where *orai* means 'going and coming,' that is 'communication' and *mono* means 'thing.' During the Tokugawa period more than 7,000 textbooks were published. In Edo alone more than 10,000 *terakoya* were founded in that period. It is estimated that about 40% of the boys and from 2% to 17% of the girls of each age group received some kind of systematic education. It should be noted that this attendance level compares favorably with Western Europe and the United States at the time and was far higher than that of Eastern Europe and other parts of Asia.

Secondary education on a more advanced level was provided in two kinds of schools. The sons of the warriors of local feudal governments attended local government fief schools called *hankoo* which were under the jurisdiction of the *daimyoo* or lords. (*Han* means 'fedual clan' and *koo* means 'school.') Occasionally the sons of commoners were also admitted to these schools. They studied Chinese philology, Confucian writings in Pure Classical Chinese, as well as the Sino-Japanese written language. Some schools also taught Dutch.

The other type of institution of secondary education were the *shijuku*, that is 'private schools' run by famous scholars. At these schools students were provided with a training in Chinese philosophy and educated to develop their own thoughts and opinions on philosophical as well as political matters.

A nationwide system of general education was established by the new government immediately after the Meiji Restoration. The Ministry of Education was created in 1871, three years after the Restoration, and a year after that the organization of a modern system of public education was detailed in the famous 'Education Edict.' In 1873 more than 12,500 primary schools were founded which accommodated more than 1,145,000 pupils. The overall school attendance rate had then reached some 28%. Although historians have yet to provide us with exact data for the number of teachers employed at these schools, it is obvious that the government was able to expand the teaching staff very rapidly.

The success of the government in establishing a new system of general education was a key factor in the rapid modernization of Japanese society during the first two decades of the Meiji period. More research is needed about the relationship between social and linguistic development at the time. However, to conclude, I would like to emphasize that the high level of general education at the beginning of the Meiji period must be seen as a fundamental pre-condition of the rapid development of the modern written colloquial style of Japanese.

Reference

Maejima Hisoka 1866. Kanji gohaishi no gi [A Case for Abolishing Chinese Characters]. In Yamamoto Masahide (ed.) 1978. *Kindai buntai keisei shiryoo shyusei* [A Collection of Historical Sources on the Formation of a Modern Style]. Tokyo.

8 Lexical aspects of the modernization of Japanese

SEIJU SUGITO

Introduction

In this chapter, I shall present a brief overview of the modernization of the lexicon of the Japanese language over the past hundred or so years, that is since the Meiji Restoration. Since the issues included under this rubric cover a broad range, the discussion will focus on the role that *kanji* (Chinese characters) have played in the modernization process, in particular on the increase of *kango* in the Japanese language.

Most Japanese scholars since the Meiji Restoration have shown a persistent preference for learning primarily through the Japanese language. Of course, we have made some effort to acquire new knowledge from foreign cultures through the study of foreign languages. However, for the most part, we have chosen to study through Japanese translations of foreign materials. In our studies we have avoided the active use of foreign languages. In other words, we have taken a 'passive attitude' in our acquisition of new knowledge from foreign sources. I use the term 'passive attitude' to refer to this tendency to use direct translation into Japanese, that is to view foreign materials through Japanese, as opposed to an 'active attitude,' which would involve attempting to use a foreign language as a native speaker does. It is the persistence of this passive attitude towards foreign languages over the past two hundred years since the limitation of foreign studies to Dutch learning in the Edo period (see chapter 7) which is responsible for the current condition of the Japanese language.

Some remarks on the Japanese writing system

As shown in figure 8.1 (see also chapter 7), Japanese can be represented using the following four types of letters:

> *hiragana*
> *katakana*
> *kanji* (Chinese characters)
> *romaji* (Roman alphabet)

Hiragana	あいうえお　かきくけこ　さしすせそ　たちつてと
Katakana	アイウエオ　カキクケコ　サシスセソ　タチツテト

Kanji   日本語　([nihongo] = Japanese language)

         雲　([kumo] = cloud)　山　([yama] = mountain)

         言語　([gengo] = language)　世界　([sekai] = world)

Romaji   a　i u e o　ka ki ku ke ko　sa shi su se so

Figure 8.1. Four types of letters in the Japanese writing system

Of these four types, the Roman alphabet is normally not included in the orthography of Japanese, although it is of course possible to write the syllables of Japanese in the Roman alphabet, for example:

(1)   *arigatoo* (thank you)
     sayoonara (goodbye)
     Sugito Seiju (a name)

However, usage of the Roman alphabet in such cases as (1) is restricted to written materials for foreigners who cannot read the other Japanese letters.

The combined use of the remaining three writing systems makes up most of Japanese orthography. Figure 8.2 illustrates current usage with an example from a newspaper. As the example shows, the three types of letters are intermixed in the Japanese written language.

It is possible to represent all the syllables of Japanese using *hiragana* and *katakana*, that is the language can be written entirely in either of these two syllabaries. However, the normal practice and the official orthography is to use a mixture of Chinese characters (*kanji*) and *hiragana*. In general, word stems are written in *kanji*, while inflectional endings, other suffixes, grammatical particles, etc. are written in *hiragana* or *katakana*.

Differentiation in the usage of *hiragana* and *katakana* is as follows. *Hiragana* are used for writing indigenous Japanese words and suffixes in normal daily writing. *Katakana*, on the other hand, are used for non-Chinese loanwords, that is loanwords from Western Europe and America, onomatopoeia, emphasized words, and the names of flora and fauna, etc.

In the Japanese writing system, the same Chinese character can be used to write a variety of different words, but the distinction between the *on* and the *kun* readings, the two basic pronunciations assigned to characters, should always be borne in mind. The *on* (sound-based) readings consist of Japanese imitations or approximations of the sound of the original Chinese syllable. The *kun* (meaning-based) readings correspond to the native Japanese translational equivalent of the Chinese word associated with the respective character. Thus *kun* readings stand for the meanings of the characters as expressed by original Japanese words.

ＩＩＩＩＩＩＩＩＩＩＩＩＩＩＩＩＩＩＩＩＩＩＩＩＩＩＩＩＩＩＩＩ

60年前の借金、千倍で返す

【シアトル二十五日＝ＵＰＩ共同】高級チョコレートで知られる神戸の製菓会社「コスモポリタン」の社長、バレンタイン・モロゾフさん（七五）＝写真＝がこのほど、約六十年前の少年時代、シアトルの新聞社から借りっ放しになっていた一ドル五十㌣の借金を、利息分にインフレを加算して千倍の千五百㌦（約二十五万円）にして返した。

モロゾフさんは「シアトルという町の名を聞くといつも気になってしょうがなかった」と話している。

モロゾフさんは一九二〇年代、シアトルで地元紙「シアトル・ポスト・インテリジェンサー」の新聞売り少年をしていた。あるとき、一束の新聞の販売代として一ドル五十㌣を前払いでもらったが、一家が急きょ日本に引っ越すことになり、これを返せぬままになったという。

新聞社には特にこの貸金の記録は残っていなかったが、「志を尊重して」受け取り、同社の基金に組み入れることにした。

Figure 8.2. Example of orthography from a Japanese daily newspaper

For example, the following characters all have the *on* reading *kaku* [kakɯ]:

a	b	c	d	e	f	g	h
獲	拡	革	角	確	覚	各	格

In addition to the *on* reading, [kakɯ], each of the above characters have one or two *kun* readings:

a	獲	*toru*	(to catch, to gain)
b	拡	*hirogeru*	(to widen)
b	拡	*hirogaru*	(to spread)
c	革	*kawa*	(leather)
d	角	*kado*	(a corner)
d	角	*tsuno*	(a horn)
e	確	*tashikameru*	(to make sure)
f	覚	*oboeru*	(to feel, to sense)

It is important to make a distinction between the two kinds of readings as well as to grasp the relation between them. First, *kun* readings, such as *toru* and *hirogeru*, are originally Japanese native word forms, in other words *kun* readings express the meaning of the character using original Japanese words. On the other hand, *on* readings are phonetic readings based on Chinese pronunciations and therefore one cannot make a direct association between the *on* reading and the meaning of the character in Japanese. Second, it should be stressed that even when a given character is read in the *on* reading, the reader can create an image and associate the meaning of the character through recall of the *kun* reading of the character:

	on reading		*kun* reading		the meaning
(革)	*kaku*	→	kawa	→	leather
	read [kaɯa]		recall [kaɯa]		associate 'leather'

Thus, although *on* readings are phonetic readings based on the Chinese pronunciation of the character, they can be easily associated with the meaning of the character through recall of the *kun* reading.

The classification of Japanese vocabulary

Japanese words are typically classified into the following four classes.

wago: Japanese native words (*yamato-kotoba*)
kango: words of Chinese origin
gairaigo: loanwords from English and other European languages
konshugo: mixed words (*wago* + *kango, kango* + *gairaigo, wago* + *gairaigo,* etc.)

In the above terminology *-go* means 'word,' *wa-* in *wago* means 'Japanese,' *kan-* in *kango* means 'Chinese,' *gairai-* in *gairaigo* means 'coming from a foreign language,' and *konshu-* in *konshugo* means 'mixed.'

The relation between the above classification and the usage of the four types of letters can be described as follows:

Vocabulary class	Written with
wago	*hiragana* or *kanji* in their *kun* reading
kango	*kanji* in their *on* reading
gairaigo	*katakana*
konshugo	mixture of *hiragana, katakana* and *kanji*

Kango is basically a class of words of Chinese origin, and is often referred to as 'Sino-Japanese,' especially by foreign scholars. *Kango* words are read in the *on* reading, that is based on the Chinese pronunciation of the characters. It is important to note that Sino-Japanese does not necessarily consist of pure loanwords from Chinese. Many *kango* have been created in Japan by combining two or three *kanji* in their *on* reading. For example, the following *kango* were created in Japan during the Meiji period:

人力車   *jin-riki-sha* (man-power-vehicle)
希望   *kiboo* (hope)
停戦   *teisen* (stop-war)

Since Sino-Japanese (*kango*) is read in the *on* reading, it is rather difficult to recall the meaning of a *kango* hearing only from its pronunication.

On the other hand, as already mentioned, an *on* reading can be associated with the meaning of a character through the character's *kun* reading. For example:

人	力	車	希	望	停	戦
hito	*chikara*	*kuruma*	*negau*	*nozomu*	*tomeru*	*ikusa*
man	power	vehicle	to hope	to desire	to stop	battle.

Through the *kun* readings, such as *hito*, *chikara*, *kuruma*, one can recall the meaning of the characters, character by character, and then, by summing up the meaning of each character, one can create the meaning of the word itself. In other words, though written and pronounced in Chinese style, *kango* (Sino-Japanese) stands as a class of Japanese words since the meaning of a *kango* can easily be recalled through the *kun* readings of its characters. Thus, although the majority of *kango* are direct loanwords from Chinese, they are understood through the Japanese language and thus reflect the passive attitude towards foreign knowledge mentioned above.

The distribution of *wago* and *kango* in Japanese vocabulary: some results of quantitative lexicography

An overview of the modernization of the lexicon of the Japanese language, especially during the Meiji Restoration, indicates that the percentage of *kango* in Japanese vocabulary increased significantly during the Meiji Restoration. The statistical data which support this observation are summarized below.

Research on 90 magazines issued in 1961

Table 8.1 indicates the results of a quantitative survey of 90 magazines issued in 1961. This survey, carried out at the National Language Research Institute (N.L.R.I.), Tokyo, comprises the most exhaustive statistical data available on the daily written Japanese language. The survey examined a total of 420,000 words of running text, which consisted of 30,000 different words. A large percentage of the words were *kango*, 41.3% of the running words and 47.5% of the different words. These figures reflect the high number of Sino-Japanese words in today's daily written language. The percentage of *wago* among the running words (53.9%) was considerably greater than that among the different words (36.7%). This is because *wago* include a great number of the fundamental words which are used frequently in all contexts, for example words like *suru* (to do), *iru* (to be), and *aru* (to be).

Table 8.1. *Distribution of* wago, kango, gairago, *and* konshugo *in 90 magazines issued in 1961*

	Running words (%)	Different words (%)
Wago	53.9	36.7
Kango	41.3	47.5
Gairaigo	2.9	9.8
Konshugo	1.9	6.0
Total	*c*. 420,000 words	*c*. 30,000 words

Source: N.L.R.I. 1962, 1963, 1964.

An historical overview of the 1,000 words used most frequently in magazines in 1961

Figure 8.3 gives a historical overview of the percentage of the different classes of vocabulary observed in a variety of texts since the eighth century. This graph, based on the same data as given in Table 8.1, gives a macro-historical overview of the shift in the ratio between *kango* (Sino-Japanese) and *wago* (native Japanese words). Specifically, the data are based on a list of the 1,000 words that appeared most frequently in 90 magazines issued in 1961. The distribution of the four Japanese vocabulary classes among the 1,000 words studied was as follows:

wago	*kango*	*gairaigo* (loan word)	*konshugo* (mixed word)	Total
584	383	17	16	1,000

The numbers given at each point in Figure 8.3 specify the percentage of the words from the list of the 1,000 most frequently occurring words mentioned above that each text contained. The texts studied are given below the graph.

For example, the earliest text studied was the *Man'yooshuu*, the oldest anthology of Japanese poems, which consists of 4,500 poems edited in the Nara period (eighth century). In the *Man'yooshuu*, 326 of the 1,000 most frequently occurring words were observed and all of these 326 words were *wago*. *Kango* and *gairaigo* did not appear at all. Thus the percentage of *wago* in text A was 100%. In text F, *Kenkyuusha's English–Japanese Dictionary*, 992 of the 1,000 words were observed. Of these 992 words, 580 were *wago*, 382 were *kango*, 16 were *gairaigo*, and 14 were *konshugo* (mixed words). Thus the percentage of *wago* was 58.5% (580/992) and that of *kango* 38.7% (382/992).

Figure 8.3 illustrates two interesting tendencies. First, the percentage of *kango* has increased, while the percentage of *wago* has decreased steadily since the eighth century. Second, this tendency was highly pronounced in the Meiji

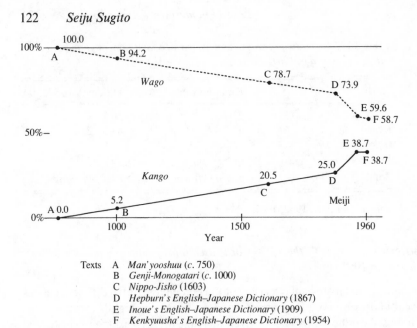

Texts A *Man'yooshuu* (c. 750)
       B *Genji-Monogatari* (c. 1000)
       C *Nippo-Jisho* (1603)
       D *Hepburn's English–Japanese Dictionary* (1867)
       E *Inoue's English–Japanese Dictionary* (1909)
       F *Kenkyuusha's English–Japanese Dictionary* (1954)

Figure 8.3. A historical overview of the 1,000 words used most frequently in magazines in 1961 (Miyajima Tatsuo 1967)

period. Note that text D (*Hepburn's English–Japanese Dictionary*) was published in the last year of the Edo period (1867). In summary, over the course of the history of the Japanese language the percentage of *wago* has gradually decreased, while that of *kango* has increased, and in particular the speed of the shift accelerated significantly during the Meiji period.

As mentioned above, *wago* contain the most fundamental words of the Japanese language and therefore one would not expect *wago* to drop out of the Japanese vocabulary. We consequently interpret the tendency indicated in Figure 8.3 to be the result of an increase in *kango*.

Changes during the Meiji period

General vocabulary as observed in English–Japanese Dictionaries of the Meiji period. Figure 8.4 gives a more detailed picture of the above mentioned tendency in the Meiji period. This graph indicates the distribution of *wago* and *kango* in English–Japanese bilingual dictionaries edited and published during the Meiji period. The ratio of *kango* exceeded that of *wago* between the time when dictionary C (1882) and dictionary D (1888) were published. During this period, the distribution of *kango* and *wago* changed drastically.

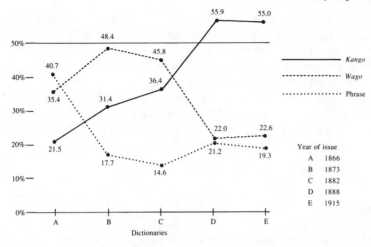

Figure 8.4. *General vocabulary as observed in English–Japanese dictionaries of the Meiji period (Morioka Kenji 1969)*

Table 8.2. *Distribution of technical terms in the bilingual glossaries of some specialized disciplines (%)*

	Year of issue	*Wago*	*Kango*	*Gairaigo*	*Konshugo*	Phrase	Total
Mathematics	1891	5.3	85.2	3.1	1.9	4.4	1,089
Physics	1888	20.2	41.7	20.7	7.3	10.0	955
Mineralogy	1890	1.7	76.1	16.6	5.5	0.0	937
Philosophy	1884	1.1	96.5	1.7	0.2	0.5	1,322

Source: Morioka 1969.

The distribution of wago *and* kango *among technical terms in the bilingual glossaries of some specialized disciplines.* Table 8.2 illustrates the distribution of *wago* and *kango* in the vocabulary of several specialized disciplines. During the Meiji period, many bilingual glossaries were edited and published in a variety of disciplines. *Kango* was dominant in the majority of these glossaries.

The distribution of vocabulary items varies across the disciplines studied. Philosophy was the discipline in which *kango* was most dominant (96.5%). In contrast, in physics, *wago* was rather strong (about 20%) and *kango* relatively weak (about 40%). This latter tendency can be attributed to the dominance of vocabulary items which express natural phenomena in physics. Since these are words for natural phenomena which tend to be used not only academically but also in daily life, it follows that the percentage of *wago* should be relatively high in physics.

Types of kango (*Sino-Japanese*). The above statistics indicate an increase in Sino-Japanese during the Meiji period. This increase was primarily due to the introduction of new knowledge from foreign countries, that is this increase in *kango* came about as a result of an increase in the translation of foreign languages into Sino-Japanese (Chinese characters in their *on* reading).

Extensive research has been done on the manner in which these translations were achieved. Although it is not possible to present the results of this research in much detail, it is worth giving a brief overview of the five patterns on which these translations were based (see Morioka 1969).

1   Translation into existing close Japanese equivalents.

   e.g. people   *choonin*   町人
      servant   *kerai*   家来

   Choonin and *kerai* have been used since the Edo period, that is since before the Meiji Restoration.

2   Translation into obsolete close Japanese equivalents.

   e.g. deduction   *en'eki*   演繹
      absolute   *zettai*   絶対

   These examples illustrate the revival of dead words that had been used in Chinese classical texts.

3   Translation into existing word forms, changing the existing readings of the characters.

   e.g. to honor   *sonkyoo*   *sonkei*   尊敬
      a male   *nanshi*   *danshi*   男子
      a female   *nyoshi*   *joshi*   女子

   Sonkyoo, nanshi, and *nyoshi* have been used since the start of Western learning in the Edo period. *Sonkei, danshi*, and *joshi* are new readings which were given to these forms during the Meiji Restoration.

4   Introduction of mainland Chinese forms as translational equivalents of corresponding foreign terms.

   e.g. arithmetic   *suugaku*   数学
      cube root   *rippookon*   立方根
      charge   *inin*   委任

   These mainland Chinese forms were taken from the *English–Chinese Dictionary* published in China in 1866.

5   Creation of new forms.

   e.g. earth   *chikyuu*   地球
      (*chi* (soil) *kyuu* (ball))
      pressure   *atsuryoku*   圧力
      (*atsu* (to press) *ryoku* (power))

Various patterns were followed in creating these new forms. However, due to space limitations, they will not be discussed here.

Conclusion

This chapter has focussed on the increase in the use of *kango* (Sino-Japanese) in the vocabulary of the Japanese language over the past hundred or so years since the Meiji Restoration. Although some differences among the types of *kango* have been observed, they all have the following common characteristic: their meanings can be created by association through the *kun* readings of the characters they are composed of. This characteristic of *kango* was the most important factor for the introduction of so many new *kango* words since the Meiji Restoration, when Japanese intellectuals embarked on the study of foreign cultures and scientific disciplines that were then new to them.

The educational background of the scholars who were engaged in the study and translation of foreign materials was another factor which led to the increase in *kango*. Their education was centered around the Chinese classics, *kangaku* (Chinese study). Thus one would expect them to be very familiar with the types of translation mentioned above.

From the viewpoint of the Japanese language itself, the co-existence of *kun* and *on* readings, and the connection between the *kun* reading and the meaning of the character, has played an important role in the adoption of vast numbers of *kango* words. It is possible that this unique relationship between the Japanese and Chinese writing systems is responsible for the persistence of a passive attitude among the Japanese towards the incorporation of foreign knowledge.

Appendix: The most recent stage of modernization of the Japanese lexicon: a brief note on the increase of *gairaigo*

In a discussion of the modernization of Japanese since the Meiji Restoration, especially after World War II, one cannot overlook the dramatic increase in the use of *gairaigo* (loanwords from Western languages).

For example, Table 8.3 illustrates the increase of *gairaigo* in the field of mechanical engineering. In four technical glossaries edited during the 70 years from 1886 to 1955, both a decrease in *kango* and an increase in *gairaigo* can be observed. We interpret this increase in *gairaigo* as the most recent stage in the modernization of the Japanese lexicon.

Although our discussion must be brief, it is important to note that *gairaigo* are usually written with *katakana* (or the Roman alphabet in some cases). However, since *katakana* lacks such keys for interpretation as the *kun* reading for *kanji* (Chinese characters), it is difficult to associate a meaning with a *gairaigo* one comes across for the first time. Information about the word formation of *gairaigo*, for example the meaning of morphemes and the patterns of their composition, is for the most part unfamiliar to the Japanese. These factors suggest that the increase of *gairaigo* plays a different role for the modernization of the Japanese lexicon today than *kango* did during and after the Meiji Restoration.

Table 8.3. *Shift of vocabulary in the field of mechanical engineering in four technical glossaries during the 70-year period from 1886 to 1955 (%)*

Year of issue	*Wago*	*Kango*	*Gairaigo*	*Konshugo*	Total (words)
A (1886)	13.6	79.9	0.0	6.5	184
B (1909)	29.8	36.4	7.6	26.2	225
C (1932)	29.4	38.0	11.3	21.3	221
D (1955)	20.0	42.1	21.0	16.9	195

Source: N.L.R.I. 1981.

Note

I would like to thank my colleagues at the conference in Bad Homburg, especially Konrad Ehlich, Florian Coulmas, and Makoto Takada, for their comments on the draft of this paper. I am also deeply grateful to Polly Szatrowski for her comments and her help with the English wording.

References

Ishiwata Toshio 1985. *Nihongo no naka no gairaigo* [Loan Words in the Japanese Language]. Tokyo.

Iwanami (ed.) 1977. *Goi to imi* [Lexicon and Meaning]. Iwanami Kooza Nihongo 9. Tokyo.

Miyajima Tatsuo 1967. Gendai goino keisei [Realization of Modern Japanese Lexicon]. In N.L.R.I. *Kotoba no kenkyuu* [Study of Language], vol. 1.3. Tokyo.

Morioka Kenji 1969. *Kindai-go no seiritu* [Realization of Modern Japanese]. Tokyo.

N.L.R.I. (National Language Research Institute) 1962. *Zasshi kyuujusshu no yoogo yooji* [Vocabulary and Chinese Characters in Ninety Magazines of Today], vol. 1. Tokyo.

　1963. *Zasshi kyuujusshu no yoogo yooji*, vol. 2. Tokyo.

　1964. *Zasshi kyuujusshu no yoogo yooji*, vol. 3. Tokyo.

　1981. *Senmongo no shomondai* [A Study of Specialized Terminology. The Problems of Technical Terms]. Tokyo.

Sakakura Atsuyoshi (ed.) 1971. *Goi-shi* [History of Japanese Lexicon]. Kooza kokugo-shi 3. Tokyo.

Suzuki Takao 1975. On the Twofold Phonetic Realization of Basic Concepts: In Defence of Chinese Characters in Japanese. In F. C. Peng (ed.) *Language in Japanese Society*. Tokyo.

9 The transition from Latin to German in the natural sciences and its consequences

UWE PÖRKSEN

Summary

The gap between natural sciences and humanities today makes it worthwhile to take a look at the development of national languages used in the field of science. Except for Olschki's studies in *Geschichte der neusprachlichen wissenschaftlichen Literatur*, little has been done so far to work out this aspect of language history, and there is still no general survey of the relationship between Latin and the European modern standard languages.

The 'nationalizing' of the various sciences has positively and negatively influenced both international communication and the popular use of theories. The work of Thomasius and posthumous essays by Leibniz are regarded as important steps towards the use of vernacular language in the sciences in Germany. A statistical survey based on the books owned by the Herzog August Bibliothek in Wolfenbüttel shows the slow increase in the use of German compared to Latin in book production between 1500 and 1800.

A look at the foundation of scientific academies and societies in Florence, Paris, and London, and at the use of vernacular languages by European scientists, shows that Germany was a late-comer in this respect.

Closer attention is paid to the sociological conditions of the change and the early founders of mathematical language, Albrecht Dürer, Johannes Kepler, and Christian Wolff.

The transition from the use of Latin to the use of German in the natural sciences has so far not been studied. There is nothing to compare with Olschki's spendid three-volume history on the vernacular scientific literature of Italy between Leonardo da Vinci and Galilei, which was written between 1918 and 1927.

Two factors might explain why Olschki failed to execute his plan of providing a similar study of the transition from Latin to German. First of all, the body of that literature is enormous and disparate. Second, it is a-synchronous: the political, religious, and academic splintering of German between the seventeenth and the nineteenth centuries created a fractured linguistic landscape. Furthermore, C. P. Snow's (1964) 'gap' between the 'two cultures'

127

deepened in Germany at the beginning of the nineteenth century at the very moment when the German language was becoming the subject of a new science. This new science, the *Germanische Philologie*, concentrated on the language of poetry, of old arts and crafts, and on German dialects, while almost totally neglecting the study of language forms that were coming into being in the new natural sciences. Even twentieth-century dictionaries sometimes neglect this area.

In this unexplored ocean I shall sketch the outlines of five islands which may serve as points of orientation in the discussion.

Dürer, Kepler, and Wolff

In 1525 Albrecht Dürer, the artist, published an 'Instruction for Measurements by Means of Compass and Straightedge.' The booklet was meant as a practical guide for apprentices who had to approach drawing and painting with 'geometric exactitude.' In this guide Dürer proposes a new German terminology. He shuns the otherwise common loan translations that ape, step by step, the composition of Greek and Latin models. In speaking about the diameter of a circle he does not use the word *Durch-Messer*, but searches for a strong vernacular term and comes up with *Zwerch-Linie*. *Zwerch* means 'across' in Old German, and we still use it in *Zwerch-Fell* (*Fell* meaning that raw skin for which English has 'pelt,' *Zwerch-Fell* meaning 'diaphragm'). Ellipsis he calls *Eier-Linie*, 'egg-line,' a line that resembles an egg. The parabola he calls a 'burn-line,' *Brenn-Linie*, because a parabolic mirror causes a fire to kindle. 'And the hyperbola shall be called the fork-line, *Gabel-Linie*.' Like his contemporary Luther he tries to incorporate the new concepts into the genius of the vernacular language.

In 1616, Johannes Kepler published an 'Art of Measurement' according to Archimedes. Its purpose was eminently practical: the calculation of the content of vats. At the time Kepler wrote this guide he was working for the Austrian government. His booklet was destined for use by official wine-testers, and was part of an attempt to establish supra-regional norms. In the German version which he prepared himself, Kepler drew heavily on Dürer. Kepler, too, wanted to elaborate a German terminology with concepts cast in concrete and clearly visual descriptions. He was a Swabian, born near Stuttgart. For segment he says *Schnitz*, a word which means 'splinter' or 'split,' but which is still used by my Swabian wife when she refers to a slice of orange. For Kepler the cylinder is a 'round column' and the pyramid is a 'pointed' one. For the tangent, which just touches the circle, he invented the term *Anstreicher* – derived from *streichen*, which here means 'a slight touch or stroke.'

In Latin the texts by Dürer and Kepler became European bestsellers. The German versions, however, had at best local influence and were not reprinted. Only after 1700 did German mathematics become generally acceptable, and

Christian Wolff may be considered its originator. He was a professor of Mathematics, Natural Sciences and Philosophy in the Prussian town of Halle. In 1734 he published a mathematical dictionary whose vocabulary was made up in almost equal parts of Latin and of German terms, some of which were taken from Dürer and Kepler. Wolff published on many different subjects and he did so in a new style: it is clear, it shuns emotionality, and it uses defined concepts as building blocks for carefully and economically constructed sentences. It avoids both redundancy and anything that might inspire the imagination of the reader. Through his writings Wolff had a considerable impact on public discourse. His style is the first German example of one-dimensional language.

Thomasius's groundwork

We cannot but ask: How did Wolff's writings on philosophy and natural sciences in German come to have such an impact on the German language? In Halle Wolff was a colleague of Thomasius, the first German academic ever to announce a lecture in German. That happened in 1687 in Leipzig. That year, at the age of 32, Thomasius had already upset his colleagues in Leipzig by wearing civilian dress (*Kavalierskleidung*) at a lecture, instead of the traditional cap and gown. Then, on Easter Sunday, he again scandalized Leipzig by pinning on the university noticeboard a public announcement which stated that he would lecture on Garcian in German. The calculated affront to tradition must have come as a great shock. Thirty years later, as a famous professor, Thomasius still remembers his apprehension that his horrid announcement would be washed from the venerable bulletin-board with holy water:

Denckt doch! ein teutsch programma an das lateinische schwartze Bret der löbl. Universität. Ein solcher Greuel ist nicht erhöret worden, weil die Universität gestanden. Ich muste damals in Gefahr stehen, dasz man nicht gar solemni processione das löbliche schwartze Bret mit Weyhwasser besprengte.[1]   (Hodermann 1891: 18)

This was indeed the first solemn *intimatio* to be published in German, and Thomasius had shrewdly planned his step by choosing the right theme. Obviously the French were ahead of the Prussians. In France, fifty years earlier, the hold of the Latinist humanists on the curriculum had been shaken. The court had replaced the university as the forum of high prestige. The worldly and practically useful *honnête homme* had cast a shadow over the Latin humanist. Thomasius set out to obtain an analogous shift in Germany by redefining a university's goals. To pursue his purpose, he announced a discussion on the ways and means of following, on this point of language, the French way of life by discussing Garcian's rules on 'How to live reasonably, wisely and decently.' To suggest that a university ought to teach how to live was quite an innovation. In retrospect, the university he wanted looks like a sophisticated eighteenth-century Knigge – or perhaps Ann Landers – and the appropriate kind of discourse made it necessary to abandon Latin. (During the same period Leibniz wrote two essays demanding a transition from Latin to the vernacular, but he never published them.)

In his writings Thomasius demonstrated that neither philosophy nor morals nor education were prisoners of Latin. Quite the contrary, he argued: Latin could easily become an obstacle to their pursuit. The Latin university was frozen in an antiquated curriculum, and its stiff procedures distorted the mind. Understandably, Thomasius did not survive at Leipzig. He switched to Halle, where he succeeded in introducing German, in addition to Latin, as a medium of instruction, and he did so despite a Prussian decree forbidding the use of German. Thus it was Thomasius who prepared the milieu within which Christian Wolff, his contemporary, could spread his 'scientific' prose.

From Latin to German in printing

The demands formulated by Thomasius and Leibniz are reflected in publishing trends. It was only 150 years after Luther, in 1680, that for the first time more titles were printed in German than in Latin. This shift did not happen at once; it took some 300 years. In 1500, only 10% of all printed material was in German. Even at this early time there were quite a number of technical books in German, using the terminology of the arts and crafts. By 1800, no more than 4% of all books printed in Germany were in Latin. This transition from Latin to German as the language of printing did not follow a smooth pattern: for well over a century it was a neck-and-neck race. A clear decision in favor of German came only in the final decades of the eighteenth century, at least as far as mathematics and science were concerned. So far no statistics have been analyzed to document this shift, but from two major sources that I have studied – the sales catalogues of the Frankfurt and Leipzig bookfairs that were published continuously from 1590 onwards, usually every six months, and the Wolfenbüttel library catalogue – the trend becomes quite clear.

The sales catalogues have two shortcomings. They are not exhaustive of the year's total production, and not even a single copy of half of the items mentioned in them during the Thirty Years War in Germany has survived. Nonetheless they do allow some generalizations, as Jentzsch already noticed in 1912. What we learn from the sales catalogues is confirmed by the catalogues of new acquisitions at the Herzog August Bibliothek in Wolfenbüttel. In this quiet town not far from Hannover and several miles from the border that now cuts through Germany, Prince August of Braunschweig founded a library of exceptional beauty. Among its chief librarians rank Leibniz and Lessing. An examination of its catalogues shows that in 1780 Latin still clearly dominates the natural sciences, but only twenty years later five out of six books in the sciences are in German.

The goal: vernacular science. The role of academies

The transition from Latin literacy to vernacular science happened everywhere in Europe, but not everywhere at the same pace. I am tempted to compare the decline of Latin with a horse-race giving the following results. Italy is far ahead, followed by France. In the middle of the field Holland vies with England; they are both well in front of Germany and Switzerland. The back-markers are Sweden, Austria, and Poland, amongst others. I have prepared a list of key authors in mathematics and the natural sciences, comparing their publications in Latin and the vernacular. The pattern described above emerges clearly from an examination of several dozen authors. In addition, it is confirmed by looking at the history of the academies that were founded during this period in several European countries.

In 1541 Cosimo I ordered the University of Florence to open its doors to the civil community and give public lectures in Italian. He intended to legitimize his position as prince by gaining the support of a citizenship rooted in the language of everyday intercourse. He ordered professors to give public talks in Italian beginning with a sentence of the *Divine Comedy* which had to be explained and interpreted. In the same year Florence established the first academy, which came to be known as the Accademia della Crusca. Almost a hundred years later, in 1635, the Académie Française was established; the Royal Society came into existence another thirty years later. Not until 1700 did Prussia get her Berliner Sozietät.

These foundations were crucial for the transition from Latin to the vernaculars in the sciences because, except in Prussia, the vernacular was the language of the academy. The academies were intended as a contribution to the popularization of learning and to the public pursuit of the applied sciences. Governments supported them and benefited from their growth. Over and over again strong feelings surfaced in the academies, feelings directed against the cloistering of the sciences in the walls of the university and their imprisonment in the Latin language. Thus the natural sciences did not only develop independently of the grip of the Church; they also grew up outside the university, having their roots in the crafts, the *artes mechanicae* and *artes magicae* of the Middle Ages. Under the pressure of the emerging nation state and its interests they became equally detached from the tradition of humanistic literacy. The gap between the 'two cultures' can be traced back at least as far as this cleavage between the sciences and the humanities.

The race towards vernacular science reflects the rivalry and competition between the European nations, which at that time were taking on their modern form of nation states. The 'nationalization' of Europe cannot be separated from the creation of science in national tongues. It is a true race, a race towards modernity. In France, the Pléiade attempts to outdo Italy. England and France compete. In Germany Leibniz berates the backwardness of science and the lack of any German terminology capable of serving scientific purposes.

New horizons and their cost

Understandably, the feud between the advocates of Latin and the proponents of the vernacular language in the sciences was violent. It was a change with serious consequences and one can only be amazed at how little scholarly attention it has attracted to date.

No doubt, in this process new horizons were opened:

1   The new right to express one's scientific view of the world in one's native tongue made it possible to look beyond the blinkers imposed by Latin convention. Science comes closer to everyday life.

2   The new obligation, imposed on the scientific author, to cast his argument in his native tongue enables his common-sense reader to unmask its fallacies. In this way science also becomes more democratic.

3   The new exigency to formulate scientific observations and arguments in the national tongue yields a new kind of elegance in nineteenth-century prose. Science becomes a kind of literature.

4   With its most outstanding works this new prose becomes a touchstone and challenge for literary texts. The language of science is imitated in other genres.

5   The displacement of Latin by the vernacular levels the barriers between academy and city. Cosimo succeeded.

6   Finally, the words and concepts borrowed from science enrich everyday language and enable it to roam far beyond its traditional confines.

However, these new horizons were created at a heavy cost:

1   The universal European tongue that had lasted for many generations – the *lingua Europeae universalis et durabilis ad posteritatem* of Leibniz – no longer existed. And science ceased to be universal for some time.

2   As a result, science often became a national, not infrequently a nationalistic, enterprise.

3   Paradoxically, the new openness of the scientific enterprise invited a new kind of supervision, – of management and exploitation – that made science into a tool of power. Latin had functioned as a 'wall' of protection, as in the case of Galileo Galilei. As long as Galileo published his ideas in Latin, there was no danger. But as soon as he began to write in the vernacular, the Inquisition went into action.

4   The 'language of science' lost its pristine character of a pliable tool that could be used unambiguously within any chosen field. An artificial Latin language, stripped of all vernacular associations and connotations, was lost and increasingly substituted for by a new universal language of algorithms which is no longer language, or by a new mixture, made up of vernacular and scientific language.

5   As the learned man became the new scientific author, he found himself faced with a dilemma. Every modern language can be divided into two or more codes, which on the surface appear to constitute a seamless whole, but which in reality derive from heterogeneous principles. As a result, the writer could not avoid addressing a general public when formulating a description in-

tended for his peers. Thus the terms he used acquired a new kind of duplicity: they are chosen to do their job as technical terms, yet inevitably they resonate in an often totally different register within ordinary speech. They constantly tempt the author to calculate their effect and – willy nilly – turn into literally 'cockeyed' concepts.

6   When scientific codes are constructed in this kind of language, they have the tendency to act as dominant myths that overshadow everyday lives. They become suitable for use as instruments and, as instruments, change from hypothesis to doctrine. 'Marxism,' 'Darwinism,' and 'Freudianism' are just some of the labels for such domineering codes.

7   Even the use of sundry bits from these terminological loanwords in everyday speech can conjure up these powerful myths. Thus they overshadow simple conversation and, surreptitiously, empty it of all concrete, personal referents.

Thus scholarly language is increasingly using the vernacular to its own advantage, thereby plundering all the power and prestige for itself. Sometimes the vernacular language might look like Gregor Samsa in Kafka's story *Metamorphosis*, who one morning found himself transformed into a gigantic insect, and was later bombarded by his father with apples. Gregor did not cease to love those who had transmuted him: 'The rotting apple in his back and the inflamed area around it, all covered with soft dust, hardly troubled him any more. He thought of his family with tenderness and love.'

Note

1 Imagine! a German announcement on the Latin notice-board of the esteemed university. Such abomination has been unheard of since the university's founding. At the time I had to fear that the esteemed notice-board would be sprinkled, *solemni processione*, with holy water.

References

Bach, Adolf 1965. *Geschichte der deutschen Sprache*, 8th revised edn. Heidelberg.

Bezzel, Imgard 1974. Das Verzeichnis der im deutschen Sprachbereich erschienenen Drucke des 16. Jahrhunderts. Ein bibliographisches Unternehmen in München und Wolfenbüttel. *Zeitschrift für Bibliothekswesen und Bibliographie*, 21: 177–85.

Blackall, Eric A. 1959. *The Emergence of German as a Literary Language 1700–1775*. Cambridge. German translation *Mit einem Bericht über neue Forschungsergebnisse 1955–1964 von Dieter Kimpel*. Stuttgart 1966.

Busch, Wilhelm 1933. *Die deutsche Fachsprache der Mathematik*. Giessener Beiträge zur deutschen Philologie 30. Giessen.

Drozd, L. and Seibicke, W. 1973. *Deutsche Fach- und Wissenschaftssprache. Bestandsaufnahme, Theorie, Geschichte*. Wiesbaden.

Dürer, Albrecht 1525. *Underweysung der messung mit dem Zirkel un richtscheyt, in Linien ebnen und gantzen corporen durch Albrecht Dürer zusammen getzogen ...* Undated new edition Nördlingen.

1527. *Etliche underricht, zu befestigung der Stett, Schlosz und Flecken.* Undated new edition Nördlingen.

1528. *Hierin sind begriffen vier bücher von menschlicher Proportion, durch A. D. von Nürnberg erfunden und beschrieben.* Undated new edition Nördlingen.

Düsterdieck, Peter 1974. Buchproduktion im 17. Jahrhundert. Eine Analyse der Messekataloge für die Jahre 1637 und 1658. *Archiv für Geschichte des Buchwesens*, 14: 163–218.

Engelsing, Rolf 1974. *Der Bürger als Leser. Lesergeschichte in Deutschland 1500–1800.* Stuttgart.

Götze, Alfred 1919. Anfänge einer mathematischen Fachsprache in Keplers Deutsch. *Germanische Studien 1.* Berlin.

Grimm, Gunter E. 1983. *Literatur und Gelehrtentum in Deutschland. Untersuchungen zum Wandel ihres Verhältnisses vom Humanismus bis zur Frühaufklärung.* Tübingen.

Heidelberger, Michael and Thiessen, Sigrun 1981. *Natur und Erfahrung. Von der mittelalterlichen zur neuzeitlichen Naturwissenschaft.* Reinbek.

Hodermann, Richard 1891. Universitätsvorlesungen in deutscher Sprache um die Wende des 17. Jahrhunderts. Doctoral Dissertation, University of Jena.

Jentzsch, Rudolf 1912. Der deutsch-lateinische Büchermarkt nach den Leipziger Ostermesskatalogen von 1740, 1770 und 1800 in seiner Gliederung und Wandlung. *Beiträge zur Kultur- und Universalgeschichte 22* (Leipzig).

Keil, Gundolf and Assion, Peter 1974. *Fachprosaforschung. Acht Vorträge zur mittelalterlichen Artesliteratur.* Berlin.

Kepler, Johannes 1616. *Außzug auß der Uralten Messekunst Archimedis.* Linz.

Kühlmann, Wilhelm 1980. Apologie und Kritik des Lateins im Schrifttum des deutschen Späthumanismus. Argumentationsmuster und sozialgeschichtliche Zusammenhänge. *Daphnis*, 9: 33–63.

Leibniz, Gottfried Wilhelm 1916. *Deutsche Schriften*, ed. Walther Schmied-Komarzik. Leipzig.

    1976. Informal Thoughts regarding the Use and Improvement of the German Language. Translated by C. and B. Wunderlich in R. Calinger, *Gottfried Wilhelm Leibniz. With an Essay by Leibniz on the German Language.* Trey, New York.

Matthias, Adolf 1907. *Geschichte des deutschen Unterrichts.* München.

Michel, Gerhard and Ratke, Wolfgang 1976. Die Muttersprache in Schule, Stadt und Wissenschaft. In A. Schöne (ed.), *Stadt, Schule, Universität, Buchwesen und die deutsche Literatur im 17. Jahrhundert.* München.

Olschki, Leonardo 1927. *Geschichte der neusprachlichen wissenschaftlichen Literatur*, 3 vols. Leipzig, Florence, Rome, Geneva, Heidelberg, Halle.

Pörksen, Uwe 1986. Deutsche Naturwissenschaftssprachen. Historische und kritische Studien. *Forum für Fachsprachenforschung* (Tübingen), 2: 42–71.

Schirmer, Alfred 1912. Der Wortschatz der Mathematik nach Alter und Herkunft untersucht. *Zeitschrift für deutsche Wortforschung*, 14: supplement.

Snow, C. P. 1964. *The Two Cultures and a Second Look. An Expanded Version of the Two Cultures and the Scientific Revolution.* Cambridge.

Thomasius, Christian 1970. *Deutsche Schriften*, ed. P. von Düffel. Stuttgart.

Ward, Albert 1974. *Book Production, Fiction, and the German Public 1740–1800.* Oxford.

Zachert, U. (ed.) 1976. *Wolfenbüttler Verzeichnis medizinischer und naturwissenschaftlicher Drucke 1472–1831*, vols. 5–7, Chronologischer Index. Nendeln.

10 Greek and Latin as a permanent source of scientific terminology: the German case

KONRAD EHLICH

Typological and diachronic aspects

The linguistic situation in Europe is unique: it consists of a set of cognate languages which are organized, or can be regarded as being organized, in the form of a 'language family.' Three main branches – the Romance, the Germanic, and the Slavonic – comprise the major languages of this family. The family as a whole constitutes the Western group of the Indo-European languages to which also belong languages like Greek and Albanian which are not part of the three main branches.

Taking into account the diachronic perspective we notice further aspects of this uniqueness. I will discuss eight such aspects.

1   The three main branches of Indo-European languages account for the bulk of the historical development of languages in Europe.

2   Only a few languages not belonging to these branches had any impact on Europe's general 'cultural' development. The most important group is the Celtic branch. Its main contributions to the formation of present-day Europe have been restricted to two fields, one linguistic and one cultural: (a) name formation (especially toponymy) and (b) lore and literary heritage (Arthurian legend, etc.). A third important Celtic contribution, the Irish Christianization of the north of Europe, was not a linguistic one because it was mainly dependent on the medium of Latin.

3   There are two important occurrences of large-scale linguistic contacts between the Romance and the Germanic branch: the 'Franconian' one on the continent, and the 'Norman' in England. The first, occurring in the early medieval period, did not leave many traces. The second one, brought about by the Norman conquest of England in 1066, produced a blending of the two branches into a single language characterized by a stratum of basic Anglo-Saxon vocabulary and grammar, and a superimposed structure of Romance vocabulary and morphology.

4   There is a Roman basis to the European linguistic development in nearly all culturally important domains. Building on the cultural infrastructures

which had been developed during the Roman Empire, and which had covered all of Europe except the north and parts of the east, the Church was responsible for the spread of culture in Europe. The missionaries crossed political borders and spread the influence of Latin to the north. The spread of culture included the art of writing and reading, which were then mainly bound to the Latin language. Of the indigenous writing systems that had been developed before or in conjunction with Latin only a few survived.

5   The Roman culture inherited most of what we know as its achievements from the Greeks. This cultural transfer implied a variety of linguistic needs. For many theoretical and practical achievements which had found their manifestation in the Greek language it was not difficult to develop corresponding forms in Latin.

This holds for vocabulary, word formation strategies, the precision and explicitness of grammatical relations, and complex sentence formation. It did *not* hold, however, for communication techniques and the means of elaborating theoretical questions. The close structural relationship between Greek and Latin facilitated the process of cultural transfer. It helped the Church to take over the mediating function with regard to the Greek-based Latin culture after the Roman Empire declined around A.D. 410. A necessary prerequisite had been the fact that between A.D. 200 and A.D. 400 the previously Greek theological tradition had been transposed into Latin, to the effect that a genuine Latin theological development took place out of very simple beginnings. The Latin theological tradition was of enormous importance for the theoretical development of (Western) Europe.

6   Christianity is a religion which is essentially based on a literate culture involving three main languages – Hebrew, Greek, and Latin.

The difficult transfer of the Hebrew into the Greek tradition had been achieved before Christianity came into being (the Septuagint, Philo Alexandrinus). This process of transfer brought into contact two types of world concepts and resulted in a revolution of Greek philosophical thinking, affecting, amongst others, the concepts of time, *archē*, and world.

7   The achievements of Greek theorizing and science were handed down to Western Europe in different ways:

(a)   through the Roman tradition (fourth to ninth centuries);
(b)   through the Aramaic (Syrian) and Arabic tradition (twelfth and thirteenth centuries); and
(c)   through an original re-encounter with the *fontes* (sources) after 1453.

After A.D. 500 the Greek world developed into a mere traditionalism which lasted until 1453. This traditionalism was obviously a reaction to a permanent external threat which lasted for centuries.

The expansion to the north-east of Europe brought ('orthodox') Christianity and a genuine writing system to the Slavonic peoples, a development which had few consequences, however, for the linguistic development of Western Europe.

The Arabic transmission of Greek culture left few traces in European languages. However, the details of these encounters are not very well understood yet. The Renaissance movement led to a thorough re-acquisition of the Greek language and put original 'sources' in this language at the disposal of Western European scholarship. The *ad fontes* movement and its importance for the Protestant religion inspired scholarship in Greek and to some extent also in Hebrew, a concern which has been maintained to the present.

8   As of 1492, in the course of imperialistic and colonial expansion, the European countries started to carry their cultural traditions to other parts of the world. This process had two main linguistic consequences:

(a)   a threat to, and/or the extinction of, many non-Indo-European languages (in Central and South America, North America, Australia, and parts of Africa); and

(b)   the functional expansion of European languages as official or hegemonial languages in the conquered territories, to the effect that

most parts of North America speak English;

some parts of North America speak French (Quebecois);

most parts of Central and South America speak Spanish;

one extensive part of South America speaks Portuguese;

most parts of Australia and New Zealand speak English;

English, French, Spanish, and Portuguese were/are the hegemonial languages in large parts of Africa and Asia;

Russian is the common language in the U.S.S.R., that is in the northern parts of Asia.

The effects of the development described above are manifold. To sum up, the European linguistic situation is unique in that a small number of cognate languages have been the vessel and tool of some of the world's most important scientific and cultural developments.

These developments include a first 'flourishing' period in classical Greece; a period of productive tradition in the Roman and medieval world (the latter having had the center of genuine productivity in the Arab world); and a second 'flourishing' period since the humanistic and Renaissance movements.

The developments are characterized by a multilinear and complex continuity which enabled the groups involved, and their languages, to incorporate revolutionary developments and even breaks of tradition. A powerful adaptation mechanism allowed for the integration of alien traditions on a large scale and put cultural achievements of other areas of the world at the disposal of the peoples of Europe. While the economic form of this adaptation process was one of direct exploitation, the cultural mechanisms of adaptation ranged from assimilation to a self-threatening admiration of foreign cultures.

The picture sketched above becomes yet more coherent when we consider the development of scholarship. In the Latin period there were two processes, one of consolidation, and a second one in the course of which the 'treasures of knowledge' were collected and put into the form of an encyclopedia by Isidor. In the medieval period there were the processes of tradition and the spread of the 'treasures of knowledge' throughout Western Europe. In the post-medieval period the traditions were 'nationalized' research area by research area (religion: Hus, Wyclif, Luther and the Reformation; grammar; philosophy: Descartes, Vico; *jus*: Thomasius; natural sciences; medicine).

This process called for a new language of science and theory. Its basis was Latin, the common ground of European scientific language. Latin had facilitated the development of academic institutions since Alcuin and the creation of a highly mobile European scientific community, with its own organizational infrastructures (travelling, *Landsmannschaften*, etc.) and a unique medium of communication. The transposition of that language of science and theory into national languages was a process that took about 400 years.

I will not discuss the external, that is the social and socio-economic aspects of this process here, though they seem to be of great importance for its beginnings, rigor, and its powerful continuity, but will confine myself to characterizing some of the internal conditions and consequences of this process, taking German as an example.

Structural aspects

Several of the diachronic features of the European languages have a direct bearing on present-day scientific language formation. Namely:

> the structural relatedness of the languages involved;
> the close proximity of word formation patterns; and
> the presence of relevant parts of 'foreign words' in the languages involved.

From a linguistic point of view, these aspects are of major importance and I will illustrate them, with German, in this section.

German is a Germanic language. The relationship to Latin and Greek is thus a third-order relationship (see Figure 10.1).

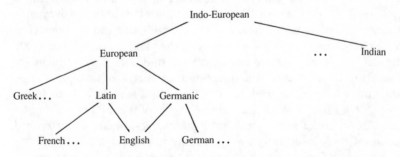

Figure 10.1. The relationship between German and Latin and Greek

This relationship entails a certain stock of common roots or stems, many of which are, however, not recognized as such by the ordinary speaker. List 1 gives some obvious examples.

(1)

Greek	Latin	German	English
patēr	pater	Vater	father
poys	pes	Fuß	foot
deka	decem	zehn	ten
(f)oida	videre	wissen	(to know/to see; cf. wit)
hals	sal	Salz	salt
hex	sex	sechs	six
kephalē	—	Giebel	gable
—	caput	Haupt	head

I call a relationship of this type a 'covert etymological relation.' Though there are hints of this relationship in the form of the words of these four languages, only linguistic expertise can avoid folk etymology. Covert etymological relations are not directly relevant to word formation. Their importance lies in a different domain. Stems coming from another language are experienced as non-alien by a speaker of one of these languages. There is thus an important difference between these words and others which are derived from languages such as Arabic (*Alchimie*); Korean/Japanese (*Taekwondo*), Chinese (*Taoismus*) or Polynesian (*tabu*).

The second aspect, the close proximity of word formation patterns, makes it possible to draw permanently on the stock of Latin and Greek stems for the formation of new words. This concerns most of all the formation of nouns and verbs and the transfer of linguistic items from one of these classes to another. Expansion of the lexical stock can be achieved by a variety of strategies. Latin and Greek, as well as German, French, and English, generally do not coin new stems. Rather, the set of stems has remained relatively constant through the ages. The most productive strategy for expanding the lexicon is the application of prefixes and suffixes (see lists 2 and 3). Consider as an example the Greek stem *the, them, thek, thes* (to put). List 4 gives derivations of this stem that can be identified in German. The semantic range of these words is very wide; nevertheless, the semantic relationship to the Greek term 'put', on the one hand, and to the semantic domain of the prefixes which are involved, on the other and, is obvious in all cases.

(2a)   PREFIXES

Greek	English	German
a-	(negation)	(verneinend)
ana-	1 upwards	1 hinauf
	2 repeated	2 wieder
ant(i)-	against	gegen
ap(o)	away from	von (... weg)
di-[1]	twice	zweimal, doppelt

di(a)-[2]	through	hindurch
dys-	bad	schlecht
ekto-	out of	außerhalb
en-	into	in (... hinein)
endo- ento-	inside	innen
ep(i)-	on	dar(auf)
ex-	from	aus
hyper-	hyper	über (mäßig)
hypo-	under/beyond	unter
kat(a)-	down from	herab
met(a)-	1 (change) 2 later	1 Veränderung 2 später
par(a)-	1 at 2 against	1 bei 2 gegen
peri-	around	um ... herum
syn-	together, with	zusammen, mit

(2b)   PREFIXES

Latin	English	German
ab-	away from	von (... weg)
ad-	at, to	an, zu, bei
cum-	together, with	zusammen, mit
de-	from	von (... herab)
dis-	away from, split up	auseinander
ex-	away from	aus
in-[1]	(going) into	in (... hinein)
in-[2]	(negation)	(verneinend)
inter-	between	zwischen
ob-	against	gegen
per-	by, through	durch
prä-	before	vor
pro-	for	vor, für
re-	again, returning	wi(e)der, zurück
sub-	under	unter
trans-	trans	hinüber

(3a)   SUFFIXES

Greek	English	German
-ia	-y	-ie
-ikē	-c(s)	-ik
-ikos	-ic	-isch
-ismos	-ism	-ismus
-istēs	-ist	-ist

(3b) SUFFIXES

Latin	English	German
-and- -end-	-and, -end	-and, -end
-ant -ent	-ant, -ent,	-ant, -ent
-antia -entia	-ance, -ence	-anz, -enz
-atus		-at
-ia	-y	-ie
-ion	-ion	-ion
-mentum	-ment	-ment
-tāt-	-ty	-tät
-tor	-tor	-tor
-ūra	-ure	-ur
-arius -aris	-ar	-är, -ar
-alis	-al	-al, -ell
-ilis	-ile	-il
-ivus	-ive	-iv
-osus	-ous	-ös
-are, -ēre -ire, -ere		-ieren

(4) Theke   Apotheke
     Thema   Antithese
     These   Epitheton
               Hypothek
               Hypothese
               Parenthese
               Prothese
               Synthese

In many of the Greek and Latin words employed for the formation of German expressions, there are similar expansions. This type of word formation is productive and 'natural' to speakers of German with regard to genuine German expressions. The close structural parallelism of word formation makes the application of a Latin- or Greek-based type of this word formation strategy a very simple procedure. It is only the elements which are different, not the type of their application. Native speakers of German have no serious difficulties integrating this type of word formation into their usage.

The cultural contacts between the Latin world and the German world, and, in later times, between the Romance world and the German world, can be considered as a continuous phenomenon since the beginning of the Christian era. Linguistically speaking, permanent contact has brought about a continuous flow of new Latin words into German. Many of these words

nowadays are no longer experienced as not being of Germanic origin. List 5
provides some examples (type A).

(5) A   Fenster   fenestra
         Pforte   porta
         Mauer   murus
         Frucht   fructus
         Sichel   segula
         Kohl   caulis
         Küche   coquina
         Spiegel   speculum

The incorporation of Latin words into German and their transformation
into German words is a good basis for the continuity of this process of
importation in later times. The importation of Latin words in the late Middle
Ages and in the sixteenth and seventeenth centuries shows the Latin origin of
words more directly (see list 6). Here the morph(ophon)emic structures have
been adapted only slightly to German structures, a feature which is most
obvious in the stress patterns.

(6) B   Akademie   Kommentar   Apotheke
         Universität   Autor   Medikament
         Studium   definieren   appellieren
         Grammatik   addieren   ˏ   konfrontieren
         Stilistik   multiplizieren protestieren

Words of type A exhibit a German stress pattern (main stress on the first
syllable of a noun); most words of type B do not have this stress pattern:

        Fenster   vs   Universität
        Sichel   vs   Akademie

In the case of *Universität*, the stress pattern is at variance with the Latin
nominative pattern because, like many other Latin-origin words, *Universität*
was derived from non-nominative forms (universitatis [gen.]; universitatem
[acc.]).

The non-German character of these words is most obvious in the standard
verb suffix *-ieren*. It is a sort of archi-morpheme for the (infinitive ending of
the) four Latin main verb classes:

        -are ⎫
        -ēre ⎪
             ⎬ -ieren
        -ire ⎪
        -ere ⎭

The suffix *-ieren* always carries the main stress. This makes verbs of Latin
origin highly salient in spoken German, for all German verbs belong to one
of two classes, one which comprises the verbs of Germanic origin, and one
which comprises the verbs of Latin origin. The first class of verbs has the stress

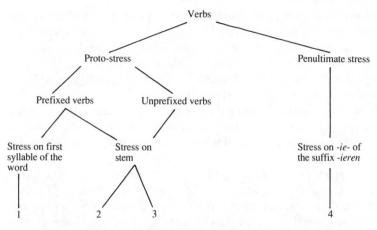

Figure 10.2. Four types of stress in German verbs. Examples: (1) übersetzen, 'to cross (a river),' (2) übersetzen, 'to translate,' (3) kommen, 'to come,' (4) regieren, 'to rule,' korrigieren, 'to correct'

on the first syllable or on the stem, and the second class has penultimate stress (see Figure 10.2).

Mater's *Rückläufiges Wörterbuch der deutschen Gegenwartssprache* of 1970 lists nearly 1,800 verbs of the second class (type 4 in Figure 10.2). The suffix *-ieren* has become the standard formative of all Latin-origin verbs. It shows a very low productivity for the derivation of hybrid forms with German stems. Examples are:

halbieren	to cut etc. into two halves
spintisieren	to dream (something) up

It *is* applied, however, to many Latin-based words which are of French origin, such as:

detaillieren	to specify
dejeunieren	to have breakfast

or of English origin, as in:

schamponieren	to shampoo
macadamesieren	to macadamize

There is no genuine morpheme to incorporate Greek verbs directly into the German language. Words of Greek origin have to be fitted into the *-ieren* formation in order to become German verbs, as in the following example:

stenotypieren	to typewrite on the basis of a shorthand manuscript

This situation is peculiar to the verbal domain, as can be inferred from the lists of prefixes and suffixes (see lists 2 and 3).

These lists of the most important formatives for the formation of Latin- and Greek-based terms in German comprise about 35 prefixes and about 26 suffixes. In the terminology of the biological sciences 71 prefixes and 122 suffixes of Greek or Latin origin could be identified (see Werner 1972). If morphological variants such as those of *ad-* illustrated in Figure 10.3 are counted separately, we arrive at a list of 111 prefixes.

In addition to formative elements, there is also a set of stemwords used for the formation of scientific terminology in German. This is an open set which can be continuously enlarged by using new, hitherto unused stems for the formation of new terms.

The use of Greek and Latin vocabulary for the formation of new terms varies greatly across scientific domains. The range of acceptability of Latin- and Greek-based neologisms seems to show great differences within the domains themselves and in the broader (academic) speech community. The closer an academic domain is to 'erudite' common sense, the lower the tolerance for neologisms (sociology, literary criticism); and, vice versa, the more specialized and the more distant a discipline, the more freely neologisms on the Greek and Latin substratum are accepted (medicine, pharmacology).

The 'importation' of words from Latin and Greek is an ongoing process. It leads to permanent renewal of terminology and supplies many languages with a specific source of adaptation to newly developing communicative needs.

Word formation has very specific repercussions upon the substratum of this process: the use of Latin and Greek semantics is not restricted to words which are actual elements of Latin and Greek. There are examples in which new

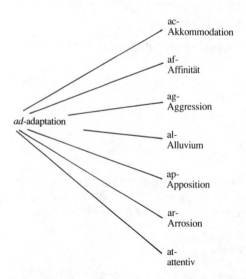

Figure 10.3. Morphological variants of Latin __ad-__

words are formed which never existed in these languages. A prominent linguistic example is the term *illokutiv*, which makes use of the negation formative *in-* (see list 2b) and applies it to the stem *loqui* (to speak). *Illoqui* does not exist in Latin. Nevertheless, the term 'illocution,' coined by J. L. Austin in English and introduced into German in the translation of his 'Lectures,' is perfectly understandable and semantically reasonable.

The use of Greek and Latin for German word formation

The derivational network

The use of Greek and Latin material for the formation of words and technical terms has been a continuous process throughout history. The communicative needs for new terms change in various stages of development of scientific disciplines. New technical terms for a given field are created either directly from Latin or Greek sources, or from Latin and Greek derivatives in other languages. Another strategy is to use terms which have been coined in other disciplines. There are various different starting points for the transfer from Greek to Latin into German, and therefore there are different types of semantic derivation. Because the transfer has proceeded along different lines, it has resulted in a highly complex structure of the lexicon. There is no simple, uni-directional development from Greek and Latin into German. Rather, there is a multi-dimensional network which can only be understood on the basis of a detailed linguistic reconstruction. An interesting aspect of this network is the fact that the semantics inherent in the Greek and Latin stems can be made use of by integrating original 'meanings' in Latin and Greek into the process of new word formation. The same holds true for those derivatives which were borrowed into other languages or for other scientific disciplines at an earlier stage.

Figure 10.4 depicts the transfer of semantic units from other languages into the German lexicon. As has been discussed in the previous section, the transfer of semantic elements of other languages into the German lexicon is not restricted to stems but comprises formatives as well. This makes the whole process and its result even more complex, because the formatives are not only applied to stems of the language from which they were borrowed, but also to stems of other languages. As an example, consider the German negation prefix *un-*. It can be applied to German stems, as in *unschön* (ugly) or *unwert* (unworthy), as well as to Latin and Greek stems, as in *unnormal* (abnormal) or in *unreell* (unfair), and *unkanonisch* (uncanonical) or *unästhetisch* (unaesthetic). Words consisting of a stem from one language and a formative of another are called 'hybrids.' While linguists dispute their status in, and desirability for, a language, speakers do not seem to care much about these problems.

Word formation processes usually make optimal use of the available means, including the possibility of hybrids. Moreover, in certain fields, such as

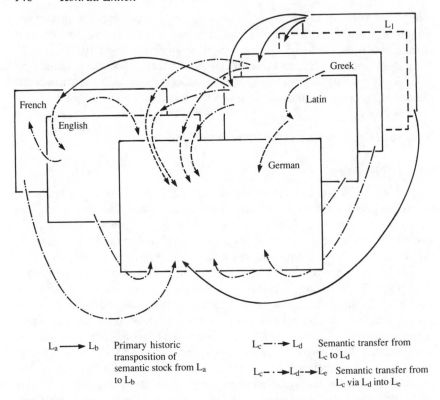

$L_a \longrightarrow L_b$ Primary historic
transposition of
semantic stock from L_a
to L_b

$L_c \, {-}\!\cdot\!{-} \, L_d$ Semantic transfer from
L_c to L_d

$L_c \, {-}\!\cdot\!{-} \, L_d \, {-}{-} \, L_e$ Semantic transfer from
L_c via L_d into L_e

Figure 10.4. Transfer of semantic units from other languages into German

chemistry, hybrids are coined and employed systematically. However, not all combinations of formatives and stems that are possible are actually used. It is impossible, therefore, to calculate the number of possible formation types on the basis of the number of prefixes and suffixes in the three languages involved. Even though certain combinations are excluded, the situation is highly complex.

A more detailed presentation of the processes involved is illustrated in Figures 10.5, 10.6, and 10.7. The old borrowing processes (see list 5) result in a specific sub-part of the lexicon, the 'loans' from Greek into Latin, and from Latin into German. (Among these loans are also parts from the Greek loans into Latin, as, for example, some expressions in the field of religion, such as Greek *episkopos* [supervisor] → Latin *episkopus* → German *Bischof* [bishop].) Figure 10.5 refers to a situation in which only these loans enter into an otherwise homogeneous picture. Figure 10.6 depicts a different situation: it represents the transfer of Greek and Latin words of the type illustrated in list 6 into German. The number of expressions which participate in this process

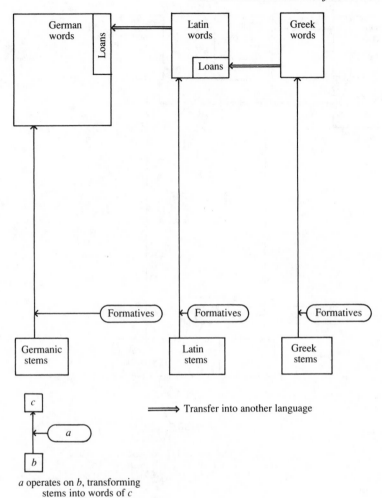

a operates on *b*, transforming
    stems into words of *c*

Figure 10.5. Greek and Latin loanwords in German

is very high, both in everyday and scientific German. Figure 10.7 includes the formation of hybrids. Obviously, the situation depicted in Figure 10.7 is highly complex. Most speakers of German are capable of using expressions belonging to all parts of the lexicon illustrated there. Not all of them are, however, aware of the complexity of their structure in the sense that they could decompose those words into their constituents. Yet their individual lexicon abounds with 'foreign' terms.

The diagrams do not represent the recursiveness of the borrowing process inherent in the history of the elements which constitute individual words. Such

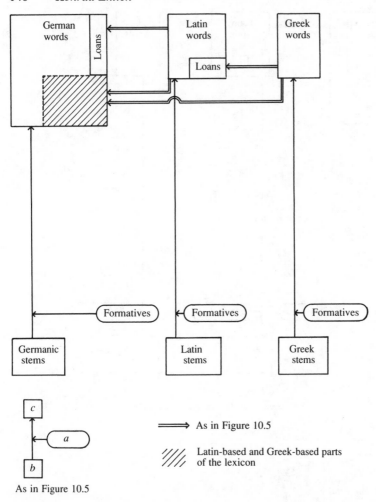

Figure 10.6. Adaptation of Greek and Latin forms to German patterns

a process of re-actualization of parts of the semantic potential means that there is a stock of knowledge which is accessible to a large number of speakers for at least passive use, and to a certain number of speakers for active use, that is for generating new words.

The history of the words of a language can often be identified by reference to the traces still present in contemporary usage. If semantic knowledge has passed the threshold of unawareness it can actively interfere with the word formation process in order to adapt a language to new needs. This is the case especially in times of semantic crisis, that is when new expressions are wanted either for designating new phenomena or for reconceptualizing phenomena

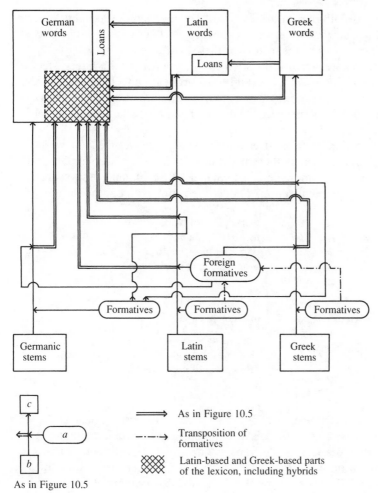

Figure 10.7. Loans and hybrid formation in German

in accordance with new perspectives or ideological needs. The availability of a tripartite pool of formatives and stems – in our case, Greek, Latin, and Germanic – is a great enrichment for the language community as well as for the individual speaker.

An example: the transfer of Greek org-, erg- into German

To illustrate some of the semantic processes mentioned above, this section discusses a Greek stem which is of major importance for German and other 'modern' European languages. The semantic field of *Organisation, organisch* is an important sub-part of the lexicon of several scientific disciplines such as biology, chemistry, political science, history, sociology, and philosophy. Let us take a closer look at the history of these expressions.

All of the expressions in question are derived from the Greek stem (0) *erg-/org-*, which in turn is part of an Indo-European root. This root, however, did not survive in a very clear shape in Greek because of the loss of the Greek 'digamma' (/w/). Together with the dropped digamma, the stem (0') (*w*)*erg-* is very close to German *Werk* and English 'work.'

The application of formatives and 'inner flexion' results in a variety of Greek expressions such as those listed in lists 7a and 7b. The application of formatives in list 7a is more opaque than in list 7b, containing 'adjectivization,' 'factivization,' 'nominalization,' and 'composition with another noun.'

(7a)	(1.1)	*ergon*	work, piece of work
	(1.2)	*ergazestai*	to work, to be busy
	(1.3)	*energeia*	potentiality, strength
	(1.4)	*organon*	tool, instrument

. . .

(7b)	(1.4)	*organon*	tool, instrument
	(1.4.1)	*organikos*	instrumental
	(1.4.2)	*organoō* ⎱	
	(1.4.3)	*organízo* ⎰	I organize
	(1.4.4)	*organósis* ⎱	
	(1.4.5)	*organopoiia* ⎰	fabrication of instrucments

. . .

Words such as those in lists 7a and 7b were at the basis of the transfer into Latin. In the case of *erg-*, there is no genuine equivalent in Latin, a fact which was favorable to a large-scale transfer into Latin. But the transfer was not brought about on the basis of the elementary meanings which are indicated in lists 7a and 7b. Other stems were available to speakers of Latin, such as *oper-*, or derivatives of *stru-* (to build), for example *instrumentum* (tool). The motivation for adopting the Greek expressions into Latin arose because of terminological needs in highly technical fields such as philosophy, medicine, and music.

Aristotle was the first to use the everyday word *organon* (tool) in a terminological sense. In his *Biology*, *organon* is used to designate parts of the body which are specified by a specific function they have to fulfill. The hand, for instance, is described as *organon pro organōn*, an 'organ for tools.' Aristotle, in a most abstract description, considers *organon* as 'mediator of movement . . . or as means to an end' (Ballauf and Scheerer 1984: 1318). In his argument, Aristotle shows that functionality is a characteristic of *organon* by means of an etymological association, since 'function' is *ergon* or (later) *energeia*. In Latin, a combination of *opus* and *instrumentum* would not be equally plausible. Aristotle's use of *organon* was adopted into Latin by Galen, a medical writer who lived more than 500 years later. The Aristotelian–Galenian tradition has survived to this very day, where one of the meanings of *Organ/* organ is 'part of the body' ([g.1][1] *Organ*$_1$).

This meaning was not the most important one, however, in Classical and Medieval Latin. Another transfer was more important, namely the application of the expression to a musical instrument: the *organum hydraulicum*, the water organ. Three derivations from this meaning are present in Latin:

(3.2)   the adjective *organalis* (of the organ);
(3.3)   the diminutive *organulum* (small organ); and
(3.4)   the noun *organarius* (organ player).

(4) This acoustic specification of the Latin form of *organon* led to another transfer which integrated the Aristotelian – Galenian use with the musical use: the human voice was also called '*organ*.'

Both uses are still present in German: Latin *organum* in the sense of 'organ' was transposed into Old High German *orgela* and is thus a very early loan word in German ([g.2] *Orgel*). (g.3) *Organ*$_2$ as 'voice' is present especially in phrases like *ein lautes Organ haben* (to have a loud voice). A German equivalent to *organarius* was derived from Medieval Latin *organista = Organist* (organ player) (g.2.2).

(5) In addition to Aristotle's biological use, there is a broad range of philosophical uses of *organon* dating back to the pre-Socratic period: various 'tools' of mental activities are qualified as *organa*, for example writing is an *organon* of memory (Gorgias), and arguments are *organa* of judgment (Plato). Here *organon* is interpreted as a 'mental tool.' This meaning became important in the post-Aristotelian tradition, where *organon* was applied to Aristotle's 'logic' as a 'tool' of philosophy. The 'logic' was termed *organon* (Andronikos?). This use of *organon* is present in Bacon's *Novum Organum* of 1620, and in a number of *Organa* in seventeenth- and eighteenth-century philosophy, down to Kant's and Schopenhauer's use (g.4) (Finster 1984). *Organisch*, the adjectival derivative (g.4.2) of the 'logical' *organon* differs in meaning from the identical form (g.1.2) *organisch*$_1$ (physical, bodily).

At the end of the eighteenth century the Greek–Latin expression experienced a real 'boom' of new uses in various disciplines. In politics, there had been a continuous importation of *organon* derivatives from the early Renaissance on. This transfer was facilitated by two more general characteristics of the time. Already in classical times the body had served as a metaphor for political entities; in the early Renaissance, medicine as a practical science of the body, its diseases, and its restitution, was regarded as a sort of leading science of the time. Consequently, less well established theories tried to constitute their own activities *per analogiam* to this highly successful science. 'Political anatomies' and theories about 'state diseases' were the result. A juridical notion of *organa* emerged at roughly the same time. Johannes Limnaeus (around 1679), for instance, attributed the ability to act to the *Reich* (empire) by speaking of its *permanente organa*.

The metaphor of a 'body' for the state and similar political entities was put into a new theoretical context in the development of the overwhelming technomorphic model of the state. Theoreticians who were opposed to this *Leitmetapher* of the seventeenth and eighteenth centuries very slowly transformed the *corpus organicum* from a mere specification of the mechanics of the technomorphic model into a new and different type of model. The term *organisatio*, which had been used in medicine from the fourteenth century onwards to designate the characteristics of *corpora naturalia* (of 'natural bodies'), changed into a concept which has to do with living entities. Living entities, which had been conceived as machines for a time, slowly came to be considered the opposite of the mechanism of the machines which were so impressive to the minds of the time. Yet, in the middle of the eighteenth century, 'organism' was still used as a special case of 'mechanism'; but in Stahl's writings (1706) against Leibniz, the very first opposition of 'mechanism' and 'organism' shows up.

In the French tradition, the opposition is developed further and a new term is coined: *anorganique*. The opposition can now be stated clearly:

organisch – mechanisch =
organisch – anorganisch   (Bonnet 1762)

The eighteenth century witnessed the emergence of two new disciplines which made the 'organic' their proper object of research: biology and chemistry. In his *Kritik der Urteilskraft* (§65), Kant provided an explanation of what an *Organismus* is which proved to be very consequential for the subsequent use of the term. The new system of opposition uses the Greek/Latin terms in a way different from what was inherent semantically in the Greek and Latin origins: *org-* is separated from the concept of 'tool' with its mechanical implications and, through the idea of the 'tools' of a living entity, gets closely linked to the concept of life. Biology, as a new science, is developed as a theory of 'organisms,' which are the wholes in which 'organs' have their functional context. In a fascinating development, the biological concepts are transposed into psychology, where they determine long periods of theorizing.

Very early in the development of biology, some of its main concepts were re-interpreted in philosophy by Schelling, who constructed his theory based on the new concatenation of the concepts of 'life' and 'organism.'

In addition to the new opposition 'organic' vs 'mechanical,' the Greek/ Latin *org-* also became important in politics. At the time of the French Revolution the main theoreticians and 'practitioners' of the Revolution used another derivative of *org-*, namely *organisation*, using the newly coined term as a weapon in the political struggle. They interpreted *organisation* in such a way, that it exposed the state and other political entities to change and active modification. An *organisation* was not God-given. This new derivative entered the German language quickly. In the context of the other semantic implications of the semantic field *org-*, the term was made functional for a variety of political aims – revolutionary, reformistic, and conservative. In Schelling's political philosophy, there are also traces of this semantic tradition.

Schelling also contributed, if rather awkwardly, to the semantic development of *organisch*, adopting, as he did, from Hölderlin the opposition of *organisch* vs *aorgisch* and transposing it into the semantics of *org-* – although this opposition is not part of that semantic system. *Aorgisch* is derived from a totally different stem, namely *org-* meaning 'wrath.' Schelling confused these two stems and was criticized for doing so by Goethe. Goethe also influenced the semantic development in a way which favored the opposition *organisch* vs *anorganisch*, in the humanities. In chemistry, the same opposition between *organisch* and *anorganisch* was introduced by the Swedish scientist Berzelius in 1806. In the following fifty years chemists learned that there is a foundation *in re* for the opposition between *organisch* and its negation *anorganisch*, namely the presence or absence of carbon compounds. The distinction proved to be valid, and it is still used in present-day chemical terminology.

The transfer of the Greek *org-* into German (and other languages) came to a peak between 1780 and 1830. As a result of the various transfers, a semantic field has come into being. The basic German terms of this field are given in list 8a.

(8a)	$(g.5_{1,...,n})$	Organ	
	(g.6)	Organismus	organism
	(g.7.1)	organisieren	to organize
	(g.7.2)	Organisation	organization
	(g.5.2)	organisch	organic
	(g.5.2.2)	anorganisch	inorganic
	(g.5.2.3)	unorganisch	non-organic

The semantic field was transferred to other theoretical contexts such as sociology, political science and economics. All of them made creative use of semantic transfer. New derivatives were, and still are, needed for very specific contexts, such as (g.8.1) *Organoskopie* in the (pseudo-)science of phrenology, or (g.8.2) *Organologie* and (g.8.3) *Organographie* in biology, to mention some examples.

Whereas earlier transfers are relatively transparent, this is not the case at present. There is a veritable network of intertwined relations and interdependencies which can only be reconstructed through detailed analysis. The transfer from the result of a previous transfer onto a new one, and the repercussions of meaning for the field of application where the new transfer has its origin can be very important. The semantic developments in some disciplines, such as sociology, philosophy, and psychology, show abundant evidence for the complexity of the processes involved.

Let us turn to linguistics now for a final example of the intricacies of the *Leitmetapher org-*. Linguistics was at the forefront of theoretical development in the first quarter of the nineteenth century. The semantic field *org-* was applied here in a very complex manner. 'Organistic' metaphors replaced a previously developed sign concept of language. The various semantic implications of the field *org-* were used in different theories of language, such as W. von Humboldt's on the one hand and Schleicher's on the other. Whereas *org-* was part of the action theoretic context in Humboldt's concepts, in Schleicher's writings we see a theoretic exploitation of the semantic potentials inherent in the biological application of *org-* (Neumann 1984; Schmidt 1986).

Linguistics also shows how a fresh start can be made in theory formation by recourse to the 'original' semantic background of a stem which had been applied before to a large number of contexts, thus having become opaque and even unclear. Karl Bühler, in his *Sprachtheorie* of 1934, re-actualized the 'quasi-etymological' semantic load of *org-* by re-establishing the term *organon* in the sense of tool. In his *'Organon-Modell' der Sprache* he interprets language as a tool or instrument.

Recently, there have been no important semantic developments of *erg-* and *org-*. The semantic potential seems to be 'exhausted.' Bühler's appeal to 'sources' of meaning of *organon* in Ancient Greek, which finds its expression in the re-actualization of the old Greek form *organon* as a 'foreign word' in German, is an act of clarification in a semantic context which is characterized by an abundant use – and abuse – of the field, in theory formation. The results, theoretical and practical, of the *org-* terminology can be analyzed by reconstructing the history of terminology formation on the Greek and Latin basis. The semantic potential in its original and in its various actualized forms is at the disposal of the speakers of German for further use.

In ordinary language, residua of the former application processes are a normal part of the lexicon, as is shown in list 8b, which, in combination with list 8a, comprises entries of the words from the field *org-* which begin with 'org-', in a dictionary of present-day German.

(8b)	(g.1)	Organ	organ (part of the body)
	(g.3)	Organ	voice
	(g.5_1)	Organ	organ (sense)
	(g.5_2)	Organ	([group of] person[s] who acts on behalf of)
	(g.$5_3/3_1$)	Organ	(journal of a party, etc.)
	(g.1.2)	Organbehandlung	medical treatment of a part of the body
	(g.1.3)	Organempfänger	receiver of an organ
	(g.1.4)	Organpräparat	transplant

(g.1.5)	Organspender	organ donor
(g.1.6)	Organtherapie	organ therapy
(g.1.7)	Organübertragung	transplantation
(g.1.8)	Organverpflanzung	transplantation
(g.7.1)	organisieren	to organize
(g.7.1.2)	organisiert	organized
(g.7.1.2.2)	Organisiertheit	the state of being organized
(g.7.1.3)	Organisierung	the act of organizing
(g.7.1.4)	organisierbar	organizable
(g.7.2)	Organisation	organization
(g.7.2.2)	Organisationsbüro	organization office
(g.7.2.3)	Organisationsfehler	organizational mistake
(g.7.2.4)	Organisationsform	form of organization
(g.7.2.5)	Organisationsgabe	talent of organization, organizing capability
(g.7.2.6)	Organisationsplan	organizational plan
(g.7.2.7)	Organisationsstruktur	organizational structure
(g.7.2.8)	Organisationstalent	(s. 7.2.5)
(g.7.2.9)	Organisationstätigkeit	organizing activity
(g.7.2.10)	Organisationswissenschaft	theory of organisations
(g.7.3)	Organisator	organizer
(g.7.4)	organisatorisch	organizational
(g.6)	Organismus	organism
(g.8)	organisch	organic
(g.8.2)	anorganisch	inorganic
(g.8.3)	unorganisch	non-organic

(Klappenbach and Steinitz 1975: 2713–2715)

Latin, Greek, and the school curriculum

An important pre-condition for using Latin and Greek for the formation of scientific terminology is a relatively widespread knowledge of Latin. As pointed out above, Latin had been the foundation of all education in medieval times. It remained the language of educated discourse for centuries after the national languages had commenced to invade areas which formerly had been restricted to Latin. During the nineteenth and the first half of the twentieth century Latin was a compulsory subject at the *Gymnasium*.

The ideology underlying the study of Latin is at variance with the actual needs of getting a thorough training in this language. The ideological justification ranges from the 'development of logical thinking' to partaking in the 'classical, humanistic' tradition, a purpose which was best achieved, it seems, by studying all the military details of Caesar's *De Bello Gallico*.

The real effect of a classical training – a good command of the basic vocabulary and the elementary word formation patterns of Latin – was not consciously regarded as an important motivation for studying Latin, but rather as a by-product of those general educational aims.

Curriculum reform discussions after World War II have led to a drastic decline of Latin teaching at high school. Latin is now by and large an optional subject which is chosen by ever fewer students. The consequences that this shift away from Latin in the schools will have on the continuity of Latin as an active substratum for scientific terminology formation and educated discourse in general are not yet clear. To many students Latin- and Greek-based technical terminology becomes opaque. Their access to, and command of, scientific terminology is seriously hampered by a lack of elementary knowledge. Learning the technical terminology is becoming a more laborious and difficult task. Another consequence is that interdisciplinary discourse has become more difficult than it has ever been. 'Languages for specific purposes' tend to produce mystifications and barriers which only the 'initiated' scholar can overcome. The perspicuity of technical terms is endangered by the absence of elementary semantic and structural information. The substratum is no longer an integral part of the active linguistic *energeia* which makes language proficiency easy and language innovation possible.

The situation of Greek is more difficult to assess. Its knowledge was less widespread, and its study was promoted later than that of Latin (as of the sixteenth century). Nevertheless, much of its semantic information has been conveyed through Latin. The problems of Latin are thus also the problems of Greek.

The present situation in Germany calls for thorough reflection on the costs and benefits of the decline of Greek and Latin at high school. It is conceivable that other languages, such as English and French (see Figure 10.1), will take over the mediating function of Latin and Greek, superseding them in their formerly indispensable function for lexical innovation. No comparative research has been done about these questions. For an understanding of the future of Latin and Greek as a permanent source and resource of terminology formation in German such research is urgently needed.

Note

1 '(g.1)' means 'German transfer product 1'; the decimal system is used to indicate a derivational relationship.

References

Adelung, J. C. 1789. *Grammatisch-kritisches Wörterbuch der Hochdeutschen Mundart.* Leipzig. Reprinted Hildesheim 1976.

Ballauf, T. 1984a. Organismus I, Biologie. In G. Ritter (ed.), *Historisches Wörterbuch der Philosophie*, 1330–1336. Basel.

    1984b. Organik. In G. Ritter (ed.), *Historisches Wörterbuch der Philosophie*, 1325–1326. Basel.

Ballauf, T. and Scheerer, E. 1984. Organ. In G. Ritter (ed.), *Historisches Wörterbuch der Philosophie*, 1317–1325. Basel.

Du Cange 1883–1887. *Glossarium mediae et infimae latinatis.* Reprinted Graz. 1954.

Dohrn-van Rossum, G. 1977. Politischer Körper, Organismus, Organisation. Die Geschichte der naturalen Metaphorik und Begrifflichkeit in der politischen Sprache. Ph.D. dissertation, University of Bielefeld.

Dohrn-van Rossum, G. and Böckenförde, E. W. 1978. Organ, Organismus, Organisation, politischer Körper. In O. Brunner, W. Conze and R. Koselleck (eds.), *Historisches Wörterbuch zur politisch-sozialen Sprache in Deutschland,* vol. 4. Stuttgart.

Dudenredaktion 1980. *Duden. Das grosse Wörterbuch der deutschen Sprache in sechs Bänden,* vol. 5. Mannheim, Vienna, Zürich.

Finster, R. 1984. Organon. In G. Ritter (ed.) *Historisches Wörterbuch der Philosophie,* 1363–1368. Basel.

Georges, K. E. 1972. *Ausführliches lateinisch-deutsches Handwörterbuch.* Hanover.

Grimm, J. and Grimm, W. 1889. *Deutsches Wörterbuch,* vol. 7, ed. M. von Lexer. Leipzig.

Jacob, W. 1984. Organologie. In G. Ritter (ed.), *Historisches Wörterbuch der Philosophie.* Basel, 1361–1363.

Klappenbach, R. and Steinitz, W. (eds.) 1975. *Wörterbuch der deutschen Gegenwartssprache.* Berlin.

Konsermann, R. 1984. Organizismus. In G. Ritter (ed.), *Historisches Wörterbuch der Philosophie,* 1358–1361. Basel.

Luhmann, N. 1984. Organisation I, Sozialphilosophie und Soziologie. In G. Ritter (ed.), *Historisches Wörterbuch der Philosophie,* 1326–1328. Basel.

Mater, E. 1970. *Rückläufiges Wörterbuch der deutschen Gegenwartssprache.* Leipzig.

Meyer, A. 1984. Organismus III, Politik und Ökonomie. In G. Ritter (ed.), *Historisches Wörterbuch der Philosophie,* 1348–1358. Basel.

Müller, K. 1984. Organisation II, Psychologie. In G. Ritter (ed.), *Historisches Wörterbuch der Philosophie,* 1328–1329. Basel.

Neumann, W. 1984. Zeichen und Organismus. Beobachtungen zum Wechsel eines Denkmusters in der deutschen Sprachwissenschaft des 19. Jahrhunderts. *Beiträge zur Erforschung der deutschen Sprache,* 4: 5–37.

Onions, C. T. (ed.) 1966. *The Oxford English Dictionary of English Etymology.* Oxford.

Pape, W. 1954. *Griechisch-deutsches Handwörterbuch.* Graz.

Roche Lexikon Medizin 1984. Munich, Vienna, Baltimore.

Ryan, L. and Seifert, A. 1984. Organisch/aorganisch. In G. Ritter (ed.), *Historisches Wörterbuch der Philosophie,* 1329–1330. Basel.

Scheerer, E. 1984. Organismus II, Kosmologie, Soziologie und Psychologie. In G. Ritter (ed.), *Historisches Wörterbuch der Philosophie,* 1336–1348. Basel.

Schmidt, H. 1986. *Die lebendige Sprache. Zur Entstehung des Organismuskonzepts.* Linguistische Studien A 151. Berlin.

A Supplement to the Oxford English Dictionary, 1972–1986, ed. E. W. Burchfield, vol. 3. Oxford.

Thümmel, W. 1984. Organonmodell (der Sprache). In G. Ritter (ed.), *Historisches Wörterbuch der Philosophie,* 1368–1369. Basel.

Wahrig, G., Krämer, H. and Zimmermann, H. 1982. *Brockhaus Wahrig Deutsches Wörterbuch in sechs Bänden.* Wiesbaden, Stuttgart.

Werner, F. C. 1972. *Wortelemente lateinisch-griechischer Fachausdrücke in den biologischen Wissenschaften.* Frankfurt.

11 *Internationalisms: identical vocabularies in European languages*

PETER BRAUN

The present chapter is a contribution towards the clarification of European language questions. Its aim is to resolve certain international language problems with the help of a reorientation in the perception and exploitation of the existing language situation. It focusses upon the loan vocabularies of several European languages to whose international status (and possible utility) only little attention has been paid up to the present. Korn (1978) took up this widely neglected topic in a leader in the *Frankfurter Allgemeine Zeitung* and pointed out the necessity of further discussion. Korn views the linguistic future of Europe as being closely related to the recognition and utilization of the existing European languages: 'The European languages are no obstacle standing in the way of European unity, rather they are the pan-European element.'

This study starts out with the assumption that this pan-European element is to be found in the identical (or similar) vocabularies of the national languages and that it is in need of linguistic investigation, and of exploitation in langauge teaching. In the following discussion German, English, and French are taken as examples.

A re-orientation in the assessment of loan vocabularies is a logical consequence of an awareness of the political situation. The eighteenth and nineteenth centuries were the era of the establishment of nation states and hence, simultaneously, of the establishment of national languages. It is easy to understand why the creation of nation states brought with it an emphasis on the idiosyncratic features of each national language, especially in view of the delayed development of a unified German language. In spite of obvious differences in the cohesion of European states (Yugoslavia, Belgium), twentieth-century Europe exhibits relatively stable linguistic conditions.

Décsy (1973: 176ff.), for example, comes to a largely positive conclusion with regard to Europe as a whole: 'Within the European state system, some 561 million members of the total population (88%) live in countries whose official language is their own, while 57 million (about 9%) are residents of countries whose official language is not their own.' In view of such positive findings, it is no longer possible to belabour twentieth-century questions with nineteenth-century answers. At the end of the twentieth century, many other problems and tasks are being approached in an international fashion. Since governments and official bodies have been trying for decades to achieve international agreement, these political efforts ought to have an effect on the treatment of national and international linguistic problems. Hence the question of the *future* of language now falls within the scope of linguistics; the linguistic *past* has been abundantly dealt with since the nineteenth century.

If we accept this historical perspective, then it becomes clear that the various epochs of linguistic borrowing have been described very one-sidedly, from the point of view of individual national languages only. It has been overlooked that the major processes of borrowing can only be understood as European linguistic movements. This holds for the Latin Middle Ages, for the concept of education during the humanistic period (Classical Latin and Greek), for cultural exchange during the seventeenth and eighteenth centuries, and for the period after 1945 (English). As yet, linguistic histories have described these European processes of borrowing almost exclusively as events limited to one language. As an expression of concern for a national language, this attitude is understandable. With respect to common European aims, however, it is politically and linguistically dubious and clearly in need of revision.

Many European languages – and not only these – possess considerable inventories of loanwords. These inventories are not the result of chance, but of international contacts with other political, cultural, and economic circumstances. From the viewpoint of a single language, they can be regarded as being a source of difficulty or a nuisance. A contrastive approach, however, reveals many linguistic enclaves with supra-national common elements. These linguistic elements common to the vocabularies of several languages are subsumed under the concept of 'internationalisms.' Many reasons can be found for the development of internationalisms in German, English, and French, among which are:

> the relatedness of the Indo-European languages;
> mutual borrowing or borrowing from other European languages;
> borrowing from non-European languages;
> linguistic conventions in supra-national institutions (e.g. the Church, official organizations);
> linguistic standardization in the international languages of science and technology; and
> exchange of information by international news agencies.

Before discussing the notion of internationalisms and the inventories of individual languages, consider some examples for illustration:

SPORTS

German	*English*	*French*
Baseball	baseball	base-ball
Basketball	basketball	basket-ball

Boxen	boxing	boxe
Derby	Derby	derby
Golf	golf	golf

MUSICAL INSTRUMENTS

Akkordeon	accordion	accordéon
Balalaika	balalaika	balalaïka
Flöte	flute	flûte
Gitarre	guitar	guitare
Gong	gong	gong

FLOWERS

Anemone	anemone	anémone
Aster	aster	aster
Dahlie	dahlia	dahlia
Edelweiß	edelweiss	edelweiss

ANTONYMS

abstrakt	abstract	abstrait
konkret	concrete	concret
aktiv	active	actif
passiv	passive	passif
defensiv	defensive	défensif
offensiv	offensive	offensif
konkav	concave	concave
konvex	convex	convexe
exportieren	export	exporter
importieren	import	importer
Altruismus	altruism	altruisme
Egoismus	egoism	egoisme

PROPER NAMES AS NAMES OF OBJECTS

Atlas	atlas	atlas
Boycott	boycott	boycottage
Celsius	Celsius	Celsius
Colt	colt	colt
Browning	Browing	Browning

TECHNOLOGY

Caravan	caravan	caravane
Chassis	chassis	châssis
Cockpit	cockpit	cockpit
Dynamo	dynamo	dynamo
Generator	generator	générateur

It would appear that linguistics, and especially loanword research, have placed too little emphasis on the concept of internationalisms. For this reason, the international vocabularies have hardly been given any attention and have not been recorded as components of the lexicon. Some compilers of dictionaries of linguistics even appear to be unacquainted with the term or to regard it as unimportant. The extant definitions range from Ulrich's (1975: 63) sober 'Word, used in many national languages, current internationally, comprehensible without translation' to Wandruszka's (1976: 8) philosophical interpretation: 'Our languages are not monosystems. Every language is a conglomerate of languages; every language is a polysystem. We are already multilingual in our own mother tongue.'

The extent of internationalization becomes clear if a comparative analysis of dictionaries is undertaken. After many years of analyzing dictionaries, I arrived at an initial inventory of identical vocabularies in the German, English, and French languages. According to my analysis of one-volume school dictionaries, the identical vocabularies encompass 3,500 words. Words from different languages are regarded as identical or similar if they show a high degree of agreement in spelling and meaning. Small graphemic deviations (such as *Tee, tea, thé*; *Oase, oasis, oasis*) were disregarded, as were minor variations in word formation (as in *exportieren, export, exporter*; *Qualität, quality, qualité*). Decisive for their inclusion was the ability of a speaker/reader to recognize these words as identical linguistic signs in the three languages in question.

Pronunciation (phonetics) was completely excluded. It is within the area of pronunciation that many languages have most clearly moved away from each other. The phonetic nature of different languages often helps to conceal identical or similar features and to emphasize dissimilarities.

The total area of identical vocabularies can be roughly divided into three areas of use: (1) everyday interaction containing words for commonly used objects (e.g. 'ball,' 'banana,' 'telephone'); (2) utility words (Pfeffer 1975: 12), which can be regarded as the core vocabularies of important conceptual and specialized areas (e.g. 'fiord,' 'service' [in tennis]) – these words are statistically not very important but are essential to denote important concepts in various referential areas; (3) languages for special purposes. This area can be divided into the three sub-areas of scientific language, workshop language or occupational dialects, and consumer or sales language. Words in scientific language (e.g. 'falsification,' 'sedative,' 'vector') frequently possess only a limited distribution and, for most non-specialists, are limited to the passive vocabulary. Knowledge of the various languages of science is, however, highly variable: the specialized vocabularies of technology, literary studies, and even medicine have up to now been more frequently popularized than those of chemistry or computer science. This is, however, only true for certain sub-vocabularies of these disciplines. This third area of usage largely embraces the university disciplines and specialized training, while the second is mainly covered by school subjects. More exact delimitations are not at present possible, especially as many of these words occur in several areas.

As the word lists show, most internationalisms do not occur in isolation but in semantically related groups. More than 75% of the internationalisms recorded can be arranged in conceptually or semantically related domains. By far the largest proportion of the vocabularies covers the domains of everyday life and school subjects, which means that about 2,700 of the international-isms given in school dictionaries can be regarded as elements of the standard language.

Sufficient information on the age of the loanwords is provided in the word histories of Maurer and Stroh (1959), Tschirch (1969), and von Polenz (1972). As regards the time of borrowing, we can say with certainty that most of the internationalisms listed in school dictionaries were borrowed before 1945. Many of these words not only occur in present-day German, English, and French, but also belong to the standard vocabularies of other European languages and form a nucleus for increasing internationalization. Here are some examples:

German	English	French	Italian	Spanish	Russian
Flamme	flame	flamme	fiamma	llama	лля́мя
Form	form	forme	forma	forma	фо́рма
Photo	photo	photo	foto	foto	фо́то
photographieren	photograph	photographier	fotografare	fotografiar	фотографи́ровать

Every year, new internationalisms are added, especially from the various languages of special purposes, since many of these languages are designed from the outset to be international. The tendency towards increasing inter-nationalization can be seen in the fact that the more recent borrowings are not assimilated or integrated to the same extent as earlier ones (e.g. English, *strike*, German, *Streik*). The retention of foreign sounds and forms can above all be ascribed to extra-linguistic factors. More than 50% of Germans state that they know a foreign language. This percentage is even higher for the younger generation.

Although the European languages have – from the genetic point of view – moved further and further away from the common languages of their origin, the inventories of internationalisms reveal tendencies towards mutual con-vergence, especially within the area of vocabulary.

Korlén (1969: 7) characterizes this internationalization of vocabulary as 'a development within the German language which has European or, more correctly, world-wide features.' And Müller (1975: 50), describing the effects of the intermingling of different languages in present-day French, emphasizes two aspects of this phenomenon: 'The tribute which each individual language must pay to the present represents the loss of a piece of individuality; the benefit gained is a mutuality over and above the individual language which is beginning to make the ancient myth of the one language of mankind a reality.' The historical, economic, and cultural reasons for linguistic borrowing were mentioned above. These extra-linguistic reasons remain without doubt the most important factors and are part and parcel of any discussion of loan-words. There must, however, be other reasons for the fact that French and

English loanwords were accepted into many European languages. Extra-linguistic reasons alone provide no satisfactory explanation of the fact that loanwords from French and English are so disproportionately represented in European dictionaries. If we take extra-linguistic factors such as history, culture, and the history of ideas, as a yardstick, then the German language appears to be under-represented. A similar under-representation seems to be the case when geographical factors are taken into account. The German-speaking area is favorably situated, having 4,850 kilometers of borders where language contact is possible, and is in close proximity to 14 other languages. Borders and proximity are synonymous with the possibility of influencing and being influenced. France and Great Britain, by contrast, are in this respect in a geographically unfavorable position.

Too little attention has been paid to the favorable morphological structure of the vocabularies of French and English, especially those features and relations determined by the hybrid nature of these languages. Such a point of view makes it necessary to include the particular characteristics of the donor languages in the discussion. With reference to the varying degrees of 'hybrid-ization,' Décsy (1973: 184f.) refers to 'hybrid languages,' 'neutral languages,' and 'introverted languages.' In hybrid languages (English, French, Ruman-ian) 'the foreign component is present to a high degree.' In introverted languages (Icelandic, Finnish, German) 'the foreign component does not attain the usual degree. The language constructs expressions for new concepts from its own resources.' The integration of Latin and Greek vocabularies and word formation elements is usually related to the degree of hybridization of various languages. To varying degrees, the Latin vocabulary has correspond-ing forms in many European languages, not least because of the borrowings from English and French. It is certainly more than a pun when the Swedish Germanist Lindkvist speaks of a linguistic development 'sub specie Latini-tatis' (Korlén 1969: 9). Korlén's interpretation goes even further (1969: 9): 'Seen from this perspective, the internal semantic structure of most European languages is indeed so similar that one is justified in speaking of an occidental linguistic convergence and levelling.' This phenomenon was re-inforced by the teaching of Latin in schools throughout Europe. Unfortunately, linguistic comparison and borrowing processes were neglected in Latin teaching. The study of Latin literature and of the monosystemic elements of grammar left little room for other aims.

French and English have become the greatest donor languages in recent European linguistic history because both these languages have integrated and activated the Latin vocabulary to a relatively great extent. For English, a west Germanic language, the percentage of direct borrowings from Latin is given as 22% to 28%, according to the dictionary consulted; in the case of borrow-ings from French, the percentage varies between 28% and 38%, giving a total Latin–Romance vocabulary of between 50% and 60% (Scheler 1977: 35ff., 52ff.). It is not surprising that a direct comparison of English and French dictionaries reveals more common features than a comparison of English and German dictionaries. This means that every page of an English or French dictionary contains internationalisms which are not present in German, for example:

English	French	German
face	face	Gesicht
faculty	faculté	Fähigkeit
fatigue	fatigue	Ermüdung
facility	facilité	Leichtigkeit

Many of these common English–French features are also to be found in other Romance areas, for example:

Italian	Spanish
faccia	faz
facoltá	facultad
fatica	fatiga
facilitá	facilidad

The vocabulary of German differs in several respects from that of other European languages. Due to a process of Germanizing loanwords, which began in the sixteenth and seventeenth centuries and which has continued up to the present, many essential elements of common European culture contained in the vocabulary have been lost. Purists such as Schottel, Harsdörffer, and von Zesen (all in the seventeenth century), and especially Campe (died 1818), tried to eradicate as many loanwords as possible by creating equivalent German words. Viewed from the present, one has to conclude that this procedure was only partly successful, since, in many cases, the loanwords continued to exist side by side with the Germanized words. Although this was not their intention, the purists contributed to an increase of synonyms in German. A few examples are: *Moment/Augenblick, Autor/Verfasser, Dialekt/Mundart, Lexikon/Wörterbuch, Tragödie/Trauerspiel, Universität/Hochschule.* Many Germanized forms differ from their models in meaning or connotation. Some examples are: *Grammatik/Sprachlehre, Melancholie/Trübsinn, Karikatur/Zerrbild.* Fortunately, not all attempts at Germanization were successful, since in many cases their pedantic exactitude becomes laughable, as, for example, in these coinages of Campe (Daniels 1959): *Poren/Schweißlöcher, Pause/Zwischenstille, Dame/Ehrenfrau, marschieren/schrittlingsgehen, fanatisch/rasegläubig.*

The above comments should not lead to rash conclusions. There are, of course, many internationalisms in the German vocabulary and it can equally well be shown that there are common German–English and German–French features which are not found in the other languages. However, internationalisms probably play a more important role in other European languages than they do in German. Another difference is the fact that they are not very highly thought of in German and are preserved in an institution which does not exist in most language communities: the foreign-word dictionary (*Fremdwörterbuch*). Unfortunately, we have to repeat here what Polenz (1967: 715) stated in a very influential essay: 'Germany is the land of foreign-word dictionaries, not because there are more of these words in German than in other modern European languages but because it has long been the practice to banish to these dictionaries those words which, in other countries, have been listed as loanwords in normal dictionaries or recorded with other "difficult words" in dictionaries of specialized terminology.' It is particularly reprehensible that the compilers of these dictionaries (contrary to the present state of linguistic knowledge) still base their decision as to whether a word is a 'foreign word' or not on its historical origin and not on its currency in the present-day language. Hence the following current and generally known words are still listed in the foreign-word dictionary published by Duden (fourth edition 1982!): *Balkon, Ball, Banane, Fabrik, Familie, Fanfare, Fasan, Ferien.* Here one can only quote the 'imprisoned words' themselves: the situation is 'fatal,' 'fanatical,' or, less seriously, a 'farce.'

An unusual example of a recently coined linguistically nationalistic word is *Fernsehen* (television), which was formed by analogy with the not very successful term *Fernsprechen* (telephone) and which is used only in German, Danish (*fjernsyn*), and Norwegian (*fjernsyn*). Most European languages use the Greco-Latin internationalism 'television': *television* (English), *televisie* (Dutch), *television* (Swedish), *télévision* (French), *televisione* (Italian), *televisión* (Spanish), *televisão* (Portuguese), телевияение (Russian), *telewizja* (Polish), *televize* (Czechoslovakian), *televizija* (Serbocroatian), *televisio* (Finnish), *televizió* (Hungarian), *televizyon* (Turkish). Non-European languages, too, have adopted the European name with the new technology, for example Arabic, Malay, Japanese, and Korean.

The Russian loanword is not a unique case. We know too little in the West today of how receptive Russian was to loanwords in many phases of its development. Décsy's comparative study (1973: 40ff.) provides us with important insights: 'Linguists are agreed that Russian is the most cosmopolitan of the Slavic languages – without a trace of xenophobia. It has always accepted foreign linguistic material willingly and abundantly. It was therefore rightly considered to be a hybrid language – a criterion that appears to be characteristic of most successful world languages.' To gain an impression of the numerous, still current internationalisms, one only has to leaf through a small Russian dictionary, for example under the letter F(Φ), to find *fabrika, fakt, fakultjet, familija, fantasija, fassad,* and many others.

To conclude, I would like to offer the following hypotheses concerning the possibilities of taking advantage of international vocabularies. Identical (or similar) vocabularies:

can facilitate everyday communication between members of different language communities;

have a multitude of applications in foreign-language acquisition and teaching;

yield information on the historical and cultural contacts between different peoples;

can be interpreted as the vocabulary of a pan-European culture; and

make an important contribution towards a differentiation of the discussion on foreign borrowings.

The first two hypotheses deserve far more attention than they have previously been given. It would appear that in foreign-language teaching the differences between the languages in contact are strongly emphasized and their identical or similar features are almost totally ignored. Apparently people have been too readily influenced by the results of research on linguistic interference, according to which structural elements from the first language can have a detrimental influence on the perception and realization of the second language. No matter how important the results of research on interference are, they can occasionally distort one's view of the possibilities for facilitating learning. Lado (1972: 17), referring to the aims and achievements of contrastive linguistics, speaks of obstructing and facilitating learning. Coseriu (1972: 45) asks whether contrastive linguistics has not placed too much emphasis on the contrasting and too little on the non-contrasting elements of individual languages.

A final comment remains to be made. The comparison of only two languages reveals much more extensive identical inventories but does not enable us to decide whether identical lexemes are also internationalisms, that is whether they occur in more than two languages. In a project at the University of Essen, German and English school dictionaries were examined for identical vocabularies and an inventory of no less than 8,000 identical or similar words was found (Braun 1979).

References

Braun, P. 1979. *Tendenzen in der deutschen Gegenwartssprache.* Stuttgart.

Braun, P. (ed.) 1979. *Fremdwort-Diskussion.* Munich.

Coseriu, E. 1972. Über Leistung und Grenzen der kontrastiven Grammatik. In G. Nickel (ed.), *Reader zur kontrastiven Linguistik.* Frankfurt.

Daniels, K. 1959. Erfolg und Misserfolg der Fremdwortverdeutschung. *Muttersprache,* 59: 46–54, 105–114.

Décsy, G. 1973. *Die linguistische Struktur Europas.* Wiesbaden.

Korlén, G. 1969. Führt die Teilung Deutschlands zur Sprachspaltung? *Der Deutschunterricht,* 21, 5: 5–23.

Korn, K. 1978. Ein Europa – eine Sprache? *Frankfurter Allgemeine Zeitung,* October 25.

Lado, R. 1972. Meine Perspektive der kontrastiven Linguistik. In G. Nickel (ed.), *Reader zur kontrastiven Linguistik*. Frankfurt.

Maurer, F. and Stroh, F. (eds.) 1959. *Deutsche Wortgeschichte*, vols. 1, 2. Berlin.

Müller, B. 1975. *Das Französische der Gegenwart*. Heidelberg.

Pfeffer, J. A. 1975. *Grunddeutsch. Erarbeitung und Wertung dreier deutscher Korpora*. Tübingen.

Polenz, P. von. 1967. Fremdwort und Lehnwort, sprachwissenschaftlich betrachtet. *Muttersprache*, 77: 65–80.

    1972. *Geschichte der deutschen Sprache*. Berlin.

Scheler, M. 1977. *Der englische Wortschatz*. Berlin.

Tschirch, F. 1969. *Geschichte der deutschen Sprache*, vols. 1, 2. Berlin.

Ulrich, W. 1975. *Linguistische Grundbegriffe*. Kiel.

Wandruszka, M. 1976. *Interlinguistik – Umrisse einer neuen Sprachwissenschaft*. Munich.

12 *International terminology*

WOLFGANG NEDOBITY

Introduction

Terminology is the only area in which moves towards the international unification of special languages can be carried out effectively. The use of planned languages, however, in the fields of science and technology, has not met with the necessary success because of a lack of pertinent terminologies.

Advantages of an international terminology

The advantages of a unification and thus an internationalization of concepts and terms are quite obvious: the understanding of subject specialists can be improved because a reading knowledge of technical texts in a foreign language can be easily acquired; the number of mistakes made in the translation of texts can be reduced tremendously because the problems of *faux amis* and the like can be eliminated. As a further consequence, technology and information transfer would no longer be hampered by communication barriers.

Technology transfer is a matter of great importance to countries with small economies. When they try to establish priorities for economic and scientific development they look for models in Western countries. As a matter of policy they have to decide how much science and technology they should develop and produce by their own efforts and how much should be imported. Developing countries usually realize that time is actually the scarcest resource when seeking to close the knowledge gap and to ease the lack of general welfare provision, and therefore they tend to opt for the fast transfer of technology from other countries.

This transfer of technology is also of great relevance to many industrialized nations because it opens new markets for products which are available everywhere in the Western world. Thus it should be in their own interests to see that there are no obstacles which might hamper the transfer of knowledge and technology. It therefore is not surprising that many international organizations have set up programs and agencies which serve this purpose. For instance, the Industrial Development Board of Unido has reiterated the high priority that it attaches to the development and transfer of technology to developing countries and the effective contribution that international action in that area could make to the industrialization of developing countries. In that context, it has stressed the particular significance of the work of Unido in transferring appropriate and advanced technologies to developing countries.

During the 1980s there have also been strong voices both in the United Nations and in Unesco calling for the establishment of a new international information order which will make it possible to close the gap between the developed and the developing countries. The value of such an information program should not be underestimated: the developing countries have to follow the industrialized countries in setting up documentation centers which hold all the major primary and secondary publications in science and technology, since these contain most of the publicly available information resulting from research in the industrial countries. Technology transfer without the accompanying information and training activities cannot be prosperous in the long run.

Many developing countries purchase patents and know-how through consultants or encourage multinational companies to set up licensed companies or genuine branches of their firms in the country in the vain hope that the advanced technology they use will generate local innovations and thus assure a technological leap for the country. But in fact the real key to successful technology transfer and a genuine improvement of the standard of living is the training of local personnel. This is certainly a most difficult task but the prize is worth the effort. If the industrial nations of our times are willing to make this effort, they can accomplish more than any previous generation: they will hand over the knowledge which is necessary to handle the new technology effectively and wisely.

Unfortunately, the current practice is still far away from this ideal, as a current report of the International Development Research Centre (1983: 111) states: 'As a rule, suppliers of technology do not train manpower unless contracts call for it. Training is usually requested in either: (1) very sophisticated technologies that are new to the country or (2) highly capital- intensive technologies involving a large amount of risk. Diffusion of these types of technology in expansion of the sector is quite limited.'

The training of key skilled personnel was undertaken in the case of new and . very sophisticated technologies, but very seldom were the 'trainers' trained by a set of directions framed for their usage. In the past the main obstacle to training native technologists used to be illiteracy, but nowadays these obstacles have become more complex – they are economic, political, and always linguistic in nature.

As regards the linguistic obstacles, terminology plays a major role in overcoming technical communication barriers. If a language lacks the necessary subject vocabularies, technological knowledge cannot be disseminated in this language and the speakers of the language become discriminated against because they have to learn a foreign language, which is a long-term process and delays development. Therefore terminological training is a prerequisite for any technical training and for the handling of technical information.

Important aspects of the General Theory of Terminology regarding international terminology

Terminology as a science explores the meaning of special languages. It has developed specific methods and principles for this purpose. Most of these principles are derived from logic, in particular from conceptology and epistemology. Generally speaking, one can say that the principal problem of information science is that of knowing how meaning is obtained from, or injected into, a text. To solve this problem it appears that one must have a detailed understanding of what meaning is and what its properties are. In special languages meanings are formulated by means of concepts and conveyed to others by means of terms. Concepts refer to objects of the inner or outer world. Individual objects can be concrete, like a table, or abstract like an innovation. Concepts can refer not only to things and events but also to properties and relations. A concept, however, is only a mental construction derived from objects. In order to communicate that mental construction, a symbol is assigned to the concept that represents it, usually a term in technical communication.

The General Theory of Terminology, which was founded by Eugen Wüster, is a very appropriate basis for practical terminology work. It is of interest to both subject specialists and teachers of special languages. For this reason, Infoterm, the Vienna-based International Information Centre for Terminology, disseminates this theory and encourages specialists in various countries to translate its basic texts into the language(s) concerned and to elaborate the section on terms, including term formation, for the language(s) concerned. Among these basic texts are the methodological standards issued by the International Organization for Standardization (I.S.O./T.C. 37). These I.S.O. specifications have to be supplemented by national standards which focus on the particularities of a given language or subject.

The standardization of terminologies can also be a substantial aid to language development for technology transfer. The terminological co-operation between technology-exporting and -importing countries can best be organized in international standardizing committees where the unification of concepts should be a priority. The formation of terms, however, is the responsibility of national committees, which are a necessity for each country interested in technology transfer. The motivation for coining terms should not be governed by purely commercial considerations and has to follow certain rules which are in conformity with the structure of the language. Otherwise there is the danger of firm- and product-specific terminology developing instead of generally accepted terminology. An example of product-specific terminology is the fact that a certain part of an I.B.M. typewriter was designated as 'golfball,' a term which does not reflect the essential character-istics of the concept in question and which was therefore not rendered into other national languages. The same problem has existed in the pharmaceutical industry for decades, where proprietary names have been used in juxtaposi-tion with non-proprietary names. Such a situation makes the terminological control more difficult and requires the compilation of appropriate works of reference. Transferring this situation to the field of commerce, one should expect, ideally, that the terminology of a warehouse catalogue should not differ from that of customs regulations.

The formation of terms can be facilitated by building up an inventory of native term elements, each reflecting a certain characteristic that could occur in a concept. Wüster compiled such an inventory for international elements mainly of Greek and Latin origin (see below).

The formation of international terms certainly offers a number of advan-tages to technology transfer, but in developing countries there are usually sociological barriers which hamper the overall acceptance of such terms. Therefore it is necessary for the government of such countries to decide on a clear-cut language-planning policy and to establish an appropriate infrastruc-ture for it. Such an infrastructure should also contain terminology courses within the respective education systems, in particular at university and post-graduate level. Infoterm supports these activities by providing advice and teaching material. A decisive step in this direction was made with the publica-tion of a terminology manual (Felber 1984) which can be used as a textbook for training courses.

Principles for the formation of international terminology

An essential principle for the unification of subject vocabularies is that it has to be carried out at several levels and should concern:

1   concepts and concept systems;
2   definitions and descriptions of concepts;
3   the internal form of terms; and
4   the external form of terms.

With regard to these four levels the methods of concept formation and term formation have to become acceptable internationally. Further, it is equally important that the same quarry of elements is used for this purpose.

Concepts and concept systems

Concepts are mental representations of individual objects. A concept may represent only one individual object or – by abstraction – comprise a set of individual objects having certain qualities in common. It serves as a means for mental ordering (classification) and with the aid of a linguistic symbol (term, letter, graphical symbol) for communication. The concept is therefore an element of thinking.

Concepts may be the mental representation not only of beings or things (as expressed by nouns), but, in a wider sense, also of qualities (as expressed by adjectives or nouns), of actions (as expressed by verbs or nouns), and even of locations, situations or relations (as expressed by adverbs, prepositions, conjunctions or nouns).

Furthermore, a concept may arise from the combination of other concepts, even without regard to reality. The number of concepts (represented by terms) which may be combined to form a new concept (term) is limited by the fact that in a proposition a concept can only be either subject or predicate, but cannot comprise both. The best way to achieve the unification of concepts is through the establishment of unified systems of concepts.

Definitions

A concept can be described either by a definition or by an explanation. If it is not possible in a certain case to provide a definition, at least an explanation of the concept should be given. The definition is the key to any scientific work.

A definition is a description of a concept by means of other known concepts, mostly in the form of words and terms. It determines this concept in a system of other related concepts. An explanation is a description of a concept without considering its position in a system of concepts.

A definition usually consists of a specification of the characteristics of the concept to be defined, that is a description of the intension of the concept. For this purpose first the nearest genus is found that has either been defined already or can be expected to be generally known. Then the genus is restricted to the correct extension by being linked to characteristics which differentiate the concept to be defined from other concepts of the same level of abstraction. These characteristics are called 'restricting characteristics.' They have to conform to the type of characteristics. This structure and the wording of definitions should be unified in multilingual vocabularies in order to see immediately if there are discrepancies in the number of characteristics.

In the Vocabulary of the International Electrotechnical Commission (I.E.C.), for example, care is taken not only over the determination of identical national concepts but also over the establishment of official definitions in English and French. Translation of such standard definitions should be introduced progressively into national standards.

The internal form of terms

Each language consists of thousands of word elements or morphemes. In addition, there are a small number of term elements which have to be used for the designation of millions of concepts. This situation is handled by combining word elements in a number of ways and by meaning transfer.

The internal form of terms is their literal or basic meaning. For instance, the widened end of a taper key has the following internal forms in various languages:

English: head
French: talon (internal form: heel)
German: Nase (internal form: nose)

If it were possible to agree in all languages on only one of these three internal forms (part of the body), such a decision would make international understanding and translation work easier. A truly international form is 'head,' for the widened end of a screw is designated in this way in all the above languages.

The external form of terms

As far as the external form of terms is concerned we can distinguish three types of international terms:

1   Terms such as 'induction' in electrical engineering are spelled and prounced differently in the various countries:
         German: Induktion
         French: induction
         Italian: indusione
         Russian: indukcija
2   The term *abies*, which is part of the international nomenclature for botany, is the Latin word for fir-tree. It is spelled the same in all countries but pronounced differently. This type is very common in the fields of zoology, botany, and medicine.
3   Terms such as 'shunt' are pronounced and spelled the same way in all countries. They are the modern type of loanwords, coming from various national languages, and are comparatively uncommon.

The need for unified spelling across languages was pointed out as early as 1932 by Verkade in his comments on the international nomenclature of organic chemistry, which was adopted in 1930. Chemists have to file thousands of international terms in alphabetical order. In spite of the fact that they are basically understandable by everyone, they cause problems because of slight spelling variants, for example the French *étyl* and the German *Äthyl*. There is still a lot of work to do in international standardization in this respect.

Affixes are also afflicted by this problem. Many of the national idiosyncrasies are due to so-called phonetic spelling. The English affix '-ity,' for instance, as in 'formality' has the German counterpart *-ität* as well as the French *-ité* and the Italian *-ità*. All these national derivations are based on the Latin prototype form *-itatem*, later *-itate*.

A national form is at the same time international if there are forms etymologically identical with it in several other languages, expecially if all these forms are similar and if the languages belong to different families. Latin-type forms are to be preferred to the internationalized ethnic forms because they are more neutral and more consistent with the majority of other international terms. They are a more suitable basis for derivation and composition. Foreign ethnic forms provoke the resistance of the language purists. The Comité d'études des termes techniques français, for instance, has suggested the replacement of the following loanwords from English with Latin-type terms:

> by-pass (technology of fluids): déviation, dérivation
> dope (chemical industry): additif
> feeder (electrical engineering): artère, conduite de transport

A modern example of unifying the external form of terms is the medical dictionary by Eschenbach (1983), which uses Latin spelling for German. An enterprise such as this will only be successful if it obtains the full support of the respective professional associations and, as a second step, of technical writers in general.

Key to international terminology

Wüster (1959) laid down the seven most important characteristics of the key to terminology as follows:

1   The key to terminology is designed to serve the needs of terminologists, not of philologists. It is to serve as a basis for the terminologies of the Romanic, Germanic, Slavic and other languages, even of planned languages such as Esperanto.

2   The term elements are to be ordered in the first instance according to concepts, that is systematically, in the second instance alphabetically.

3   The frequency of term elements has to be considered and recorded. Thus an evaluation of synonyms is possible and also a selective use of the key. Consequently the key to terminology can be taught step by step.

4   The term elements have to be spelled in the same way as is done in Latin today. This way of spelling is preserved most accurately in French and English.

5   The term elements have to be presented in a basic form (prototype form) which is free of any national variants. The prototype forms can be transformed into national forms in a systematic way.

6   In order to be able to teach and practice the key to terminology, an internationally uniform pronunciation has to be assigned to the latinized prototype forms.

7   International terms which are not Latin-type terms are to be admitted to the key in an unaltered way as 'ethnic type terms.' They are to be pronounced as in their language of origin.

There are already hundreds of thousands of international terms available in the various subject vocabularies. Most of them are formed by combining roots and affixes. There are several thousand international roots and a few dozen international affixes available for this purpose. Only a small number of principles and guidelines is necessary to describe the procedure of term formation sufficiently. If one prepares a systematic schedule of the term elements (roots and affixes), as well as of the rules for their combination, one creates a key to international terminology. The purpose of such a key is to give the various subject specialists the opportunity to understand the meaning of international concepts by analyzing their inner form and to create new terms if required. This will promote the universal comprehensibility of subject communication among specialists from all over the world.

The first organizational step towards the preparation of principles for the international unification of technical vocabularies was taken in 1936, when the International Federation of National Standardizing Associates (I.S.A.) established a technical committee for terminology (I.S.A. 37). In 1938 this committee passed a resolution concerning the 'International terminology of technology,' also known as the 'I.S.A. code.' I would like to quote two paragraphs from it:

c)   *necessity of rules*
It is deemed necessary to lay down uniform rules for the formation of code-words ... These rules constitute at the same time a kind of 'Key to Terminology' in regard to the already available international subject terminologies. It is intended to achieve with these rules the uniform, correct and purpose-oriented formation of code-words in the various disciplines. They should not lead to a forced mixture of languages nor to a distortion of terms which are already almost international in nature.

The rules for the code have to be supplemented by a list of the most important roots and affixes which are to be the formation of code-words.

g)   *Sources for code-words*
The code-words are to be very similar to the available technical expressions in the national languages, with special consideration of the three ISA-languages and related languages.   Nedobity 1982: 250ff

Before World War II the elaboration of the code system was in the hands of a small international sub-committee of I.S.A. 37. In 1946 I.S.A. 37 was replaced by the Technical Committee (T.C.) 37 of I.S.O. In 1955 the secretariat of I.S.O./T.C. 37 drafted a catalogue of principles entitled 'Principes pour l'unification internationale des notions et termes.' Largely concerned with the unification of concepts and of the inner form of terms, it served as the basis for the elaboration of the recommendation *International Unification of Concepts and Terms* (I.S.O./R. 860-1968), which is presently under revision. Work on the I.S.A. code has not been continued, however, by I.S.O. or any other international body. Nevertheless, the Austrian standardizing sub-committee Terminologie Q followed the I.S.A. 37 resolution and compiled a list of roots (*Wortstammliste*). On the basis of Eaton (1934), Wüster selected 500 concepts. Their respective forms were labeled 'crude forms' because the final forms remain to be determined.

In 1951 the *Interlingua – English Dictionary* (Gode 1971) was prepared by I.A.L.A., and this drew to a great extent on Wüster's principles for crude forms of roots. It can serve as an additional basis for future work. International subject communication will be facilitated by the creation of a key to international terminology. Even if it will not enable an immediate and precise understanding, which only definitions can provide, it will have a tremendous mnemonic effect as it uses familiar elements and combinations of these elements.

Reference

Eaton, Helen S. 1934. *Comparative Word Frequency List*. New York.

Eschenbach, K.-P. 1983. *Wörterbuch der Medicin/Dictionary of Medicine*. Neckarsulm.

Felber, H. 1984. *Terminology Manual*. Paris.

Gode, A. 1971. *Interlingua – English Dictionary*. New York.

International Development Research Centre 1983. *Absorption and Diffusion of Imported Technology. Proceedings of a Workshop held in Singapore, 26–30 January 1981*. Ottawa.

I.S.O. 1968. *International Unification of Concepts and Terms*. Geneva.

Nedobity, W. 1982. Key to International Terminology. In Infoterm, *Terminologies for the Eighties. With a Special Section: 10 Years of Infoterm*. Munich, New York, London, Paris.

Tell, B. 1983. Information Consciousness and Knowledge Enhancement in the LDCs in View of a New International Information Order. *International Forum on Information and Documentation 9*.

Unido 1984. *Newsletter* no. 195 (July).

Verkade, P. E.: 1932. La révision récente de la nomenclature des combinaisons organiques. *Recueil des travaux chimiques des Pays-Bas 51*, 850–852.

Wüster, E. 1959. Die internationale Angleichung der Fachausdrücke. *Elektrotechnische Zeitschrift*, 16: 550–552.

13 Democracy and the crisis of normative linguistics

FLORIAN COULMAS

Die Schöpfung einer einheitlichen Schriftsprache ist eine Kulturtat ersten Ranges. (O. Behaghel 1907)[1]

Two points of view concerning conscious intervention in linguistic development

Language is essentially a social phenomenon. No linguist would deny this, yet the social character of language poses a difficult problem for linguistics as a science. 'Natural language' is the key word of twentieth-century linguistics, and despite the enormous expansion and advances of sociolinguistics in the last quarter century, the scholar who investigates language from either a partly structural (synchronic) or quasi-Darwinian (diachronic) perspective as a *natural* phenomenon is widely regarded – and regards himself – as the true keeper of the Holy Grail of scientific rigor in linguistics. Even though he admits that language does not exist but in, and through, a speech community, he insists on studying it from the Olympian point of view of the unbiased observer. Most of all he refuses to get involved and make judgments or define standards of excellence. Yet this noble attitudes does not get him off the prescriptive hook, because the fundamental paradox of descriptive linguistics – that is, the inability of describing a language without providing a standard or setting a norm – is yet to be solved.

The prescriptive abstinence of linguists is a recent phenomenon, a result, one tends to think, of the overall positivist trend in the social sciences in this century. Linguists were much concerned with establishing their scientific credentials and thus tried to liberate themselves from a tradition where the grammarians were always also the norm makers.[2] They discovered what John Lyons called the 'classical fallacy,' the refuting of which became an example of scientific self-assurance and the basis of the attempt to define a new beginning for the study of language. The 'classical fallacy' had already been committed by Alexandrinian linguists. It was

the assumption that the language of the fifth-century Attic writers was more 'correct' than the colloquial speech of their own time; and in general that the 'purity' of a

177

language is maintained by the usage of the educated, and 'corrupted' by the illiterate. For more than two thousand years this prejudice was to reign unchallenged.

(Lyons 1968: 9)

And it is still upheld by virtually all people who have no linguistic training. Laymen need not really be concerned about this, but for linguists this misconception, this fallacious view about language is a real problem. For the past two thousand years, Lyons tells us, they did not do what they were supposed to do, because they fell prey to the 'classical fallacy' that some linguistic usages are superior to others. There is no reason to despair, however, because now that the fallacy has been recognized as such, most linguists would say that it is absurd to talk about languages changing for the better or the worse.[3] They change, and that is all.

There are two versions of this point of view. One is that language change can be influenced as much as the terrestrial climate. There is really no point in trying to do it. The other is that the very attempt to exercise an influence on language is unscientific and hence not what linguists are being paid for. Whether we can or cannot influence language change is unimportant; we should not do it. The metaphor of language as an organism has influenced the notion of what a language is so strongly that any attempt at influencing its natural development is morally as dubious as cloning. Most linguists have gladly adopted either the 'cannot' or the 'should not' position, and by declaring themselves incompetent in matters of 'good' or 'bad' language have relieved themselves of responsibility for the possible consequences of their own work.

The scholars' serene detachment from the object of their studies is, however, in sharp conflict with the expectations of the speech community, as well as the actual needs of modern standard languages. What is a linguist good for when he cannot give advice about good or bad language and refuses to make statements about what is good for our languages? Who else would be more qualified to make such statements? At school, students are taught their own mother tongue for ten years or more, but what happens after that? Most schoolteachers are still willing to say what is right and what is wrong, but the professional linguist, the authority at the top, is much more reluctant, nowadays. Generally, linguists have failed to appreciate the effects of generations of schooling or language academies on the development of language.

Sociologically the linguists' reluctance to prescribe usage is very interesting, because their authority was never challenged from 'below' by the speech community who rebelled against arbitrary norms, but rather they abandoned it voluntarily in the name of truth and scientific advance. What we have here, then, are two conflicting viewpoints about language and linguistics: the modern linguists, who are trying to free themselves from their predecessors' traditional role as 'language makers,' as Harris (1980) somewhat ironically calls them, on the one hand, and the authoritarian public, who have been brought up to rely on specialists in all matters of importance and thus want to rely on the language specialist in linguistic matters, on the other hand. Most laymen, after all, think of prescriptive grammars as the only possible kind. The subtle difference between *discovering* and *imposing* structures is quite beyond their interest.

In the long run the linguist who refuses to believe in the feasibility of prescribed usage and consciously guided language adaptation may be proven right. Neither Cicero nor Priscian could have averted the decline of Latin and its splitting-up into the modern Romance languages, and it would presumably be preposterous to assume that linguists today could do better. In any event, the professional linguist's refusal to take a stand about 'right' and 'wrong' or 'good' and 'bad' is unsatisfactory because he abandons his field of expertise, allowing all sorts of charlatens to rampage in it, shamans, as Bolinger (1980) calls them. Moreover, linguists today are in a better position than Cicero or Priscian, because they can enlist the support of institutions that can reach practically the entire speech community, while the effects of systematic education were restricted to a small part of the speech community in classical times. However, in a sense this also makes the linguist's task more difficult precisely because he has to reckon with a much larger speech community, and thus has to pay attention to usage on a larger scale, which he can only ignore at the risk of making suggestions that not only deviate from, but run counter to, strong tendencies of development and are therefore bound to be ineffective.

In societies with highly institutionalized infrastructures the public will not accept that 'anything goes' in language and that they themselves are the ones who decide about good and bad. But, on the other hand, propositions which are in sharp conflict with established usage do not stand a good chance of being accepted either. Law makers and judges have to make decisions about good and bad in juridical terms, and this is generally seen as an improvement in society's conduct of affairs, but while such decisions must be above, and sometimes in conflict with, public opinion, they cannot be entirely arbitrary in the sense of being at variance with both tradition and reason. The great dilemma of normative linguistics is that the equality postulate of democracy as applied to languages and language varieties has deprived linguists of a standard of what is good in matters of language and has thus called into doubt the very idea that the removal of linguistic anarchy on rational grounds can be regarded as a step forward. Linguists, of course, have been arguing for some time that the only reason why certain usages are considered 'correct' by traditional grammars and textbooks is that they have been adopted by a privileged social class in the past.[4] To a certain extent they are right, but what some of them fail to notice is that the reason *why* these usages are considered correct are less important than *that* they are so considered. The fact that a norm is established in a speech community means that there is no immediate need for the grammarian to crack the whip, but it also means that the speakers adhere to it, even if they do not always follow it in their own performance. This is demonstrated, maybe most impressively, by diglossic speech communities.

Why diglossic situations are perpetuated is one of the most puzzling questions of sociolinguistics. The fact is that the cleavage between a fossilized literary variety and the vernacular(s) characteristic of such situations is perpetuated without pressure from the socially dominant, and sometimes even against conscious attempts directed at abolishing it. What De Silva writes about Tamil diglossia may illustrate the point:

> The diglossic character has ... not been affected by the state's [Tamil-Nadu] political changes, and the high variety is still looked up to with the same respect and awe ... Even the uneducated people would not take people seriously when they attempt to address them in public using the colloquial language known to the audience.
>
> (De Silva 1976: 51f.).

Diglossia is the linguistic sediment of certain socio-historical conditions, to be sure. Being aware of these conditions, however, does not necessarily affect the situation. To be more explicit, to know that certain linguistic norms stem from social privileges and from using language as a socially dividing rather than unifying force does not necessarily diminish their potency. No matter where a norm comes from, once it is there it is a sociolinguistic fact and an effective factor of linguistic change.

De Saussure, it is well known, was one of the godfathers of the notion of 'natural language' as it came to be understood in modern linguistics. However, a historical linguist by training, he was still aware of its precariousness, which nowadays is often covered with the veil of 'necessary abstraction.' 'Is it possible,' he asked, 'to distinguish the natural, organic growth of an idiom from its artificial forms, such as the literary language, which are due to external, and therefore inorganic forces? Common languages are always developing alongside local dialects' (de Saussure 1972: 20).

Grammarians have done little to meet the challenge of this question and to determine what is and what is not natural in a language.[5] But one thing is clear: every sociolinguistic explanation of linguistic change has to reckon with the factor of language attitude, which is at the interface of the organic and the artificial, combining, as it does, elements of *Sprachgefühl* and social prestige. Speakers do have feelings about their 'idiom' which may be a powerful determinant of linguistic change, and which may be influenced consciously by political intervention. In one way or another all of the chapters of this book testify to this fact, no matter whether the language concerned belongs to the few with a classical tradition of their own that can be exploited, such as Hebrew, Arabic, or Chinese, or to those which during a period of their history have assimilated a classical stratum from another language, such as German or Japanese, or to those languages which, like Kiswahili, have no direct access to a classical language by virtue of their own tradition. As the individual chapters demonstrate, conscious intervention in natural change is both called for and feasible at crucial junctures of the history of languages of all three types. For this reason, linguists should not just step back and allow language to develop 'naturally,' waiving their right to make their opinion known in this matter and leaving a vacuum to be filled by others less competent to make a judgment.

Cultivated language

One of the axioms of modern linguistics is that all languages are equal. To be sure, this is, in principle a good axiom and a decisive advance over the times of even Bloomfield and Sapir, when unwritten languages were commonly called 'dialects,' and 'primitive language' was an inoffensive expression among linguists. It is also an advance over ideological statements as to the special beauty, power, richness, purity, etc. of a given language, so common among nationalists in the nineteenth century (Coulmas 1988). After all, the equality of all languages with respect to their potential was not generally recognized until quite recently. Bloomfield, in his article 'Literate and Illiterate Speech' of 1927, still felt the need to convince his readers that unwritten languages, too, were languages proper and not merely unintelligible gibberish, and he is to be commended for making it clear that a literary tradition is not a good criterion for distinguishing between language and dialect. Nineteenth-century European ethnocentrism did not spare linguistics. As a representative example consider the following unabashed remark by such an enlightened spirit as Wilhelm von Humboldt: 'That nations more happily endowed and under more favorable conditions should possess more excellent languages than others is grounded in the very nature of things.'[6]

There are no two ways about it, for Humboldt and many of his contemporaries some nations naturally had better languages than others. That modern linguistics has done away with good and not so good languages is an unquestionable improvement.

However, the desire to part with its ethnocentric past has led the main stream of linguistics into an egalitarian relativism,[7] blocking the view that there may be differences other than grammatical ones between languages, differences, that is, as to how the potential of a language is functionally exploited, or, to put it in economic terms, differences as to the relative productivity of languages. Insisting on the superiority of some (Western) languages is one thing, but evaluating a given language at a given historical state with respect to its relative suitability for certain forms of communication is another. There is nothing degrading in saying that, at present, Zulu, a South African Bantu language, is not a suitable medium for scientific writing in nuclear physics (Louw 1983). This is hardly surprising, because so far nobody has ever wanted to write about nuclear physics in Zulu, and the attributes that make a language fit as a medium for writing about nuclear physics are not what languages are naturally endowed with. Unless there is a functional requirement, the functional potential will not develop. Similarly, 'communicating in Arabic' for certain purposes poses a number of problems due to the particular historical circumstances in which Arabic diglossia evolved. As Ibrahim shows (see chapter 3), the Arabic language could be more suitable than it is.

To take another example, a hundred years ago, the Japanese language was not fit to express the scientific and social ideas of Western culture (Ono 1980; Coulmas forthcoming a), but today it is. While it is not a better language for that, it has overcome serious deficiencies which, at the time, made it seem doubtful that Japanese could be adapted to the new tasks. Yet it *has* been adapted to the needs of modern communication, partly by conscious effort, and now serves its speech community as an adequate means for all communicative purposes. Kindaichi, whose career as a linguist unfolded unperturbed by the value crisis of Western democracy or the sudden discovery of the 'classical fallacy,' which is only one of its many expressions, writes about this achievement:

How should we evaluate the Japanese language? ... Japanese does have various defects, but it is also true that we can say and write whatever we think in Japanese. Fortunately, we can use it to write scientific theses and business papers ...

(Kindaichi 1957: 223)

This is the result not of natural development but of co-operative reactions to pressing language problems. In the 1870s and 1880s Japanese was regarded by many Japanese intellectuals as so poorly equipped for meeting the demands of modernity that they even toyed with the idea of replacing it by a Western language. In 1873, Mori Arinori, a leading intellectual of his day who commanded tremendous prestige within Japanese society, wrote a letter to the American linguist William Whitney, soliciting his view of whether or not introducing a new national language for Japan was advisable and feasible:

The march of civilization in Japan has already reached the heart of the nation – the English language following it suppresses the use of both Chinese and Japanese. The commercial power of the English speaking race which now rules the world drives our people into some knowledge of their commercial ways and habits. The absolute necessity of mastering the English language is thus forced upon us. It is a requisite of our independence in the community of nations. Under the circumstances, our meager language, which can never be of any use outside our islands, is doomed to yield to the domination of the English tongue, especially when the power of steam and electricity shall have pervaded the land. Our intelligent race, eager in the pursuit of knowledge, cannot depend on a weak and uncertain medium of communication in its endeavor to grasp the principal truths from the precious treasury of Western science and art and religion. The laws of state can never be preserved in the language of Japan. All reasons suggest its disuse.

(Mori 1973: vol. 1, vi)

Nowadays it is hard to believe that such a suggestion was ever seriously discussed by serious people; but a hundred years ago Japanese intellectuals were intensely worried about the linguistic future of their country. Westernization in Japan was so rapid that for some time Japanese seemed inadequate for many purposes of communication. Fukuzawa Yukichi, the founder of Japan's first private university, Keio-gijuku, in 1874 observed:

Up to now, there has been the fear that it is awkward to give a speech in Japanese, and that therefore a speech cannot take a respectable form. However, after careful thought, I have come to the conclusion that there is no reason why a speech cannot be given in the Japanese language.   (Fukuzawa 1932: 206)

And further: 'You may meet anyone in Japan, and you will never find a man who can express clearly everything he means' (*ibid.*: 207). Such contemporary perceptions of the Japanese language make Mori's suggestion seem a little less bizarre.

Given this background, it is not so surprising that, some eighty years later, Kindaichi, with some relief, makes a point of saying that 'it would be neither possible nor advisable to abandon this language' (Kindaichi 1957: 223). To him it is a matter of course that a language is not only a natural object but also a cultural asset worthy of thoughtful attention:

On the one hand, a language is a natural development, but on the other, something created. Even German, which is said to be a model of a systematic language, is a creation of the German people over a period of several generations. We who are living at the present time cannot help feeling a heavy responsibility for the future of the Japanese language.   (Kindaichi 1957: 224)

What Kindaichi says about German is, of course, quite correct. As late as the turn of the seventeenth century German had a reputation as a boorish language unfit for educated discourse. German had to compete with French, which was still the preferred language of the political elite in the eighteenth century, but the intellectuals were already determined to use German as the medium of education and culture. Nothing like the Accademia della Crusca or the Académie Française ever came into existence in Germany, but a number of bourgeois grammarians like J. Bödiker (1690), J. Ch. Gottsched (1748), and J. C. Adelung (1774), as well as poets like Klopstock, Herder and others pursued the common goal of turning German into a 'cultivated language' by using it for all higher forms of writing and by pleading for its acceptance by the elites. Their contribution to adapting the German language to the requirements of higher functions of communication and thus overcoming the stigma of inadequacy was very significant indeed.

It is interesting to note in this connection that in the absence of a single prestige model, such as that of the language of the royal courts in Paris and London, the standardization of German was mediated to a much higher degree than that of French or English, by writing (Polenz 1983: 28). Despite

Luther's famous maxim of *dem Volk aufs Maul schaun* – that is, taking the vernacular as a model for the written language – the emerging standard was heavily biased by the stiff style of the chanceries, whose grammatical conventions were partly shaped on Latin paradigms. Thus German, somewhat later than French and English, became a cultivated language whose literature gained international recognition in the eighteenth century. (In government, however, it took such drastic measures as the Napoleonic wars to replace French by German.) Ever since, German has been free of all functional restrictions, serving as the means of expression in all social domains of developed communication, such as culture, technology, science, and government.

This is what the notion of 'cultivated language' means. In the sense in which it is used here it was first introduced by Grace (1981). Grace makes a distinction between 'cultivated language' and 'ordinary language' which is based on differences in language consciousness. Language is not perceived and experienced in the same way by all people at all times. Those 'natural' languages that have become objects of conscious attention on the part of their speakers are called 'cultivated language' by Grace (1981: 3). Conscious attention to matters linguistic is not restricted to neutral observation, but rather implies that the languages in question, or certain forms of them, are being shaped consciously by deliberate intervention. Learned Latin is a pertinent example.

Between A.D. 550 and A.D. 700 Latin ceased to be a natural language, that is a native language. It continued to be widely used in the world of learning (see chapter 10) and was hence of great importance to the development of advanced thought throughout the European Middle Ages. But it was nobody's mother tongue, as it became converted into a 'chirographically controlled language' (Ong 1977: 27). Other learned languages such as Sanskrit (see chapter 5), Classical Arabic (see chapter 3), Hebrew (see chapter 2), Geez (Mulugeta 1988), or *kanbun* (Coulmas forthcoming b) – that is, written Japanese[8] – had a similar fate, being reduced to writing in the literal sense. Not being native languages anymore, nobody could claim authentic intuitions about their natural feel and development. Thus the classical models of generally acclaimed written documents became ever more important. The learned languages did not only use writing, they were subdued by writing. The acquisition of these languages without baby talk became a matter of pen and ink; they were consciously learned while sitting on a school bench rather than on a mother's lap. The written standard was the only guide for correct usage, which was a great merit of the learned languages for a long time. Not being subject to regional variation, they functioned as universal media of intellectual exchange in widely separated parts of the world. That was an advantage at times of intellectual consolidation and relatively slow development. But eventually the lack of native speakers proved fatal. Stability turned into inflexibility, the reliable norm into an ossified artefact incapable of innovation and adaptation. The existence of Latin depended on the written medium exclusively. It lacked the dynamics of an oral tradition passed from one generation to the next that is characteristic of every native language. In the Renaissance, Latin had become a cultivated language only and lost the ability to change in accordance with the accelerated development of communicative needs in science, technology, and government. The written conversation of a standard thus led to atrophy.

Similarly, *kanbun*, the peculiar style of writing Classical Chinese developed in Japan (see chapter 7), which was the most highly respected written language in Japan for about a millennium and also provided the intellectuals with a means of transnational communication similar to the role of Latin in Europe, was eventually too tightly restricted by traditional norms never counterbalanced by 'natural' development, and could not be adapted to the modern forms of communication it was confronted with very suddenly in the nineteenth century. Like Latin it thus fell out of use. Nevertheless, this written language has left deep traces in the Japanese language which are comparable to those left by Sanskrit in the literary languages of India and the Greco-Latin stratum in the languages of Europe. Indeed, Sinicisms, that is Chinese-origin words which entered Vietnamese, Korean, and Japanese, as well as some minor East Asian languages through the medium of the written language, that is Classical Chinese, are the oriental counterpart (Suzuki 1987) to what in the European context have been called 'internationalisms' (see chapter 11).

What these examples serve to illustrate is that an artificial intervention in the evolution of a language may have profound effects. A point that is yet to be seriously examined, however, is the question of whether different writing systems affect language development differently. (There is no spelling pronunciation in Chinese, yet the Chinese language has been deeply influenced by its writing.)

Ferguson (1962) suggested four levels of written communication: (1) no writing, (2) writing for personal communication and literature, (3) writing on the natural sciences, and (4) writing for translating scientific texts from other languages. This classification is useful for certain purposes, but it does not distinguish languages with respect to their regimentation by writing. Writing is instrumental in language cultivation and regularization, which is not the same as language planning, but language planning too would be inconceivable without writing. Linguistic conventions become objectified in writing and can be maintained by a codified standard. However, the importance of the written form(s) of a language for the speech community at large, and consequently for the development of its language, varies greatly from case to case.

If languages were to be ordered along a scale of the relative import of writing, learned Latin would be positioned at one end and, for example, Cameroon Pidgin at the other. Latin exists as a written language only. Its soul is enshrined in the letter. Cameroon Pidgin, by contrast, is not used in writing. Moreover, no efforts are made to cultivate it, because it enjoys little prestige, although it is very practical in a multilingual country like Cameroon and, despite the government's French–English bilingual education policy, still serves as an important link language between different regions, social classes, and age groups (Todd 1984: 88ff.). Like Latin it is nobody's mother tongue, but while Latin is a sacrosanct literary language whose classical texts are respected like the letter of the law, Cameroon Pidgin is like an outlawed bastard whom nobody respects and everybody feels free to treat as he pleases. In between these two extremes of a language in the Procrustean bed of writing that straightens every deviation and hence innovation, on the one hand, and the uncontrolled promiscuity of a language answering every *ad hoc* communicative need by bending or expanding the rules, on the other hand, there are various degrees of flexibility, regularization, and conformity of the spoken language with a written standard, which, in historical terms, can be seen as either linguistic convergence (of the spoken with the written form) or divergence. The modern European standard languages are the result of convergence. Diglossic languages, such as Tamil, Sinhalese, or Arabic, are a result of divergence. Both cases can be defined in terms of writing, written norm, and literacy.

Writing is not the only factor in language cultivation. As for example the history of Vedic civilization teaches us, language cultivation can go a long way without writing (see chapter 5). However, if writing is perhaps not a necessary condition of language cultivation, it surely is an important intervention in the history of any language that acquires a written form, especially in deliberately steering its adaptation to novel communicative needs or ideological purposes.

Language cultivation requires certain language attitudes, such as the willingness of an elite to use language as a means of social control and unification, as a barrier to outsiders, and as a symbol of national identity. Thus language cultivation is likely to become, and often has become, a political issue. Whenever this happens, there is a good chance that other than reasonable criteria come to bear on attempts at influencing linguistic development. This is, I believe, a major reason why linguists should not abstain, under the pretext of misunderstood democratic ideals such as egalitarianism, relativism, and anti-normativism, from dealing with 'good language' and 'bad language.' Linguists have no monopoly on shaping a language – in as far as it can be shaped – but they are better qualified than others to distinguish between linguistic and non-linguistic matters and make judgments that are not emotionally and ideologically biased.

Our language is going down the drain

Language is often instrumentalized for purposes of political socialization (see Coulmas 1985). To a greater or lesser extent, the representatives of states or nations feel an obligation to imbue their citizenry with a respect for their culture, of which language is seen to be a part. Among the most common ideologemes exerted in this connection is the authenticity maxim: our heritage is authentic and therefore good.[9] Its correlate, of course, is xenophobia: the alien is bad. When applied to language, linguistic purification results. Loan-words are perceived as contaminating the purity of the language, which in turn is regarded as a threat to cultural identity. Once such an ideal gains public recognition, a purification movement is born, and this is the other side of the coin of language cultivation.

An interesting case is that of the purification of German, which was gradually cleansed of foreign words, or, to put it differently, whose vocabulary was split by the custodians of purity into two parts, only one of which was recognized as German proper. This movement began early in the nineteenth century when, under the influence of the Napoleonic wars, hostility to France encouraged opposition to the *Verwelschung* of the German language. Early leaders in this movement were writers, philosophers, lexicographers, and political activists, among them Herder, Fichte, Campe, Arndt, and Fouqué.

Since then, opposition to foreign words has never entirely ceased. Its intensity grew markedly at times of nationalism, for instance after the Franco-Prussian War of 1870–1871 or during World War I (see Polenz 1972). The focus was on French and English loanwords, but what was recognized as foreign was determined by the respective purist's knowledge and resourcefulness (see chapter 11). Many words which most innocent citizens would never have suspected of having an un-German origin were unmasked and black-listed, household words such as *Karotte*, *Paket*, *Papa*, *Insekt*, *Kilo*, to name just a few.[10]

Had the advice of the purifiers been followed more scrupulously, German would surely be a much purer language, but one that could hardly cope with the demands of modern communication. Obviously a book like *Zur Kritik der politischen Ökonomie* could never have been written without the subversive words. Of the title, only the two shortest words would survive a purifying revision. 'So much the better for the German language and the German people,' is the way one might be tempted to paraphrase the purist's argument. However, politically the assessment of language purism is not so simple, that is to say the political left was not always immune against it either.

Nor was Germany the only prominent case. The French have a glorious tradition in this regard, and so have many others. The pejorative title of Etiemble's (1964) book *Parlez-vous franglais?* is only one of many, and it was only as recently as 1985 that *L'Express* published a long feature article 'Sait-on encore parler le français?' Of Arabic an observer, anxious about the incorporation of many Western loanwords into its vocabulary, reports:

The modern Arabic mind is becoming an offshoot of the modern Western mind and is retaining fewer and fewer of the rigidly Semitic thought habits ... It may take no more than two or three generations for it to become a highly integrated member of the Western cultural linguistic family, sharing fully in a common modern linguistic spirit.   (Stetkevych 1970: 119, 122)

Language purity is often seen as a value of and by itself, but it is also credited with remarkable power. In considering the problems of language modernization in some South-East Asian countries, del Rosario argues against lexical borrowing from Western languages on the grounds that

> consistent and intelligent modernization of their national languages would enable the Malaysians, the Indonesians and the Filipinos to overtake and eventually surpass in science and technology the Western nations, whose national languages are burdened with large numbers of terms derived from Latin and Greek, combining forms which are no longer consistent with the home and community languages spoken by their children. Japan, with her consistent Nippongo, is demonstrating that this can be done
>
> (del Rosario 1968: 16).

Maybe the Europeans and Americans, too, should take this to heart, but it is hard to believe that this will be the unexpected solution to their trade frictions with Japan. For one thing, whatever can be said about Nippongo, it certainly is one of the prime examples of hybrid languages (see chapter 8). Some 50% of the vocabulary is of Chinese origin or coined with Chinese-origin morphemes, and since the Meiji Restoration there has been a heavy influx of Western loanwords. Since the end of World War II English loans have entered the language at a breathtaking rate. Yet Japanese is a language with a unique identity that sets it apart from almost all other languages. Its genius is its ability to adapt and assimilate without losing its identity.

'The reason of a language to exist and to survive resides in its original way of giving expression to the social facts of humankind,'[11] writes Massignon (1954: 15). There is some truth in this remark; however, this 'original way of giving expression' has nothing to do with the purity of a language, as Japanese very clearly demonstrates, or English for that matter.

The above ideas on the virtues of purity are fundamentally misguided because they are based on faulty notion of what a language is. They are based on the assumption that a language is a nomenclature. Languages incorporate nomenclatures, but they are not nomenclatures. Even heavy lexical borrowing does not necessarily affect a language's identity, if there is such a thing. In one sense, the identity of a language is much like that of a river in Herodotus's sense: you cannot step into the same river twice. But linguists also have more sophisticated notions of what a language is. Like the bed of a river which may be stable for long periods of time while the water flowing through it is never the same, the basic features of a linguistic system may support the stream of speech through the ages without changing much. Only occasionally are the elements of this stream of ever new words sedimented on the bottom of the river bed in such a way that it eventually alters its course. The opposite is also possible. Parts of the bed may be washed away. For example, Ehlich (see chapter 10) argues that the Greco-Latin stratum of German is in the process of losing its potency because too little attention is being paid by the speech community to its maintenance.

Speech communities are not always indifferent to such developments. Rather, they often find them desirable or deplorable, as the case may be, and deem it essential to correct them if necessary. If they do, they should be able to rely on linguists who know how this can be done. The business of linguists is, among other things, to distinguish the essential from the contingent in language, to show which is solid rock and which quicksand. Their knowledge of various languages – their structures and history – furthermore puts them in a position to make an informed judgment as to what kind of support structure is necessary for canalizing the stream of a given language, to determine whether it carries enough water to provide for the enlarged fields of its speech community, or whether and how a sluice can be opened to enrich it with the waters of another.

As the chapters of this volume demonstrate, there are rational ways of going about these matters. How terminologies should be structured in order to (1) blend in with the language in question, while at the same time (2) offering a maximum of cross-linguistic communicability is a scientific question which linguists more than anyone else are qualified to answer (see chapter 12). Thus I find myself in agreement with Greenbaum, who in a recent article about English criticizes that '"prescriptivism" is often used pejoratively, especially among linguists and scholarly grammarians' (Greenbaum 1986: 195) and stresses the grammarians' responsibility for their language. Yet a lack of linguistic expertise in terminology formation processes is unfortunately common (see chapter 4), a sad fact for which partly at least linguists themselves are to blame.

Among the reasons why modern linguistics as a discipline has by and large abstained from taking a stand in normative questions, the most important ones, I think, are that language standards have been 'unmasked' as mere dialects of power; that there is no scientific basis for making judgments in terms of 'good' and 'bad'; and that conceding one variety a privileged status is anti-egalitarian and thus bad. However, in thus denying the intrinsic value of a cultivated standard language, the proponents of these ideas have thrown out the baby of proper linguistic care together with the bathwater of social prejudice.

What is called for in normative linguistics is prudence, not resignation. The ability of linguists to influence usage is, and should be, limited, but they are better prepared than others to keep purists' ideologically informed guidance in check. The difficult task is to avoid both the Scylla of exaggerated protection of the established standard, on the one hand, and the Charybdis of unqualified acceptance of actually occurring usage as the only yardstick for defining a standard, on the other hand. This can only be achieved by linguists who have a thorough understanding of how natural tendencies can be exploited and supplemented by artificial additions with a chance of success. This is what language adaptation is all about. If linguists are willing to recognize more than they have done in the recent past that languages not only grow naturally, but are also made by their speakers and, where necessary, consciously adapted to novel needs, they may be less reluctant to voice their respective opinions about good language and bad language. In a world where technological innovation is rapid and rapidly trickles down to the nonspecialist public, deliberate language adaptation is more necessary than ever.

Notes

1 'The creation of a uniform literary language is a cultural achievement of the highest order.'

2 The following statements from the prefaces of Lowth's grammar of English and Gottsched's grammar of German can be seen as typical of the prevailing view of the purpose of grammar in the Renaissance.

> The principle design of a Grammar of any Language is to teach us to express ourselves with propriety in that Language; and to enable us to judge of every phrase and form of construction, whether it be right or not.   (Lowth 1775: xi)

> Eine Sprachkunst überhaupt ist eine gegründete Anweisung, wie man die Sprache eines gewissen Volkes, nach der besten Mundart derselben, und nach der Einstimmung seiner besten Schriftsteller, richtig und zierlich, sowohl reden, als auch schreiben solle. (Gottsched 1748/1978: 37)
>
> (In general, a grammar is a well-founded prescription of how to speak and write the language of a given people correctly and elegantly, in accordance with its finest vernacular and the consensus of its best writers.)

3 Laymen usually think that linguistic change is bad. Linguists, nowadays, take a more distanced view, refraining from evaluating language change. Again, this is a very modern view. In the past, it was common not only to regard some languages as better, richer, more refined, more rigid, etc. than others, but also to look at language change in qualitative terms.

Leibniz was worried about the impoverishment of German and wrote his famous 'Admonition to the Germans' (1683). At roughly the same time, the Royal Society in London appointed a committee 'for improving the English language.' In 1712 Swift published a 'Proposal for Correcting, Improving and Ascertaining the English Tongue.' Renaissance grammarians often stated as their explicit goal the making of their language as good as others, especially Greek, Latin, and Hebrew.

4 This attitude is exemplified in a typical way by the following statement:

> It all boils down, really, to a question of acceptability in certain classes of our society, in those classes which are socially dominant and which set the tone for others. Whether a form is accepted or rejected does not depend on its inherent merit ... 'Correct' can only mean 'socially acceptable,' and apart from this has no meaning as applied to language.   (Hall 1950: 12–13).

This is a very radical position, as it denies the possibility of the 'inherent merit' of a linguistic form, that is, for instance, its systematic coherence. For a long time, however, structuralist linguists thought there was no other solution to the problem of linguistic correctness.

5 See the section 'Natural versus Artificial' (pp. 15–20) in the introductory chapter.

6 'Daß Nationen von glücklicheren Gaben und unter günstigeren Umständen vor-züglichere Sprachen, als andere, besitzen, liegt in der Natur der Sache selbst' (Humboldt 1830–1835: 20).

7 A good example is Miller's explicit remark 'There are no such things as an inadequate or a false and treacherous language' (1982: 104) which he made in criticizing 'irrational' arguments of Japanese linguists about the shortcomings of their language.

8 *Kanbun* is the earliest form of written Japanese which evolved from applying the Chinese script to the Japanese language, a tradition that originated in the sixth century A.D. and continued until the nineteenth century.

Notice, for instance, what Nishi Amane, a leading intellectual of the Meiji period, said about Japanese as late as 1874: 'In our letters at present, however, it is improper for us to write as we speak as well as improper to speak as we write since the grammar of speech and writing in our language are different' (Nishi 1874/1976: 5).

9 The delusion of authenticity and linguistic purity seems to become a public issue either as a reaction to excessive borrowing or in conjunction with a nationalist movement. It is thus a recurrent theme of sociolinguistic history. In 1561 Sir John Cheke wrote about English: 'Our language should be written clean and pure, unmixed and unmangled with borrowing of other tongues, wherein if we take no heed by time, ever borrowing and never paying, she shall be fain to keep her house as bankrupt' (quoted from Moore 1910: 5). Cheke, for one, should have been aware of the difficulty of fulfilling his request, as he was a professor of Classics at Cambridge. Yet 'unmixed' is hardly unmixed and 'pure' not pure in his sense.

The German poet Klopstock, in his polemical treatise *Die deutsche Gelehrten-republik*, brands as treason and 'contrary to the nature and the good old customs of our language' to 'mix foreign words in the language without need' (1774/1975: 25). His exasperation was understandable, however, because the German language was still held in little respect by the social elites. What Voltaire wrote home from Potsdam in 1750 testifies to its inferior status: 'L'allemand est pour les soldats et pour les chevaux.'

10 The following is a list of some arbitrarily selected foreign words with their suggest-ed German replacements from Eduard Engel's (1918) *Verdeutschungswörterbuch* [Germanification dictionary]. Many of the German substitutes have a humorous effect, testifying to the author's courage as much as to the misguidedness of his proposals:

Loanword	*Proposed alternative*
Karriere	Dienstlauf, Stufenleiter
Karikatur	Verzerrung
Kapital	Vermögen, Hauptgut
kapieren	begreifen
Karotte	Möhre
Installation	Einrichtung, Leitlegung
Ingenieur	Werkherr, Oberwerker
immanent	einhaftend
transzendent	überirdisch, jenseitig

Triangel	Dreieck
Epigone	Nachkomme
Enfant terrible	Hecht im Karpfenteich
Energie	Kraft
Echo	Rückschall
Duell	Ehrenhandel
Diplomat	Staatsmann
dionysisch	edelrauschig
demonstrativ	außenwirksam
alphabetisch	abecelich
Ultimatum	letztes Wort
Zynismus	Schamlosigkeit

11 'La raison d'être, et de survivre, d'une langue, réside dans son mode original d'expression des faites sociaux humains' Massignon (1954: 15).

References

Behaghel, Otto 1907 *Die Deutsche Sprache.* Vienna, Leipzig.

Bloomfield, Leonard 1927. Literate and Illiterate Speech. *American Speech*, 2: 432–439.

Bolinger, Dwight 1980. *Language the Loaded Weapon.* London.

Coulmas, Florian 1985. *Sprache und Staat.* Berlin, New York.

—— 1988. What is a National Language Good for? In F. Coulmas (ed.), *With Forked Tongues.* Ann Arbor.

—— (forthcoming a) Language Adaptation in Meijii Japan. In Brian Weinstein (ed.), *Language Planning and Political Development.* Norwood, N.J.

—— (forthcoming b) The Function of Written Language in East Asia. In U. Ammon (ed.), *Function and Status of Language.* Berlin, Amsterdam, New York.

De Silva, M. W. S. 1976. *Diglossia and Literacy.* Mysore.

—— 1982. Some Consequences of Diglossia. In W. Hass (ed.), *Standard Languages, Spoken and Written.* Manchester.

del Rosario, Gonsalo 1968. A Modernization–Standardization Plan for the Austronesian-Derived National Languages of Southeast Asia. *Asian Studies*, 6: 1–18.

Engel, Eduard 1918. *Entwelschung. Verdeutschungswörterbuch.* Leipzig.

Etiemble, R. 1964. *Parlez-vous franglais?* Paris.

Ferguson, Charlges A. 1962. The Language Factor in National Development. *Anthropological Linguistics*, 4, 1: 32–70.

Fukuzawa Yukichi 1932. *Den* [Biography of Fukuzawa Yukichi], 4 vols., ed. Ishikawa Kammei. Tokyo.

Gottsched, Johann Christop 1748. *Deutsche Sprachkunst. Ausgewählte Werke*, ed. P. M. Mitchell, vol. 8. Berlin, New York. 1978.

Grace, George 1981. Ordinary Language. MS, Linguistics Department, University of Hawaii.

Greenbaum, Sidney 1986. English and a Grammarian's Responsibility: The Present and the Future. *World Englishes*, 5: 189–195.

Hall, R. A. Jr 1950. *Leave your Language Alone.* Ithaca, New York.

Harris, Roy 1980. *The Language Makers.* Ithaca, New York.

Humboldt, Wilhelm von 1830–1835. Über die Verschiedenheit des menschlichen Sprachbaus und ihren Einfluß auf die geistige Entwicklung des Menschengeschlechts. *Werke in fünf Bänden*, vol. 3. Stuttgart 1963.

Kindaichi Haruhiko 1957. *Nihongo* [The Japanese Language]. Tokyo.

Klopstock, F. G. 1774. *Die Deutsche Gelehrtenrepublik*, ed. Rose-Marie Hurlebusch. Berlin, New York. 1975.

Leibniz, G. W. 1683. Ermahnung an die Deutschen. In *G. W. Leibniz Deutsche Schriften*, ed. W. Schmied-Kowarzik. Leipzig 1916.

1697. Unvorgreifliche Gedanken betreffend die Ausübung und Verbesserung der Teutschen Sprache. *Die Philosophischen Schriften von G. W. Leibniz*, ed. C. J. Gerhardt. Berlin 1896.

Louw, J. A. 1983. The Development of Xhosa and Zulu as Languages. In J. Fodor and C. Hagège (eds.), *Language Reform, History and Future*, vol. 2. Hamburg.

Lowth, Robert 1775. *A Short Introduction to English Grammar*. London.

Lyons, John 1968. *Introduction to Theoretical Linguistics*. London.

Massignon, Louis. 1954. Reflexions sur la structure primitive de l'analyse grammaticale en Arabe. *Arabica*, 1: 4–16.

Miller, Roy Andrew 1982. *Japan's Modern Myth*. New York, Tokyo.

Moore, J. L. 1910. *Tudor–Stuart Views on the Growth, Status, and Destiny of the English Language*. Halle.

Mori Arinori 1973. *Education in Japan. A Series of Letters Addressed by Prominent Americans to Arinori Mori*. New York.

Mulugeta Seyoum 1988. The Emergence of the National Language in Ethiopia: An Historical Perspective. In F. Coulmas (ed.), *With Forked Tongues*. Ann Arbor: Karoma, 101–144.

Nishi Amane 1874. Writing Japanese with the Western Alphabet. *Meiroku Zasshi*, 1. Quoted from *Meiroku Zasshi* [Journal of the Japanese Enlightenment], translated by W. R. Braisted. Tokyo 1976.

Ong, Walter 1977. *Interfaces of the World*. Ithaca, New York.

Ono Susumu 1980. *The Japanese Language and Modernization in Japan*. Tokyo.

Polenz, Peter von 1972. *Die Geschichte der deutschen Sprache*. Berlin.

1983. Sprachnormierung und Ansätze zur Sprachreform im Deutschen. In J. Fodor and C. Hagège (eds.) *Language Reform, History and Future*, vol. 3. Hamburg.

Sacy, Silvestre de 1808. Critique de E. Quatremère, recherches sur la langue et la littérature de l'Egypte. *Magasin Encyclopédique*, 4: 241–282.

Saussure, Ferdinand de 1972. *Cours de linguistique générale. Edition critique préparé par T. de Mauro*. Paris.

Stetkevych, Jaroslav 1970. *The Modern Arabic Literary Language. Lexical and Stylistic Developments*. Chicago.

Suzuki Takao 1987. Kokusaigo toshite no kango to kanji. In M. Hashimoto, T. Suzuki and H. Yamada *Kanji minzoku no ketsudan*. Tokyo.

Todd, Loreto 1984. *Modern Englishes: Pidgins and Creoles*. Oxford.

Name index

195

Subject index